Praxis Core Academic Skills for Educators

Includes Subtests
Reading 5713
Writing 5723
Math 5733

NavaED

10600 Chevrolet Way #107
Estero, FL 33928

Praxis Core Academic Skills for Educators

Includes Subtests

Reading 5713
Writing 5723
Math 5733

ISBN: 9781696955652

Table of Contents

This page is intentionally left blank.

PRAXIS® CORE ACADEMIC SKILLS FOR EDUCATORS: READING

This page is intentionally left blank.

You will have 85 minutes to complete 56 selected response (multiple-choice) questions based on a variety of readings and stimuli (charts, graphs, pictures).

The *Praxis*® Core reading subtest has four types of reading passages: short passages, long passages, double passages, and charts/graphs. These readings cover a variety of academic subjects and are simple enough that you won't need a great deal of prior knowledge of the subject matter to understand the readings. The questions are based directly on the readings.

There are two basic categories of questions on the *Praxis*® Core reading subtest exam:

1. **Content questions** require you to understand the explicit information presented in the readings. These are what many teachers call 'right there' questions—you can point to them directly in the text.
2. **Analysis questions** require you to analyze the readings for deeper understanding. In these questions, the answers are NOT explicitly stated in the passage and require the reader to use inference to answer the questions.

Quick Tip!
Inference is when the reader comes to a logical conclusion based on the information in the passage. While inference questions are not explicitly stated in the text, the reader must use information in the text to answer inference questions correctly.

All questions in the *Praxis*® Core reading subtest are selected response questions. Some questions will require you to choose multiple answers by clicking multiple boxes or *all that apply*.

Test at a Glance	
Test Name	Core Academic Skills for Educators: Reading
Test Code	5713
Time	85 minutes
Number of Questions	56 selected-response questions
Format	Selected response questions based on reading passages
Test Delivery	Computer delivered

Content Categories	Approximate number of questions	Approximate percentage of the exam
I. Key Ideas and Details	17-22	35%
II. Craft, Structure and Language Skills	14-19	30%
III. Integration of Knowledge and Ideas	17-22	35%

You will see several types of reading passages on the *Praxis®* Core reading subtest exam. Understanding how to navigate the different passages will help you succeed on the test. We have outlined the different passaged and some suggested strategies for tackling these passages.

Short passages

Short passages are single paragraphs and are followed by one to two selected response questions. These passages will be written on a variety of subjects—both informational and narrative. The questions will be focused on author's opinion, tone, purpose, vocabulary in context, etc. The questions may ask you to make inferences or to analyze a particular aspect of the text. We suggest reading the question(s) or question stem(s) first before reading the passage. This sets the purpose for reading. Do not read the answer choices because there are incorrect answers there, and you do not want to fill your brain with useless information. However, quickly looking over the questions first can help you be more efficient as you read. Then read the passage completely. It is important to read each passage completely because failing to do so will make it difficult to answer contextual and main idea questions.

Strategy for Short Passages

1. Set the purpose for reading. **Read the question(s) or questions stem(s) first**. Do **NOT** read the answer choices. Just read the questions or question stems.

2. Read the passage in its entirety.

3. As you read, think about these things.

   - What is the tone of this passage?

   - Why would the author write this?

   - Is this an opinion piece or is it informational?

4. Answer the question(s) using the process of elimination (exclude wrong answers), and your understanding of the passage.

The following is an example of what a short passage will look like on the *Praxis®* Core reading subtest.

Example

Heart of Darkness

by: Joseph Conrad

The sea-reach of the Thames stretched before us like the beginning of an interminable waterway. In the offing, the sea and the sky were welded together without a joint, and in the luminous space the tanned sails of the barges drifting up with the tide seemed to stand still in red clusters of canvas sharply peaked, with gleams of varnished sprits. A haze rested on the low shores that ran out to sea in vanishing flatness. The air was dark above Gravesend, and farther back still seemed condensed into a mournful gloom, brooding motionless over the biggest, and the greatest, town on earth.

The tone of the above passage can be described as:

A. optimistic as the author gazes at the greatest town on earth.
B. restless as the author is anticipating an upcoming voyage.
C. oblivious as the author is unaffected by the scenery.
D. ominous as the author is cautious about the surrounding area.
E. terminal as the author is sure he will die.

Explanation: If we read the question stem first, we understand that as we read, we should be paying attention to the tone or overall feeling of the passage. From the title—*Heart of Darkness*—and the descriptions in the text—*vanishing flatness, air is dark, a mournful gloom*—we can infer that this passage is probably not optimistic or relentless because those words do not fit here. Oblivious means unaware, but the author seems very aware of his surroundings. Terminal is too strong of a word here, and we cannot infer that the author is *sure he will die*. That is what we call strong language, and choices containing strong language are typically not the correct answers. Therefore, **D** is the best answer here. Ominous can mean gloomy, and the word gloom is used in the last sentence.

Long passages

The long passages contain multiple paragraphs that are either fiction or non-fiction. These passages will be written on a variety of subjects from a variety of perspectives. These longer passages will be followed by 3-6 multiple-choice questions that relate directly to the piece. The same strategies should be applied here. Read the question(s) or question stem(s) first—do NOT read the answer choices. Then read the passage, keeping in mind the overall feeling of the passage, the purpose of the passage, and anything specific that stands out in the passage.

Strategy for Long Passages

1. Set the purpose for reading. **Read the questions first**. Do **NOT** read the answer choices. Just read the questions or question stems.

2. Read the passage in its entirety.

3. Take notes on your scratch paper as you read. We recommend taking a quick note after each paragraph that summarizes the paragraph. This is called active reading and can help you remember important information and help you stay focused on the passage.

4. As you read, think about these things.

    • What is the tone of this passage?

    • Why would the author write this?

    • Is this an opinion piece or is it informational?

5. Answer the questions using your notes, process of elimination (exclude wrong answers), and your understanding of the passage.

The following is an example of a long passage like the ones you will see on the *Praxis*® Core reading subtest.

Example:

The Art of Cross-Examination

By Francis L. Wellman

An amusing incident, leading to the exposure of a manifest fraud, occurred recently in another of the many damage suits brought against the Metropolitan Street Railway and growing out of a collision between two of the company's electric cars.

The plaintiff, a laboring man, had been thrown to the street pavement from the platform of the car by the force of the collision, and had dislocated his shoulder. He had testified in his own behalf that he had been permanently injured in so far as he had not been able to follow his usual employment for the reason that he could not raise his arm above a point parallel with his shoulder. Upon cross-examination the attorney for the railroad asked the witness a few sympathetic questions about his sufferings, and upon getting on a friendly basis with him asked him "to be good enough to show the jury the extreme limit to which he could raise his arm since the accident." The plaintiff slowly and with considerable difficulty raised his arm to the parallel of his shoulder.

"Now, using the same arm, show the jury how high you could get it up before the accident," quietly continued the attorney; whereupon the witness extended his arm to its full height above his head, amid peals of laughter from the court and jury.

In a case of murder, to which the defense of insanity was set up, a medical witness called on behalf of the accused swore that in his opinion the accused, at the time he killed the deceased, was affected with a homicidal mania, and urged to the act by an *irresistible* impulse. The judge, not satisfied with this, first put the witness some questions on other subjects, and then asked, "Do you think the accused would have acted as he did if a policeman had been present?" to which the witness at once answered in the negative. Thereupon the judge remarked, "Your definition of an irresistible impulse must then be an impulse irresistible at all times except when a policeman is present."

Which of the following statements would the author of the passage agree?

- ❑ It is easy to trick a plaintiff during a cross examination when the attorney becomes friendly with the plaintiff.

- ❑ To trick a witness in a cross examination, it helps to ask preliminary questions before asking the questions that will prove your case in court.

- ❑ A case of fraud and a case of murder are two different situations and require different approaches in cross examination.

- ❑ Cross examinations can be very amusing, especially when the plaintiffs or witnesses don't catch on to the tactics of the cross-examining attorney or judge.

- ❑ Fraud and insanity are hard to prove, and attorneys can easily discredit witnesses who rely on those defenses.

Explanation: The best answers are the **2 and 4**. In both instances, the author mentions the cross-examining attorney preparing the plaintiffs or witnesses with preliminary questions to trick them into saying what the attorney needs to win the case. In the first instance, preliminary questions were, "to be good enough to show the jury the extreme limit to which he could raise his arm since the accident." In the second case, preliminary questions were, "The judge, not satisfied with this, first put the witness some questions on other subjects, and then asked, 'Do you think the accused would have acted as he did if a policeman had been present?'" In both cases, the stories are humorous. Therefore, the 4th choice can also be correct. The 1st answer choice has elements of the passage but for only one part of the passage, the dislocated shoulder case. Answers 3 and 5 are not applicable to the passage.

For what type of publication would the passage be best suited?

A. A textbook for a criminal law course.

B. The classified section of a local newspaper.

C. A newspaper op-ed piece.

D. A biography about a famous attorney.

E. A non-fiction book about famous criminal trials.

Explanation: The answer is choice **E**. The witness examination outlined in the piece is meant to show the reader the sometimes-humorous side of very tense criminal cases. You are much more likely to find anecdotes such as these in a non-fiction book than you would find in a textbook or academic piece of writing. Op-eds are opinion pieces; therefore, choice C is incorrect because the author is not discussing his opinion—he is simply telling stories. Choice B does not work because classified sections of newspapers are for advertisements and announcements. Choice D sounds good, but the author is discussing cases not an individual who tried the cases.

Double passages

During the *Praxis®* Core reading subtest, you will be presented with two passages covering the same topic in different ways. Remember, read the question(s) and question stem(s) first. That will set the purpose for reading. Then read each passage. Once you've read each passage, you will be presented with several multiple-choice questions. Some of the questions will ask about the passages individually, but several will ask you to make connections between the two passages. Again, it's very important that you read each passage in its entirety in order to understand main ideas, organization, and context for each passage individually and how they relate to each other.

Strategy for Double Passages

In the double passages, we recommend breaking up the questions into only passage 1 questions, only passage 2 questions, and 1 and 2 questions. If you read all of passage 1 and all of passage 2 and then go through the questions in order, you will probably forget a lot of what you read in passage 1. Reading the questions for 1 first, then reading passage 1, and answering passage 1's questions will limit the number of times you have to go back and reread the passage. You are essentially breaking the passages up into two distinct passages with their own questions.

1. Set the purpose for reading for each passage. **Read only the questions for passage 1 first.** Do **NOT** read the answer choices. Just the questions or question stems.

2. Read passage 1.

3. Use your scratch paper to jot down important information.

4. Answer passage 1 questions.

5. **Read the questions for passage 2 next.** Do **NOT** read the answer choices. Just the questions or question stems.

6. Read passage 2.

7. Use your scratch paper to jot down important information.

8. Answer passage 2 questions.

9. Now answer the questions that have to do with both passages.

10. As you read, think about these things.

    - What is the tone of this passage?

    - Why would the author write this?

    - Is this an opinion piece or is it informational?

11. Answer the questions using your notes, process of elimination (exclude wrong answers), and your understanding of the passage.

The following is an example of a double passage like the ones you will see on the *Praxis®* Core reading subtest exam.

Example:

Passage 1

The Tennessee Valley Authority (TVA) was tasked by President Franklin D. Roosevelt to build the Pickwick Dam, which would be a significant producer of hydroelectric power for the region. During the Great Depression, the towns of Waterloo and Riverton were sacrificed as a result of the construction of the dam. More than a loss of property, it was a sacrifice of community for the greater good. The people were happy to sacrifice their property in order to see their region prosper. This act resulted in a better region allowing for the creation of jobs, economic security, recreational facilities and a better quality of life for the residents of the Tennessee Valley. As in other lost towns throughout the region, these communities and the families living in them dedicated their properties, homes and histories to the creation of a vastly improved region and a stronger nation for their children and grandchildren.

Passage 2

When people talk about the great success of the Tennessee Valley Authority (TVA)—it helped ease some of the economic hardship not only in the state of Tennessee but also in parts of Kentucky, Alabama, Georgia, North Carolina, and Virginia—they often fail to consider those who lost everything to the government. These people are often billed as land and business owners who sacrificed their homes and livelihood for the future of the nation. The place where my grandparents raised my mother is now underwater, and the result of their sacrifice: they lost everything and nearly starved to death during the depression.

> **Quick Tip!**
>
> Notice how the question for passage 1 only is the 3rd question in the set. That is a tactic test makers use to make answering these questions difficult. If you read the passage in order and answer the questions in order, you will probably forget important information in the first passage and have to reread it to get #3 correct. That's why we recommend finding passage 1's questions, reading passage 1 and answer that question first. It saves time and helps you beat the test makers at their own game!

1. The main purpose of both passages 1 and 2 is to do which of the following?
    A. To determine the amount of work put in to building the Pickwick Dam.
    B. To celebrate the Tennessee Valley Authority.
    C. To show the reader the importance of sacrifice for one's community.
    D. To show that sacrifices were made to forward the progress of a region.
    E. Explain the massive success of the Pickwick Dam.

Explanation: The answer is **D**. Each of the passages show local landowners had to sacrifice their land and livelihood for the good of the region. Passage 2 has a negative view of the history of the TVA. Choices A and B are not discussed. Choice C is more aligned with passage A only.

2. In passage 2, the term *billed* means which of the following?
    A. asked for payment
    B. offered a settlement
    C. are charged
    D. described as
    E. are beaked

Explanation: The correct choice is **D** because *billed*, in this instance, means to describe someone or something. Choices A, C and E are referring to different uses of the word billed that do not work in this context. Choice B doesn't work because a settlement is the opposite of being billed.

3. In passage 1, the author's position on the topic is which of the following?
    A. The landowners did not deserve to be treated the way they were.
    B. The landowners made a great fortune from their sacrifice.
    C. The Tennessee Valley Authority failed in their endeavors.
    D. The farms around the river were not very valuable.
    E. The landowners understood that their sacrifice was for the good of the region.

Explanation: The correct answer is **E**. In the passage the author states that, "The people were happy to sacrifice their property in order to see their region prosper." Choice A shows the opposite opinion. B is incorrect because the landowners made a sacrifice without mention of financial restitution. C is incorrect because the TVA is mentioned as being quite successful in the region. D is unknown.

4. Which of the following statement summarizes the overall tone and structure of both passages?

- Passage 1 generalizes favorably at the TVA, while passage 2 expresses a cynical personal experience of the TVA.

- Passage 1 draws from enjoyable personal experience of the TVA, while passage 2 expresses a generalized anger toward the project.

- Passage 1 extends is a cautious warning of the TVA, while the passage 2 expresses doubt of the TVA's success.

- Passage 1 is pessimistic about the TVA and other projects, while passage 2 is cautiously optimistic about the results of the TVA.

- Passage 1 praises the sacrifice of the government during the TVA, while passage 2 blames the government for people's suffering during the TVA.

Explanation: The answer is choice A. Passage one is favorable, so you can eliminate any answer choices that indicate passage 1 is negative; therefore, eliminate choices C and D. Only passage 2 draws on a personal experience; therefore, choice B is out. Choice E is close; however, passage 1 does not talk about the government's sacrifice, but rather the community members' sacrifices; therefore, E is out. This leaves you with choice A as the best answer.

Graphs and charts

On the *Praxis*® Core reading subtest, you will be required to evaluate data and information from a chart, graph, picture, etc. These are referred to as *visual-information* questions. These visuals will contain a variety of information: business trends, changes in the weather, survey results, daily timetables, monthly calendars, etc. Each piece of visual information is followed by one or more questions.

Strategy for visual information (charts & graphs) questions

1. Look at the question stem(s) first. Knowing what you should be looking for in the graph will focus your approach.

2. Look over all the elements of the graph or chart—the title, legend, and information.

3. Pay attention to the *x*- and *y*-axes. There will be important information there, including the increments the data is presented. For example, on the *x*-axis it may go from month to month or every 5 years, and on the *y*-axis, information may be presented in thousands, millions, etc.

4. Identify trends in the data and any patterns.

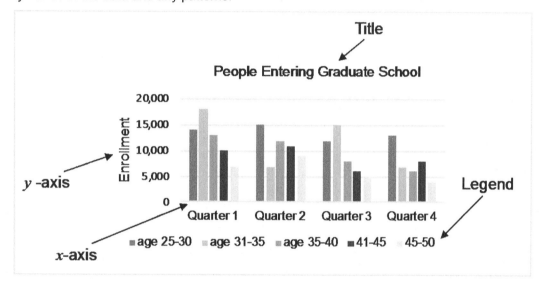

1. The university above has a limited budget for marketing, and only has enough money to market for one quarter and towards one age group. According to the graph above, where should the limited marketing budget be used to increase enrollment?

   A. School officials should use the marketing budget during quarter 2 for the 25-30 age group.

   B. School officials should use the marketing budget during quarter 4 for the 45-50 age group.

   C. School officials should use the marketing budget during quarter 1 for the 20-30 age group.

   D. School officials should use the marketing budget during quarter 3 for the 31-35 age group.

   E. School officials should use the marketing budget during quarter 2 for the 31-35 age group.

Explanation: The correct choice is **B**. Because quarter 4 and the age group 41-50 have the lowest enrollment, marketing dollars would be best spent for that quarter and age group.

2. According to the graph, the age group with the most consistent enrollment is:

   A. age 25-30

   B. age 31-35

   C. age 35-40

   D. age 41-45

   E. age 45-50

Explanation: Answer choice **A** is the best choice here. Look at the trends in the data and you will see that the age group 25-30 enrollment stays relatively the same over all 4 quarters compared to the other age groups.

Types of Reading Questions

Content questions

Content questions are based on information that comes directly from the passage.

- **Detail questions:** Detail questions ask you to correctly identify specific pieces of information in the passage.

  These questions usually include phrases like

  - *...according to the passage/author...*

  - *...the passage/author/sentence suggests...?*

  - *...which of the following...?*

  These questions are asking you to identify specific information that can be found in the passage. However, the answer choice will not appear exactly as it does in the text. Look carefully to find a re-wording of a detail.

- **Main idea questions:** You will be asked to identify the main idea of a statement, passage, or pair of passages. Main idea questions are always a general description of the text.

  Any questions asking you to identify *main idea, main purpose*, and *summary* are all looking for the same thing—you're being asked to identify the most general description of the passage (not a detail). This is the "umbrella" idea which covers the piece as a whole. The answer stem will have several choices that offer specific information (details, examples) from the text, you will be able to eliminate these options immediately because the main idea will not have random, specific details scattered within it.

- **Vocabulary in context:** This kind of question asks you about the meaning of an important word from the reading. The word will be highlighted in the text, and it's important to identify the context in which the word is being used, as often times you will be looking for a synonym, not a strict dictionary definition.

  Strategy: Context is key. You must read the piece completely if you are going to answer vocab context questions correctly. Once you've identified the word and the meaning of the passage, eliminate the choices that don't make sense. Replace the word in question with the remaining choices to see if they could work in the context of the passage.

- **Organization questions:** These questions require you to understand how different pieces of information are arranged together. In most cases, organization questions will directly mention the organization of the passage. Organization questions may also ask about the relationship between two ideas, sentences or paragraphs. Pay attention to text structures when answering these questions—chronological order, cause and effect, compare and contrast, etc.

Analysis questions

With analysis questions, you'll need to look at the deeper meaning of what you're reading—at anything not directly stated in the content. You will want to make sure to read the piece in its entirety; reading from beginning to end is essential when gathering the information required to answer main idea, contextual, opinion/attitude, and inference questions.

- **Inference questions:** these questions ask you to identify ideas that are not explicitly stated but are strongly suggested by the author. Key phrases that mark inference questions include:

  - *it can be inferred that...*

  - *the passage suggests...*

  - *the author would likely agree....*

- **Tone questions:** With these questions, you need to understand the author's personal opinion or attitude toward the subject of the passage. Tone questions are usually worded in the following ways, *the author's attitude…, how does the author feel…, or this passage would appear in…* These types of questions require you to understand the overall felling of the passage.

- **Point of view questions:** Identifying the point of view will help you understand the passages purpose, intended effect, and what type of publication it might have appeared in.

  1. **First-person** narrative is when the author is talking about herself or himself. This point of view is rarely seen in academic or informative/expository writing; however, this style is quite common in fictional narratives. For example, *"I've been to many countries, but I've never been to New York."*

  2. **Second-person** point of view is when the writer is directly addressing the reader with *you, your* and *yours*. For example, *"You open the door to find the keys in the ignition and the engine running."*

  > **Quick Tip!**
  >
  > In academic/informational/expository writing, a third person perspective is used to give an objective, unbiased point of view. For example, "Congress voted to give itself a raise in salary for the third consecutive year," is written in 3rd person.

  3. **Third-person** is when the author is talking about other situations or people. This point-of-view provides a certain amount of flexibility for the writer. In a creative piece, the author employs a third person perspective to access the minds of all characters across without being limited by geographical distance and/or timelines. For example, *"Sally thought about her mother as she opened the old letters."*

- **Argument analysis questions:** These questions require you to understand all that is stated in the text and determine the main argument. When you do get questions like this, you'll need to carefully think about the structure of the author's claims. Then, you need to identify a new piece of information that—if true—would either weaken or strengthen the argument in the passage. You can identify an argument question by the language used in the question:

  - *Which of the following, if true, would most strengthen the argument?*

  - *Which of the following, if true, suggests an alternative hypothesis?*

At Home Practice Plan

The best way to improve your reading skills is to read as much as you can. You should set-aside 10-20 minutes each day to read. Find websites, books, and magazines that offer light academic reading. The *Praxis®* Core reading subtest offers passages on a variety of academic subjects; however, none of the passages require more than a superficial knowledge of the subject.

While you're reading, begin to identify main ideas, details, specific examples, and organization. You should also practice identifying vocabulary based on the context of the piece—if you don't understand a word, try and figure out the meaning based on the piece as whole and the words surrounding it before you look it up. It is important that you understand what the test will be asking you to do and incorporating that information into your practice. The best way to improve your timing and accuracy is to practice with the test structure in mind.

Quick Tip!

While this book has many great passages to practice from, you may need more support. We recommend using released ACT or SAT reading passages to practice. The questions are similar to the ones you will see on the *Praxis®*. Released tests can be found on ACT and The College Board websites, and they are FREE. Just Google, "released ACT tests" or "released SAT tests," and you should have no problem finding them.

Practice Plan

If you are studying for the reading, below is a study plan to help you focus your approach. Just like anything else, getting better at reading for a standardized test takes practice. Reading 20-45 min a day can improve your reading skills exponentially.

Weekly Practice Plan for Reading

Day	Total Time	Practice
Monday	20 – 30 min	1 ACT Passage (unlimited time) – Analyze your answers; your goals should be accuracy.
Tuesday	45 min	2 SAT Passages (unlimited time) – Identify the main idea questions and key details questions.
Wednesday	20-30 min	1 ACT Passage for time – 10 min. Shoot for > 70% accuracy. Analyze your answers. Evaluate why certain answers are correct and incorrect.
Thursday	45 min	2 ACT Passages for time – 20 min. Shoot for >70% accuracy. Analyze your answers. Evaluate why certain answers are correct and incorrect.
Friday	20-30 min	1 SAT Passage for time – 10 min. Shoot for >80% accuracy. Analyze your answers. Evaluate why certain answers are correct and incorrect.
Saturday	20-30 min	Read anything you want: news article, reading passage, book, etc.
Sunday	0 min	Take the day off. Get back to it in 24 hours.

This page is intentionally left blank.

Questions 1-2 refer to the following passage.

Adapted from *Heart of Darkness* by Joseph Conrad

It was in 1868, when nine years old or thereabouts, that while looking at a map of Africa of the time and putting my finger on the blank space then representing the unsolved mystery of that continent, I said to myself, with absolute assurance and an amazing audacity, which are no longer in my character now: "When I grow up I shall go there."

1. Which of the following statements would the narrator most likely agree?

    A. Regret is unproductive; one must look to the future.

    B. Young people are full of adventure and conviction, something desperately needed later in life.

    C. To live life fully, one must travel often.

    D. Exploring blank spaces is something people should do when they're young.

    E. Examining one's past and present character can be heartbreaking.

2. The narrator of this passage can be described as:

    A. a 17th century explorer looking back on his life with regret over not having gone to Africa.

    B. a young adult explaining his travel plans for when he grows up.

    C. a grown man looking back at his younger self with admiration.

    D. an old man explaining his biggest regret to his grandson.

    E. a child who is curious about the world.

Questions 3-4 refer to the following passage.

Adapted from *Free as in Freedom: Richard Stallman's Crusade for Free Software* by Sam Williams

The New York University computer-science department sits inside Warren Weaver Hall, a fortress-like building located two blocks east of Washington Square Park. Industrial-strength air-conditioning vents create a surrounding moat of hot air, discouraging loiterers and solicitors alike. Visitors who breach the moat encounter another formidable barrier, a security check-in counter, immediately inside the building's single entryway.

3. The description above would most likely appear in:

    A. a brochure for new students to use as they enter New York University's campus for the first time.

    B. a newspaper article outlining the university's $2.8 million construction project that was finished last the fall.

    C. a novel about a college student's experience on New York University's campus.

    D. a flyer promoting the computer science department.

    E. An instruction manual about the security check-in at New York University's campus.

4. By using the phrase "breach the moat," the author is trying to convey what effect?

    ❑ anger at the fact that the computer science building is so difficult to get into

    ❑ sarcasm in explaining that getting into the computer science building is like breaking through an almost impossible barrier.

    ❑ humor in describing the image of industrial-strength air-conditioning blowing solicitors away from the doors.

    ❑ persuasion in getting people to see the importance of the barriers to the computer science building.

    ❑ cause and effect in showing how a moat and security check-in can cause restrict entrance to the building.

Questions 5-6 refer to the following passage.

Adapted from *The Art of Journalism: An Interview with Hunter S. Thompson* by Douglas Brinkley

Hunter Thompson carved out his niche early. He was born in 1937, in Louisville, Kentucky, where his fiction and poetry earned him induction into the local Athenaeum Literary Association while he was still in high school. Thompson continued his literary pursuits in the United States Air Force, writing a weekly column for the base newspaper. After two years of service, Thompson endured a series of newspaper jobs—all of which ended in disaster—before he took to freelancing in Puerto Rico and South America for a variety of publications. The vocation quickly evolved into a compulsion.

5. The main purpose of this passage is to:

    A. celebrate the accomplishments of a great American writer.

    B. chronical a brief history of a great American writer.

    C. explain what makes writers leave the U.S. for other countries.

    D. show how military service can lead to exciting opportunities abroad.

    E. describe a great American writer and his niche.

6. Which of the following can be assumed of Hunter Thompson?

   A. He enjoyed the adventure the United States Airforce brought him and used that in his weekly column.

   B. He spent years trying to figure out his purpose.

   C. While in high school, he developed a love for poetry.

   D. When he tired of his newspaper jobs he left the U.S. and moved to Puerto Rico.

   E. While he was not fond of his newspaper jobs, he became obsessed with writing as a freelancer.

Questions 7-8 refer to the following passage.

Adapted from *The Adjunctification of New York State Universities* by Justin Vibbert

The defining moment for the City University of New York (CUNY) came in 1976. The city, which was quickly sinking into bankruptcy, struck a deal with the state that required CUNY institutions to charge tuition for the first time in the system's history. The influx of cash via tuition would be used to subsidize the loss of funds that were needed to keep the city afloat. At the time, there were roughly 11,000 faculty members and 250,000 students.

Since then, CUNY—its principal funding source remains the state (50%), then tuition (39%), and the city (11%)—has seen its faculty drop to 7,000 while the student population has risen to 266,000. State funding has been unpredictable for the past two and a half decades and flat since 2011, putting many state and city schools in difficult financial situations.

"As a result, only 46 percent of CUNY classes are now taught by full-time faculty," said Dr. Steven London, Vice President of the Professional Staff Congress of CUNY, the largest faculty and staff union. "The biggest problem is the continuing adjunctification of the universities. At the end of the day what this is about, delivering quality education… and professional staff."

7. The term **subsidize** (reproduced in the excerpt below) as it is used in the passage means:

   The influx of cash via tuition would be used to subsidize the loss of funds that were needed to keep the city afloat. At the time, there were roughly 11,000 faculty members and 250,000 students.

   A. replace

   B. reduce

   C. increase

   D. exempt

   E. finance

8. Which of the following sentences, if added to paragraph 2, would support the argument that faculty membership has been significantly reduced because of funding?

   A. Visitors to campus have also decreased, causing lower sales at bookstores on the CUNY campus.

   B. Alternative funding coming from grants has also been reduced because of the lack of personnel qualified to facilitate the grand process.

   C. Students are feeling the cutbacks as new programs are not supported.

   D. Most of CUNY classes will now be taught online.

   E. The student population is predicted to triple by school year 2022-2023.

Questions 9-12 refer to the following passage.

Born in 1893 in the Georgian village of Baghdadi (later renamed Mayakovsky), Vladimir Mayakovsky was the son of a forestry officer. By the time of the 1905 revolution, Mayakovsky was already working with the local social democrats, and when his family moved to Moscow a couple of years later, he joined the Bolsheviks. He wrote propaganda for the party until his arrest in 1908, which resulted in an imprisonment of eleven months.

The imprisonment was crucial to his artistic and political development, as he spent the time reading the classics of world literature. Nevertheless, upon leaving prison, he became a key figure of the artistic avant-garde in Moscow, becoming a Futurist, an artistic movement resolutely opposed to all that was old and bucolic, and which praised the city, speed and modernity. As their manifesto said: "We alone are the face of our time. Time's trumpet blares in our art of words. The past is stifling... Throw Pushkin, Dostoevsky, Tolstoy, etc., overboard."

From this time until the revolutions of 1917, Mayakovsky was one of the most visible members of the Russian artistic scene. He wrote rough, declamatory poetry and cultivated the image of a hooligan. *A Cloud in Trousers* and *I* were among the most important works of the time.

9. The author of this passage would most likely agree that:

   A. Mayakovsky was a radical artist creating works that were innovative and impressionable in his time.

   B. Mayakovsky, while talented as an artist, did not let politics infiltrate his work.

   C. Pushkin, Dostoevsky, and Tolstoy are too bucolic and should not be considered great authors.

   D. The imprisonment of Mayakovsky stifled his writing ability and interest in politics.

   E. Being the son of a forester impacted Mayakovsky art and political positions.

10. The word **bucolic** (reproduced in the excerpt below) most likely means:

   Nevertheless, upon leaving prison he became a key figure of the artistic avant-garde in Moscow, becoming a Futurist, an artistic movement resolutely opposed to all that was old and bucolic, and which praised the city, speed and modernity.

   A. modern

   B. artistic

   C. rural

   D. innovative

   E. dreary

11. It can be inferred the author wrote this article to:

   A. exploit the works of a little-known poet to show how socialism ruined a country.

   B. explain how the poetry skills of a socialist author helped to bring down a regime.

   C. persuade people to focus on modern, urban poetry rather than old-fashioned prose.

   D. outline the tumultuous life of a radical poet who helped shape a movement.

   E. present a cautionary tale of what can happen when one decides to go against the status quo.

12. Based on what is presented in the article, the poem *A Cloud in Trousers* mentioned in the passage most probably depicts:

    A. subjects of love, revolution, religion and art.

    B. a life in prison and lessons learned.

    C. a focus on the old-world order.

    D. images of the Russian countryside.

    E. style that is indicative of the time before the revolution of 1905.

Questions 13-16 refer to the following pair of passages.

Passage 1

Adapted from *Young Conservatives like me care about climate change. The GOP needs to take notice* by Danielle Butcher

As a young conservative woman in my early 20s, I'm often met with surprise when people learn that environmentalism is a top political concern for me. Like many millennial conservatives, I believe the Republican Party has been slow to address environmental challenges, even though many environmental solutions fit well within a belief in free market solutions. The economic and national security benefits of prioritizing climate change are concepts the GOP can and should embrace; they're consistent with its ideology. While the left and right may have different reasons behind prioritizing eco-friendly reforms, such reforms are in everyone's collective interest.

Passage 2

Adapted from *Actually, Republicans do Believe in Climate Change* by Leaf Van Boven and David Sherman

It is widely believed that most Republicans are skeptical about human-caused climate change. However, a national survey of more than 2,000 respondents on the issue of climate change found that most Republicans agreed that climate change is happening, is threating humans, and is caused by human activity—reducing carbon emissions would assuage the problem. This research suggests the problem is not so much that Republicans are skeptical about climate change, but that Republicans are skeptical of Democrats—and that Democrats are skeptical of Republicans. This tribalism leads to political fights over differences between the parties that either do not exist or are vastly exaggerated.

13. The authors of passage 1 and 2 would most likely agree that (check all that apply):

❑ whether it is the environment or market issues, conservatism and environmentalism do not mix.

❑ even though there is a divide between democrats and republicans, environmentalism is important to everyone.

❑ even though Republicans implement strict environmental policies, their efforts are overshadowed by a heavily politicized environment.

❑ Rather than focus on the differences in politics, Democrats and Republicans should work together on environmental policy.

❑ Republicans and Democrats will never be able to agree on environmental policy unless they compromise their politics.

14. It can be inferred from the first sentence of passage 1 (reproduced below), that Republicans are seen as being:

As a young conservative woman in my early 20s, I'm often met with surprise when people learn that environmentalism is a top political concern for me.

A. indifferent about the environment.

B. concerned about the environment.

C. indignant regarding the environment.

D. overwhelmed regarding the environment.

E. anxious about the environment.

15. The term *assuage,* as used in passage 2 (reproduced below), means:

However, a national survey of more than 2,000 respondents on the issue of climate change found that most Republicans agreed that climate change is happening, is threating humans, and is caused by human activity—reducing carbon emissions would assuage the problem.

   A. exacerbate

   B. embellish

   C. intensify

   D. mitigate

   E. hasten

16. Both passages imply that Republicans care about the environment. However, only one passage has support for the claim that Republicans do, in fact, care about the environment. Identify which passage has support for the claim and an example of that support.

   A. Passage 1: "Like many millennial conservatives, I believe the Republican Party has been slow to address environmental challenges, even though many environmental solutions fit well within a belief in free market solutions.

   B. Passage 1: "The economic and national security benefits of prioritizing climate change are concepts the GOP can and should embrace; they're consistent with its ideology."

   C. Passage 2: "It is widely believed that most Republicans are skeptical about human-caused climate change."

   D. Passage 2: "However, a national survey of more than 2,000 respondents on the issue of climate change found that most Republicans agreed that climate change is happening..."

   E. Neither passage 1 nor passage 2 contains support for the claim Republicans care about the environment.

Questions 17-19 refer to the following passages

Adapted from *Darwin's Polar Bear* by Michael Engelhard

As any good high school student should know, the beaks of Galápagos "finches" (in fact the islands' mockingbirds) helped Darwin to develop his ideas about evolution. But few people realize that the polar bear, too, informed his grand theory.

Letting his fancy run wild in *On the Origin of Species*, the man accustomed to thinking in eons hypothesized "a race of bears being rendered, by natural selection, more and more aquatic in their structure and habits, with larger and larger mouths, till a creature was produced as monstrous as a whale." Darwin based this speculation on a black bear the fur trader-explorer Samuel Hearne had observed swimming for hours, its mouth wide open, catching insects in the water. If the supply of insects were constant, Darwin thought, and no better-adapted competitors present, such a species could well take shape over time.

17. What is the main idea of the passage?

    A. Finches were not the only species to inform Darwin's theory of evolution.

    B. Galápagos finches were the best evidence of natural selection.

    C. Land animals can evolve to become aquatic in nature.

    D. When food supplies are sparse, natural predators will take over.

    E. Whales have large mouths because of evolution.

18. Why does the author use quotations and parenthesis in the first line (reproduced below) of the passage?

As any good high school student should know, the beaks of Galápagos "finches" (in fact the islands' mockingbirds) helped Darwin to develop his ideas about evolution.

    A. to emphasize an important aspect of Darwin's research.

    B. to provide an anecdote about Galápagos finches.

    C. to provide an image of what the Galápagos looks like.

    D. to clarify a previously stated phrase.

    E. to support a claim made by Darwin.

19. The tone of the passage can best be described as:

    A. cautionary

    B. skeptical

    C. curious

    D. indignant

    E. endearing

Questions 20-21 refer to the following chart of data.

Ms. Rodriquez is collecting data to see how her students scored on a state test. The test has multiple sections—math, English, reading, and essay. A score of 200 is the passing score for each section.

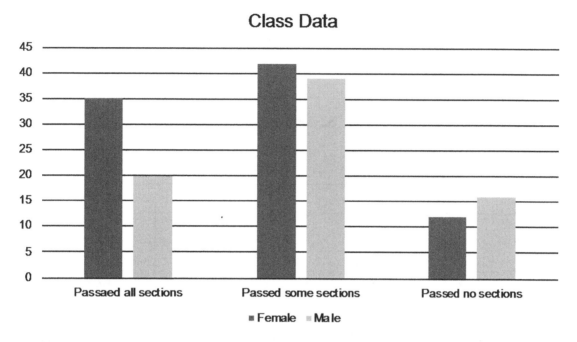

Class Data

■ Female ■ Male

20. What can Ms. Rodriguez assert based on the data above? Select all that apply.

   ❑ Female students, as a whole, had a harder time passing some sections of the exams than male students.

   ❑ Fewer males than females passed no sections on the exam.

   ❑ There was a bigger gap between student performance for those who passed all sections than between those who passed some sections.

   ❑ Male students outperformed female students 1:3 in passing all sections of the exam.

   ❑ Female students outperformed male students 2:1 in passing all sections.

21. Which of the following statements below is supported by the data?

   A. Even though females passed all sections of the exam at higher rates than males, more males than females passed some sections of the exam.

   B. More males than females scored a 200 on some sections of the exam.

   C. More females than males scored below a 200 on all sections of the exam.

   D. While more females than males passed all sections and some sections of the exam, more females than males took the exam.

   E. While more females than males passed all sections and some sections of the exam, more males than females took the exam.

Questions 22-23 refer to the following chart of data.

A local coffee company, Kind Koffee, sells regular coffee and fair-trade coffee for distribution within the US. Below is the data collected for the 3rd and 4th quarter of the year.

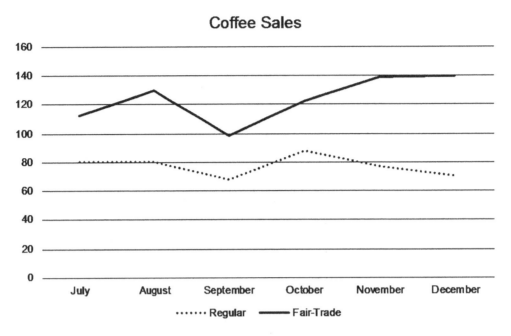

22. The biggest difference in the sales between fair-trade coffee and regular coffee happened in the month of:

    A. August

    B. September

    C. October

    D. November

    E. December

23. What can be inferred about the coffee business based on the data in the graph?

    A. Kind Koffee's best month for regular coffee was November.

    B. Kind Koffee's worst month for fair-trade coffee was July.

    C. Kind Koffee sold the least amount of regular coffee and fair-trade coffee in September.

    D. Kind Koffee sold the most fair-trade coffee and the least regular coffee in July.

    E. Kind Koffee's fair-trade coffee sales steadily declined in the months of July through September.

Question 24 refers to the following passage.

Adapted from *When Chocolate was Medicine* by Christine A. Jones.

In the seventeenth century, Europeans who had not traveled overseas tasted coffee, hot chocolate, and tea for the very first time. For this brand-new clientele, the brews of foreign beans and leaves carried within them the wonder and danger of far-away lands. They were classified at first not as food, but as drugs — pleasant-tasting, with recommended dosages prescribed by pharmacists and physicians, and dangerous when self-administered. As they warmed to the use and abuse of hot beverages, Europeans frequently experienced moral and physical confusion brought on by frothy pungency, unpredictable effects, and even (rumor had it) fatality.

24. Based on the information in the passage, how would the early Europeans most likely react to today's energy drinks?

   A. They would prohibit the consumption of energy drinks.

   B. They would over-indulge in the use of energy drinks.

   C. They would test the effects of energy drinks extensively before drinking.

   D. They would accept the energy drinks as a miracle potion.

   E. They would cautiously drink the energy drinks.

Question 25-26 refer to the following passage.

Adapted from The Complexity of Fear: Are you experiencing anxiety, or is it fear? by Mary C. Lamia, Ph.D.

You find a time machine and travel to 1920. A young Austrian artist and war veteran named Adolf Hitler is staying in the hotel room next to yours. The doors aren't locked, so you could easily stroll next door and smother him. World War II would never happen.

But Hitler hasn't done anything wrong yet. Is it acceptable to kill him to prevent World War II?

This is one moral dilemma researchers often use to analyze how people make difficult decisions. Most recently, one group analyzed answers from more than 6,000 subjects to compare men's and women's responses. They found men and women both calculate consequences such as lives lost. However, women are more likely to feel conflicted over what to do; having to commit murder is more likely to push them toward letting Hitler live.

"Women seem to be likely to have this negative, emotional, gut-level reaction to causing harm to people in the dilemmas, to the one person, whereas men were less likely to express this strong emotional reaction to harm," Rebecca Friesdorf, the lead author of the study, tells *Shots*. A master's student in social psychology at Wilfrid Laurier University in Waterloo, Ontario, Friesdorf analyzed 40 data sets from previous studies. The study was published Friday in the *Personality and Social Psychology Bulletin*.

25. Which of the following best summarizes the findings of the on male and female decision making?

    A. Both men and women think it's acceptable to kill Hitler to prevent World War II?

    B. Women are less capable than men to make hypothetical decisions.

    C. Women and men differ in their approaches to making moral decisions.

    D. Men are more likely to calculate consequences of the decision.

    E. Women will make decisions based on the easiest answer possible.

26. How is this passage organized?

    A. Second person narrative is used to convey a hypothetical situation, and the passage goes on to outline research related to that situation.

    B. First person narrative is used to convey a hypothetical situation, and the passage goes on to outline research related to that situation.

    C. A chronological account of a story is used in the first part of the passage, and the passage goes on to support that chronological account.

    D. Cause and effect are used to outline an issue in world history, and the passage goes on to describe that time in world history.

    E. A research study is introduced, and the passage goes on to outline important researcher's and their work in the study.

Questions 27-28 refer to the following passage.

From *The Forgotten Tales of the Brothers Grimm* by Jack Zipes

The greatest irony of the numerous world-wide celebrations held in 2012 to honor the 200th anniversary of the first edition of the Grimms' *Kinder-und Hausmärchen*, published in two volumes in 1812 and 1815, involves the discovery that most people really don't know the original Grimms' tales or much about their lives. That is, most people have no clue that the Grimms' first edition of 1812/15 is totally unlike the final or so-called definitive edition of 1857. The Grimm brothers published seven different editions from 1812 to 1857, and they made vast changes in the contents and style of their collections and also altered their concept of folk and fairy tales in the process. Even so-called scholars of German literature and experts of the Grimms' tales are not aware of how little most people, including themselves, know about the first edition, and ironically it is their and our "ignorance" that makes the rediscovery of the tales in the first edition so exciting and exhilarating. Indeed, there is still much to learn about the unique contribution that the Grimms made to folklore not only in Germany but also in Europe if we return to take a closer look at the first edition, for it was this edition that sparked the pioneer efforts of folklorists throughout Europe and Great Britain to gather tales from the oral tradition and preserve them for future generations.

27. According to the passage, all the following are true except

    A. The first edition of Grimms' *Kinder-und Hausmärchen* is quite dissimilar to later editions.

    B. Most people know very little about the lives of the Grimm brothers.

    C. The fact that people are unaware of the first edition makes its rediscovery uninteresting.

    D. The first edition inspired folklorists throughout both Germany and Great Britain.

    E. Even the experts of German literature do not understand how little society knows about the Grimm brothers and their first edition.

28. Which of the following statements is based on fact rather than an expression of opinion?

    A. Indeed, there is still much to learn about the unique contribution that the Grimms made to folklore.

    B. Even so-called scholars of German literature and experts of the Grimms' tales are not aware of how little most people, including themselves, know about the first edition.

    C. They published seven different editions from 1812 to 1857.

    D. it is their and our "ignorance" that makes the rediscovery of the tales in the first edition so exciting and exhilarating.

    E. The greatest irony of the numerous world-wide celebrations held in 2012 to honor the 200th anniversary of the first edition of the Grimms' *Kinder-und Hausmärchen* involves the discovery that most people really don't know the original Grimms' tales or much about their lives.

Questions 29-30 refer to the following passage.

From *Man's Violent Destiny and His Struggle Against the Natural Universe in McCarthy's Blood Meridian* by Justin Vibbert

The 19th century westward expansion of the American south can be identified as the inception point of southern Gothic literature. Cormac McCarthy's novel is a meticulously researched reimagining of these dark origins of the southwest expansion before the Civil War and the violence that accompanied that expansion. McCarthy examines a mélange of religious, mystical, and supernatural beliefs of the time period that are common themes found in much of southern Gothic literature. In the novel, the Glanton Gang operates as a microcosm of the ultra-violent nature of man. The gang is flanked by two extremes: the war-like wrath of the Judge and his universal—at times supernatural—knowledge of the men and world around him, and The Kid, who sits at the opposite edge of the spectrum, representing man's last chance: a child constantly wavering somewhere on the edge of good and evil.

29. Which of the following statements best summarizes the main idea of the passage?

    A. McCarthy's novel is responsible for the revival of southern Gothic literature.

    B. McCarthy's novel delves deep into the violent side of the southwest culture, beliefs, and customs during the 19th century westward expansion.

    C. In McCarthy's novel, he uses the Judge and the Kid to symbolize the constant fight between good and evil where he believes most people waver.

    D. McCarthy wrote his novel in order to exemplify the conflicting religious beliefs found within the unsettled southwestern portion of the country.

    E. Violent and supernatural themes, like the ones in McCarthy's novel, are common of southern Gothic literature.

30. The term mélange (as produced below) most likely means a(n):

    McCarthy examines a mélange of religious, mystical, and supernatural beliefs of the time period that are common themes found in much of Southern Gothic literature.

    A. long list

    B. depth of understand

    C. unit of measurement

    D. art form

    E. variety

Questions 31-35 refer to the following passage.

This Side of Paradise

F. Scott Fitzgerald

CODE OF THE YOUNG EGOTIST

Before he was summoned back to Lake Geneva, he had appeared, shy but inwardly glowing, in his first long trousers, set off by a purple accordion tie and a "Belmont" collar with the edges unassailably meeting, purple socks, and handkerchief with a purple border peeping from his breast pocket. But more than that, he had formulated his first philosophy, a code to live by, which, as near as it can be named, was a sort of aristocratic egotism.

He had realized that his best interests were bound up with those of a certain variant, changing person, whose label, in order that his past might always be identified with him, was Amory Blaine. Amory marked himself a fortunate youth, capable of infinite expansion for good or evil. He did not consider himself a "strong character," but relied on his facility (learn things sorta quick) and his superior mentality (read a lotta deep books). He was proud of the fact that he could never become a mechanical or scientific genius. From no other heights was he debarred.

Physically—Amory thought that he was exceedingly handsome. He was. He fancied himself an athlete of possibilities and a supple dancer.

Socially—here his condition was, perhaps, most dangerous. He granted himself personality, charm, magnetism, poise, the power of dominating all contemporary males, the gift of fascinating all women.

Mentally—complete, unquestioned superiority.

Now a confession will have to be made. Amory had rather a Puritan conscience. Not that he yielded to it—later in life he almost completely slew it—but at fifteen it made him consider himself a great deal worse than other boys... unscrupulousness... the desire to influence people in almost every way, even for evil... a certain coldness and lack of affection, amounting sometimes to cruelty... a shifting sense of honor... an unholy selfishness... a puzzled, furtive interest in everything concerning sex.

There was, also, a curious strain of weakness running crosswise through his make-up... a harsh phrase from the lips of an older boy (older boys usually detested him) was liable to sweep him off his poise into surly sensitiveness, or timid stupidity... he was a slave to his own moods and he felt that though he was capable of recklessness and audacity, he possessed neither courage, perseverance, nor self-respect.

Vanity, tempered with self-suspicion if not self-knowledge, a sense of people as automatons to his will, a desire to "pass" as many boys as possible and get to a vague top of the world... with this background did Amory drift into adolescence.

31. It can be inferred from the passage that the author most likely believes Amory Blaine is generally

    A. shy

    B. conceited

    C. trustworthy

    D. sad

    E. charming

32. Which of the following would strengthen the author's assessment of Amory Blaine's personality?

    A. Amory Blaine believed he could easily win the heart of the most beautiful woman in his town.

    B. Amory Blaine lived life as a hermit away from society.

    C. Amory Blaine did not attend school

    D. Amory Blaine hid his physique under heavy coats.

    E. Amory Blaine became extremely nervous when he socialized with his superiors.

33. According to the author, the only time that Amory Blaine displayed self-doubt was during which of the following social interactions?

    A. with family

    B. with females

    C. with older boys.

    D. with church clergy

    E. with teachers

34. The passage above suggests that Amory Blaine would have agreed with which of the following statements?

    A. Some of the brightest people today are found within the Science Department of the local state university.

    B. Puritan beliefs are far more accurate than the non-secular beliefs among many young people in modern days.

    C. All humans are created equal.

    D. Success is achieved through the survival of the fittest.

    E. Intelligence is acquired through learned skills and trades.

35. Which of the following conclusions is best supported by the passage?

    A. Amory Blaine's adopted code to live by earned him many admirers.

    B. Amory Blaine's overall intelligence and physical appearance was something that most young men continue to strive for even to this day.

    C. Amory Blaine's transition from childhood was marked by uncomfortable situations.

    D. Amory Blaine was, above all, egotistical in his opinion of himself.

    E. Amory Blaine remained stuck in his childhood fantasies for many years into his young adult life.

Questions 36-37 refer to the following passage.

This Side of Paradise

F. Scott Fitzgerald

The time is February. The place is a large, dainty bedroom in the Connage house on Sixty-eighth Street, New York. A girl's room: pink walls and curtains and a pink bedspread on a cream-colored bed. Pink and cream are the motifs of the room, but the only article of furniture in full view is a luxurious dressing-table with a glass top and a three-sided mirror. On the walls there is an expensive print of "Cherry Ripe," a few polite dogs by Landseer, and the "King of the Black Isles," by Maxfield Parrish.

Great disorder consisting of the following items: (1) seven or eight empty cardboard boxes, with tissue-paper tongues hanging panting from their mouths; (2) an assortment of street dresses mingled with their sisters of the evening, all upon the table, all evidently new; (3) a roll of tulle, which has lost its dignity and wound itself tortuously around everything in sight, and (4) upon the two small chairs, a collection of lingerie that beggars description. One would enjoy seeing the bill called forth by the finery displayed and one is possessed by a desire to see the princess for whose benefit—Look! There's some one! Disappointment! This is only a maid hunting for something—she lifts a heap from a chair—Not there; another heap, the dressing-table, the chiffonier drawers. She brings to light several beautiful chemises and an amazing pajama but this does not satisfy her—she goes out.

36. Which of the following best describes the organization of the passage?

  A. The first paragraph offers a general description of a typical young woman's room of the time period, while the second paragraph analyzes specific features that gives the reader clues about the young woman's recent activities.

  B. The first paragraph sets the scene for the piece, while the second paragraph offers supporting details to the argument presented.

  C. The first paragraph makes a general observation, while the second paragraph criticizes the clothes of the era.

  D. The first paragraph offers a general description of setting, while the second paragraph provides a specific observation of the young woman.

  E. The first paragraph provides a description of the room in general, while the second paragraph focuses only on the dresses she wears.

37. Which of the following can be inferred based on the description of the bedroom from the passage? Select all that apply.

  ❑ The recent occupant was disorganized and messy, throwing things about the room.

  ❑ The author is hiding somewhere in the room and assessing his surroundings.

  ❑ The state of the room suggests that a young woman was recently getting ready for an important social function.

  ❑ The maid was angry when she couldn't find what she was looking for and stormed out of the room.

  ❑ The author was implying that the recent occupant was promiscuous by mentioning the street dresses and lingerie found in the messy room.

Questions 38-41 refer to the following passage.

Adapted from *The Harp* from The Irish Penny Journal Vol. 1 No. 2 July 11, 1840

The harp was the favorite musical instrument, not only of the Irish, but of the Britons and other northern nations, during the middle ages, as is evident from their laws, and from every passage in their history in which there is the least allusion to music. By the laws of Wales, the possession of a harp was one of the three things that were necessary to constitute a gentleman, that is, a freeman; and no person could pretend to that title, unless he had one of those favorite instruments, and could play upon it.

In the same laws, to prevent peasants from pretending to be gentlemen, it was expressly forbidden to teach or to permit them to play upon the harp; and none but the king, the king's musicians, and gentlemen, were allowed to have harps in their possession. A gentleman's harp was not liable to be seized for debt, because the want of it would have degraded him from his rank and reduced him to a peasant.

The harp was in no less estimation and universal use among the Saxons and Danes; those who played upon this instrument were declared gentlemen by law; their persons were esteemed inviolable and secured from injuries by very severe penalties; they were readily admitted into the highest company and treated with distinguished marks of respect wherever they appeared.

38. Which of the following statements best summarizes the main idea of the passage?

    A. Peasants of the time period wanted to learn to play the harp but were forbidden as the instrument was reserved for the authentic gentlemen.

    B. The harp, or music produced by the harp, was always mentioned in historical passages from the Middle Ages proving its importance at the time.

    C. The harp could not be taken by law from the owner as it would degrade the owner of his station in life.

    D. During the Middle Ages in many European countries, owning and knowing how to play a harp was a status symbol separating the upper-class gentlemen from the lower-class peasants.

    E. The reputation of the harp spread to other countries and continued to represent a distinction between classes.

39. During the Middle Ages, why were peasants prohibited from playing the harp?

    A. The king considered the peasants not capable of learning or appreciating the harp which represented the music of the upper-class.

    B. The lawmakers feared that peasants may learn to play the harp in order to gain status and pretend to be a gentleman.

    C. Only the king's men and the gentlemen were permitted the leisure time to enjoy the harp.

    D. The harp was reserved for upper-class functions only, making the talent of playing one useless for peasants.

    E. The king feared that peasants would ignore their work in order to enjoy the harp.

40. The passage above suggests that the members of nobility during the Middle Ages would agree with which of the following statements? Select all that apply.

❏ Peasants should be seen and not heard.

❏ Peasants are a nuisance to society.

❏ The harp is a symbol of socio-economic status and is reserved for upper-class members.

❏ The harp and music produced by the harp should be respected by all members of society.

❏ The harp is a complicated instrument that could not possibly be mastered by the peasants.

41. What does the term inviolable (reproduced below) mean?

*Their persons were esteemed **inviolable** and secured from injuries by very severe penalties.*

A. reprehensible

B. unbreakable

C. disgraceful

D. scrupulous

E. intelligent.

Questions 42-43 refer to the following passage.

From *The New York Writer* by Justin Vibbert

I bought my first laptop (a used Mac-Book, for which I remember paying five-hundred dollars; it seemed like—and still does—a lot of money for a used computer, but I've still got it, a decade-plus later, and it still works fine) and with the money I had left over I made a down payment on a small basement apartment on the corner of Third Street and Thompson. I had few clothes, few dollars, and many books. Most days were spent in the bar across Third Street, writing and drinking in the same leather and mahogany booths that once sheltered Fitzgerald, Zelda, Thompson, and Mamet. Looking back, I think I can safely say I successfully emulated the life of a New York writer.

42. Based on the passage, the author feels that life as a New York writer is which of the following?

A. The author believes the lifestyle can be lucrative with time.

B. The author believes that writing in New York is only enjoyable when making money.

C. The author believes the lifestyle is agonizing because the writer is not making money.

D. The author believes that writing in New York can be prosperous whether one has a new computer or not.

E. The author believes that the life of a New York writer is one with few possessions but enjoyable experiences.

43. Which of the following statements, taken from the passage, is most clearly an expression of opinion rather that fact?

A. I had few clothes, few dollars, and many books.

B. Most days were spent in the bar across third street, writing and drinking in the same leather and mahogany booths that once sheltered Fitzgerald, Zelda, Thompson, and Mamet.

C. I successfully emulated the life of a New York Writer.

D. I bought my first laptop (a used Mac-Book, for which I remember paying five-hundred dollars.

E. With the money I had left over I made a down payment on a small basement apartment on the corner of Third Street and Thompson.

Questions 44-48 refer to the following passage.

NavaED Original Work by Justin Vibbert

Passage 1

You—the writer, director, actor—enter the building from the back alley where a solid steel door materializes out of a canyon of brick. The patrons—the paying customer—are corralled under a brightly lit façade advertising the name of this *thing* you've toiled over for months and they will, probably, forget about before the end of their subway ride home. However, you understand it's the journey, not the destination, where your reward lies in the *doing*. Because once you walk through that ominous steel door, through dark hallways, tiny dressing rooms, past trays of inedible food, cold coffee and warm beer, you and your feelings no longer matter: the ticket holder must be entertained, or you have failed.

Passage 2

What is a theatre production's responsibility to the audience? In short, it has none. In the theatre the artistic integrity of a written, directed, and rehearsed piece must not be affected by the emotional, critical, or political response of the mass audience. The optimal result of a theatre going experience is to leave the theatre ravaged: by fear, guilt, joy, shock, love, or some combination. For good or ill, that result is subjective and should be of no concern to the artists.

44. The main purpose of both passage 1 and 2 is to which of the following?

    A. To determine amount of work that is needed to create a successful theatre production

    B. To argue that the effect the production has on the audience determines the success of the show

    C. To determine the best results for a theater production

    D. To debate the artist's responsibility to entertain the audience

    E. To argue that the success of a theater production is based on artwork and not the audience reaction

45. Which of the following best describes the organization of both passages?

    A. An observation is made, and both paragraphs uses evidence to support that observation.

    B. Each paragraph compares the same topic with each reaching a different conclusion.

    C. A generalization is made followed by specific examples.

    D. A specific example is made followed by generalized conclusions.

    E. The passage offers and idea and then refutes it.

46. In passage 1, the author's position on the topic is which of the following?

    A. Both the artist and the audience will feel many of the same emotions during the production.

    B. The producer's work is done once the curtain goes up.

    C. The audience's reaction to the production should not reflect onto the artist.

    D. If the audience is not entertained, then the artist has not created a successful production.

    E. The audience does not truly appreciate the time and work needed to create a theatre production.

47. According to passage 2, which argument is used to support the idea that the theatre has no responsibility to the audience's opinion about the production?

   A. The audience does not have expert knowledge of the artistic elements of the production.

   B. The audience places too much emphasis on the emotional impact of the production.

   C. The theater continues to sell tickets regardless of the audience's reaction.

   D. The audience's reaction should not be taken seriously as theater goers only wished to be entertained.

   E. The audience's judgement is simply an opinion that is not reflective of the artistic production.

48. Given the information in both passages, which of the following could be concluded about theater production?

   A. There is a debate concerning the artist's role in entertaining the audience.

   B. Artists feel pressure to create a production that brings about an emotional reaction from the audience.

   C. Theater goers judge a production based upon artistic style instead of emotional plots.

   D. Regardless of audience opinion, most theater productions are considered to be artistic.

   E. Most theater critics believe that the producer should be concerned with audience's reaction to the production.

Questions 49-50 refer to the following passage.

NavaED Original Work by Justin Vibbert

Playwright Gertrude Stein (1874-1946) stands as a major avant-garde influence primarily for her experimentation with language. Stein moved to Paris is in 1903 and would eventually become closely associated with several modernist painters such as Picasso, Matisse, George Braque, and Cezanne, sharing with them an interest in abstraction. In particular, Picasso's Cubism and Cezanne's ideas about movement in painting influenced Stein, who subsequently developed a theory of landscape theater based on ideas she had loosely adapted from the visual arts.

49. Which of the following assumptions is most likely made by the author of the passage?

   A. Gertrude Stein understood the artistic styling of many of the modernist and abstract painters.

   B. Gertrude Stein was fortunate to live near some of the famous painters of the time.

   C. Gertrude Stein copied the artistic styling of many famous painters in her work.

   D. Gertrude Stein was criticized for her work that was influenced by the painters.

   E. Gertrude Stein bought several of Picasso's paintings to use for inspiration.

50. What does the term loosely (reproduced below) mean?

   She had subsequently developed a theory of landscape theater based on ideas she had loosely adapted from the visual arts.

   A. ill-fitting, not tight

   B. falling apart

   C. unsuccessful, but accepted

   D. close, but not exactly

   E. barely noticeable

Questions 51-54 refer to the following passage.

From *Barbershop* by Justin Vibbert

My father once warned me that I should never ask a man what he does for a living upon meeting him. Eventually, I came to understand that what he meant by that was that I should never ask a question that would give me reason to judge a person without knowing them. To ask a stranger what he does for a living is tantamount to asking: *How much money do you have? How educated are you? How do you compare to me?*

I thought about this and my father as I crossed Third Avenue heading west on 27th street. My barber, Boris, opened the shop three years ago. The shop was no bigger than a small studio apartment with three barber chairs—the old school kind with big chrome peddles and chrome handle that the barbers would work back and forth to adjust each patron to the desired height. Several TV's graced the wall, usually showing a variety of international soccer games, the teams and pronunciation of the players' names mysterious to me having been raised on American football, being broadcast on some esoteric satellite network. In the corner he had a small college-boy refrigerator—the type that tempted me as a small child in high-end hotel rooms—that they kept stocked with European beer and a strange homemade whiskey that had been made by Boris' father back in Kazakhstan.

Boris' shop is an ethnic, religious, and socioeconomic, melting pot. The conversation is the conversation of men, as women did not often, I'd imagine not ever, frequent the shop. Which means the conversation typically revolved around, of course, *women*. Conversations left unfinished from the last haircut continued as if there were no two-week interruption. Men smoked cigars and made prop bets on whatever game was on at the time. They talked about guns, the pros and cons of Israeli vs. American pistols. No one discussed money, or socio-economic status, and if anyone in the shop had an abundance of either one, I didn't know about it.

51. What is the overall structure of the passage?

    A. A claim is made in the beginning that asking someone how much they make can be intrusive, and that claim is refuted by the end of the passage.

    B. An institution is described in the beginning of the passage, and examples of that institution are listed in the following paragraphs of the passage.

    C. An anecdote is mentioned in the beginning of the passages, and eventually a connection is made from what is said at the beginning to what is experienced in the barbershop.

    D. The passage is a chronological account of a young boy's experience with his father growing up going to the barbershop.

    E. The passage uses cause and effect to demonstrate the pitfalls of asking someone personal questions about money.

52. Based on the description of interaction within the barbershop, which of the following would most likely not be a topic of discussion on a typical day?

    A. The new shorter style of dresses worn by women in the neighborhood.

    B. The predicted outcome of an upcoming sports game.

    C. The best gun to use for protection.

    D. The unequal pay among ethnic groups in the community.

    E. The latest cigars on the market.

53. Which of the following, if true, would weaken the argument that the barbershop was free of discussion of tension-filled topics?

    A. Men of diverse ethnic groups favored the barbershop.

    B. Occasionally, a fistfight would erupt in the barbershop as one man insulted another's heritage.

    C. A sign on the wall stated that "all men are created equal."

    D. A famous Italian movie star patronized the barbershop.

    E. Music from all over the world was shared periodically on the shop's record player.

54. The author's attitude toward the interactions in the barbershop can be described as which of the following?

    A. disapproving

    B. confused

    C. concerned

    D. tormented

    E. intrigued

Questions 55-56 refer to the following diagram.

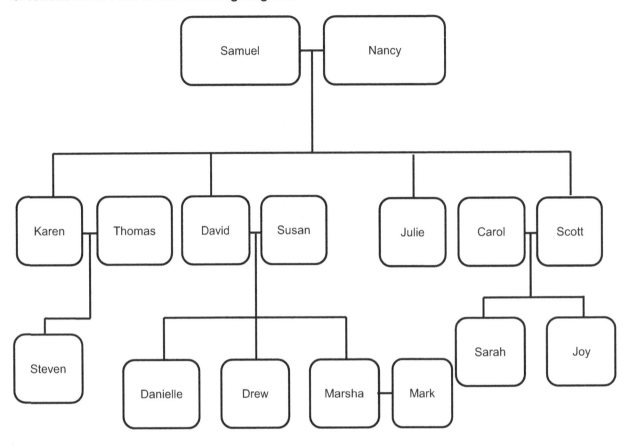

55. How many grandchildren do Samuel and Nancy have?

    A. 4

    B. 5

    C. 6

    D. 7

    E. 8

56. How many of Samuel and Nancy's children had children of their own?

    A. 3

    B. 4

    C. 5

    D. 6

    E. 7

Number	Answer	Content Category	Explanation
1.	B	I	This question requires you to understand the implied main idea of the passage. In this case, the author is looking back at a time when he believed he could go anywhere in the world. He stated that he had "amazing audacity and assurance, which are no longer in my character now." This leads to the idea that he misses this in his present adulthood age.
2.	C	I	This is an inference question that asks you to conclude information about the author from stated facts within the passage. In this case, the author states that, "when nine years old" at the beginning of the passage. Toward the end he states that this is "no longer my character now," which alerts the reader time has passed and the narrator has changed. He also uses the terms assurance and audacity favorably as he looks back at himself.
3.	B	II	This description of the new computer lab was most likely written for a newspaper. Because it mentions the computer lab, air-conditioner unit, and security check, construction project is the best subject here. If the article was written for choices A or D, it would have more of a positive tone. Choice E, a brochure, would not have any detectable tone, and this clearly does have a humorous tone to it. Choice C seems to be a good choice, but the article only focuses on the lab at the campus verses the author's overall experience.
4.	Choices 2 and 3	II	The author is using the word moat both sarcastically and humorously to describe how difficult it is do enter the building. It does not seem that the writer is angered; anger is too strong of a word here, so box 1 is out. Persuasion and cause and effect are not relevant here, so box 4 and 5 are out.
5.	B	II	This question is asking you to determine the central point of passage. Choice A is incorrect because the passage does not celebrate the author's accomplishments. Choice E is incorrect because the passage does not describe the author's characteristics or his niche. Choices C and D have nothing to do with the passage. However, the passage details, in order (chronological), the milestones throughout Hunter Thompson's life, making B the best answer.
6.	E	III	This question is asking you to assume information that is not specifically stated within the passage. We can gather clues about Thompson's feelings toward working at the newspapers. Phrases such as "ended in disaster" and "he endured" alert the reader that Thompson did not enjoy his early work. The last sentence, however, states that his freelancing work "quickly evolved into a compulsion," suggesting he could not resist this type of writing.

Number	Answer	Content Category	Explanation
7.	E	II	Subsidize means to finance or to provide funding. In this case, CUNY began to charge tuition to help *finance* the city which was sinking in debt. There is not a promise to replace, reduce, increase the revenue as choices A-C suggest. There is only mention of offering financial funding or subsidizing the city with tuition money.
8.	D	I	By adding this statement, the author could further strengthen the issue that *faculty* membership has been reduced because most of CUNY classes are being taught online, which reduces the need for full-time faculty. Choices A, B, C, and E do not offer any additional information about faculty population, making D the best choice for support.
9.	A	I	This question asks you to decide which statement the author would agree with based on the information in the passage. Choices B-E are specific facts that we cannot determine based on information given. However, choice A offers a general observation that is supported throughout the passage.
10.	C	II	Bucolic means rural. The artistic movement discussed was opposed to anything old and bucolic (rural); whereas, the movement praised anything from modern times and city life.
11.	D	I	This question asks you to determine the author's purpose for writing this article. Although the author does not specifically state this, it can be inferred based on the tone of writing and information provided within the text—Mayakosovsky was imprisoned, and he was one of the most visible members of the movement. Also, the first word on each answer choice— exploit, explain, persuade, outline, present—offers additional clues for determining the correct answer. In this case the author is outlining or presenting, so choices A, B, and C are not the best answers. This is not a cautionary tale of going against the status quo, leaving E out. Therefore, choice D is the best answer here.
12.	A	III	Because we have learned from the passage that Mayakosky was a *Futurist*, we can conclude that his works would embrace this model as well. Thus, choices B-E represent choices that include old-fashioned and/or past events.
13.	Choices 2 and 4	III	All choices suggest that Republicans and democrats are concerned with the environment to some degree. However, choice 1 suggests that the Republicans are ambivalent— unsure—about the subject, which is untrue according to Passage 1. Choice 3 suggests Republicans have implemented strict environmental policies, which was not mentioned in either passage. Choice 5 implies that Republicans and democrats will never agree on environmental policy, which is not true according to passage 2. Choices 2 and 4 are the best answers because they outline that both parties are concerned and that both parties should put political differences aside to solve environmental problems. This is addressed in the last lines of both passages.

Number	Answer	Content Category	Explanation
14.	A	III	By analyzing context clues within the statement, we can infer that Republicans are viewed as indifferent to the topic. *Indifferent* means unconcerned. The author states that she is "often met with surprise" when people learn about her concern in environmentalism. This suggests people believe Republicans do not care about the environment because they are surprised to learn the author, a Republican, does care. According to the line and passage, the author states people believe Republicans are not concerned, leaving choice A out. The words indignant, overwhelmed, and anxious are not appropriate words for the way Republicans may feel about the environment; therefore, choices C, D and E are out.
15.	D	II	Assuage means to mitigate or makes less severe. The author states that Republicans acknowledge that reducing carbon emissions will assuage, or lessen, the problem. All other choices—*exacerbate, embellish, intensify, and hasten*—suggest that it will speed up or add to the problem
16.	B	III	While both passages suggest that Republicans are concerned with the issue, only passage 1 has support for that claim by saying economic and national security are important issues for the GOP, and national and economic security are directly impacted by climate change. The terms national and economic security provide the support for the claim that Republicans do, in fact, care about the environment. Choice A simply states that people think Republicans do not care about the environment. Choice C from passage 2 only states that most people think Republicans do not care about the environment. Choice D references a survey outlining Republicans do believe climate change is happening, but it does not address that Republicans *care* about the environment.
17.	A	I	Choice A restates the main idea. While finches are the most common animal associated with Darwin's theory, he also looked at other animals like polar bears. This is the main point of the entire passage. Choices B-E are supporting ideas of the passage and too specific to be the main idea or central theme.
18.	B	II	Sometimes an author will use quotes to set-off something that is interesting or anecdotal to a word. In this case, the author wants you to know that these "finches" were more like mockingbirds than they were finches. Therefore, B is the best answer choice here. Choice A focuses on Darwin's research rather than the word finches. Choice C connects the quotes to the Galapagos Islands rather than the finches. Choices D and E do not happen in the text.
19.	C	I	The curious tone of this passage is captured in the author's description of the polar bear observation which showcases Darwin's own curiosity in the animal.

Number	Answer	Content Category	Explanation
20.	Choice 3	III	Box 3 is the only correct choice. The other choices are not factual when reviewing the data chart. The last box is tempting because females did outperform males. However, for the females to outperform the males, the female bar would have to hit 40—40:20, or 4:2, or reduced to 2:1.
21.	D	III	By using the numbers on the y axis, you can determine the number of boys and girls who took the exam. For females, approximately 35 passed all sections, 42 passed some sections, and 12 passed no sections—approximately 89 females took the exam. For males, approximately 20 passed all sections, 39 passed some sections, 16 passed no sections—approximately 75 males took the exam. This makes answer choice D the correct answer. Choice E is the opposite of D, which is incorrect. Choices A-C are also incorrect based on the chart.
22.	E	III	The difference in sales between free-trade and regular coffee can easily be determined by looking for the largest gap between the two lines and calculating the differences between the two. In this case, August and December have the biggest gaps among all the other months. However, if you look closely, you will see that both December's gap is bigger than August's gap, leaving choice E as the best answer.
23.	C	III	By viewing the yearly sales chart, we can see that both types of coffee were at lowest amount sold in September. The other choices are incorrect based on the data.
24.	E	I	This question is asking you to predict what would most likely occur in another situation not mentioned in the passage. In this passage, we learn that early European enjoyed new foreign drinks, but they also had some reservations. Thus, if they were introduced to a modern-day energy drink, they would most likely consume it with some concerns in mind.
25.	C	I	This question asks you to determine the overall point or main idea of the passage. Choices A and D are supporting ideas. Choice B and E are never stated or implied in the passage. Choice C is the main idea of the entire passage.
26.	A	I	The first word in the passage is **You**; therefore, second person narrative is used. Also, the beginning of the passage is hypothetical because it talks about a fake situation where you can kill Hitler and prevent WWII. Finally, the passage goes on to introduce a study that pertains to the hypothetical solution of whether or not to kill Hitler.
27.	C	II	This question reviews several supporting details within the passage. Choices A, B, D & E are all specifically stated. However, choice C changes the word *interesting* to *uninteresting* which is untrue according to the passage.

Number	Answer	Content Category	Explanation
28.	C	II	Choice C is the only statement that is a fact, or something that could be verified. The other choices represent the opinion of the author. Although his opinion may be accurate, it is based on his personal judgement of society's knowledge of the Grimm Brothers.
29.	B	I	For this question, you are asked to determine the main idea of the passage. Choice A, C, D, & E are all supporting ideas used to strengthen the overall point. Choice B is a general statement that includes all the elements in the passage.
30.	E	II	The term *mélange* means a variety. There were several types and varieties of beliefs during the time period when McCarthy studied the culture. Choices B, C, D do not make sense. Choice A is close, but E is exact.
31.	B	I	Based on Fitzgerald's description of Amory Blaine, we can infer that the author felt the character was conceited. He states that Blaine thought himself "exceedingly handsome," "fancied himself and athlete," "granted himself charm and magnetism, "and thought himself to have "complete, superiority" in mental capabilities.
32.	A	III	Because we know that Blaine was conceited, he would most likely feel he could win the heart of most women. Choices B-E suggest characteristics that are of someone with low self-esteem.
33.	C	I	A supporting idea of the passage is that the only time Blaine felt any insecurities was when the older boys made comments about him. We can infer then, that he remained confident in other social situations mentioned in choices A, B. D, and E.
34.	D	III	This question asks you to determine the results of a hypothetical event based on information gleamed from the passage. Choices A, B, and E can be refuted by analyzing the personality descriptions listed in the writing. Choice C can be inferred as the wrong choice because we know that Amory felt he was superior over other humans, so they could not all be created equal. He would most likely agree with the survival of the fittest notion as he felt he could excel amongst his peers as he believed he was the most fit in mental, social, and physical capacities.
35.	D	I	Based on the reading, we can conclude that Blaine was quite egotistical—it's even in the title of the piece. Choice A and B suggest that people admired his conceited behavior. Choices C and E are not mentioned or implied in the passage, making D the best choice.

Number	Answer	Content Category	Explanation
36.	A	II	The organization of the passage is one that offers a description of the room in both paragraphs but closely examines the disarray in the second paragraph, alerting the reader to clues about the occupant's recent activity. Choice B may seem like a good choice as well, yet it is incorrect as there is not an argument made in this piece. Choice C, D, E contradict the description of the passage.
37.	Choices 1, 2, and 3	I	The author is assessing the room, noticing different details, and we can assume he is hiding because the maid comes in and does not see him. We can also infer from the way the clothing and boxes were scattered about, that the occupant was messy and was probably getting ready for a social event. Choices D and E are out because while the maid came in to find something, she was not angry when she couldn't find it, and while lingerie was mentioned, it was not mentioned in a way that the author was implying promiscuity.
38.	D	I	This question asks you to determine the main idea of the entire passage. Choice A, B, C, and E are mentioned in the passage but are specific details.
39.	B	I	This question asks you to review a specific supporting idea. Choice B restates the supporting idea that the king did not want peasants pretending to be gentlemen by playing the harp. The other choices are not stated or implied in the passage.
40.	Choices 1, 3, and 4	III	Members of nobility would most likely agree that peasants should not be heard in that they did not want them playing the harp, making box 1 correct. Also, throughout the entire passage, the harp is regarded as a status symbol and that the harp should be respected as a status symbol, making box 3 and 4 correct. The other two statements, choices 2 and 5, are most likely not true as we know that peasants, although not respected, were useful to society and the king for labor purposes. Likewise, peasants were not considered too unintelligent to play the harp, as the king clearly feared they could play it and pretend to be noblemen.
41.	B	II	*Inviolable* means unchallengeable or unbreakable. The words that follow *inviolable* are *secured from injuries by very severe penalties*, which reinforces they were unbreakable, choice B. Reprehensible and disgraceful are negative words and do not fit here. Scrupulous means meticulous or thorough, which also does not fit here. Intelligent is a favorable word, but unbreakable is better here.
42.	E	I	This question asks you to determine the author's attitude. In the passage it states the author had, "few cloths, few dollars and many books." However, he enjoys writing and drinking. Choices A & D are not mentioned in the passage. Choice E states the dominant point and thought of the passage.

Number	Answer	Content Category	Explanation
43.	C	II	The author is of the opinion that he successfully emulated the lifestyle. Whether true or not, it is still an opinion. The other choices represent statements, facts, that could be verified, or judged based on concrete evidence.
44.	D	III	Be careful; the question asks you to draw from **both** passages. Both passages are debating the role the artist holds in entertaining the audience. Choice A and C talk about the amount of work in and results of a production, and those are not applicable here. Choice B may seem like a good choice; however, it matches the argument proposed only in passage 1. Likewise, choice E is stating only the issue for passage 2. Choice D, on the other hand, encompasses the main idea for both passages.
45.	B	II	For this question, you are asked to determine the organization of the entire passage. Choices A and E are incorrect because neither try to disprove or refute a statement previously mentioned in the passage. Choices C and D are wrong because both passages are written as generalizations. Choice B is the best answer because both passages are talking about the same thing but coming to different conclusions—that the artist *is responsible* for the audience's reaction, and that the artist *is not responsible* for the audience's reaction.
46.	D	I	This question asks you to determine the main argument from passage 1. Choice A is referring to information about both passages. Choice B & C are the main ideas for passage 2. Choice E is not mentioned in the passage.
47.	E	I	This question asks you to determine which statement is a supporting idea of the argument in Passage 2. Although A-D may be implied, the most accurate choice is E, as it is stated explicitly in the passage.
48.	A	III	For this question you are asked to determine the overall conclusion that can be gleamed from the information provided through **both passages together**. In this case, we can deduce that there is a debate in the theater field as to the role of the artist in entertaining the audience because in passage 1, the responsibility in entertaining the audience is the producer of the play. In passage 2, the responsibility is on the theater goer.
49.	A	I	For assumption questions, you are asked to determine unstated ideas or facts that the author accepts as true. The author, in this case, assumes that Gertrude Stein was able to understand the meanings behind the famous paintings as she continued the ideas in her own work. Choice C may seem like a good answer, but the author states that she was influenced by the painters, not that she directly copied them.
50.	D	II	The term loosely in this context means closely. Stein was able to closely mimic ideas she learned though visual arts. Choice E seems like a good choice as well but would not make sense within the sentence.

Number	Answer	Content Category	Explanation
51.	C	II	This question asks you to look at the overall structure of the paragraphs. In this case, the author mentions the advice his dad gave him about not asking another person something that would give the author reason to judge another person—money, socioeconomic status, etc. Then at the end of the passage, the author observes how these men in the barbershop never brought up such topics.
52.	D	II	For this question, you are asked to predict something about the characters or events that is *not* mentioned in the passage. Choices A, B, C, & E are all topics that were mentioned through examples. Choice D is the best choice because it is implied that the men in the barbershop avoid the subject of money amongst ethnic groups.
53.	B	III	This question requires you to understand the main idea of the passage, and then determine which statement would weaken the main point. In this case, a fistfight in the barbershop would discredit the main idea that it was a place free of tension. The other choices would all strengthen the argument.
54.	E	II	The author writes about interactions in a neutral tone, but it is obvious he is curious about the unusual occurrences for the time at the barbershop. Choices A-D lean toward a negative attitude, which is not evident based on the passage.
55.	C	III	Be careful here. Samuel and Nancy's grandchildren are Steven, Danielle, Drew, Marsha, Sarah and Joy. Marsha is married to Mark. However, Mark is not one of Samuel and Nancy's grandchildren.
56.	A	III	Samuel and Nancy had 4 children: Karen, David, Julie, and Scott. All had children except for Julie. Therefore, **3** of Samuel and Nancy's kids had children of their own.

Copyright - NavaED   52   October 2019

References

Brinkley, D. (2000). The art of journalism: An interview with Hunter S. Thomson. *The Paris review (156).*

Butcher, D. (2018). Young conservatives like me care about climate change. The GOP needs to take notice. *Vox*

Conrad. J. (1899). Heart of darkness. *Project Guttenberg.* Retrieved from https://www.gutenberg.org/files/219/219-h/219-h.htm

Engelhard, M. (n.d.). Darwin's polar bear. *The Public Domain.* Retrieved from https://publicdomainreview.org/2018/02/21/darwins-polar-bear/

Fitzgerald, S. (1920). *This side of paradise.* Charles Scribner's Sons.

Jones, C. A. (n.d.). When chocolate was medicine. *The Public Domain.* Retrieved from https://publicdomainreview.org/2015/01/28/when-chocolate-was-medicine-colmenero-wadsworth-and-dufour/

Lamia, M., C. (2011). The complexity of fear: Are you experiencing anxiety, or is it fear? *CommonLit.* Retrieved from https://www.commonlit.org/en/texts/the-complexity-of-fear

The Public Domain. (1840). The harp. *The Irish Penny Journal* (1) 2.

Van Boven, L., Sherman, D. (2018). Actually, republicans do believe in climate change. *The New York Times: Opinion – Gray Matter.*

Vibbert, J. (2007). The New York writer.

Vibbert, J. (2013). The adjunctification of New York State Universities. *City and State.*

Vibbert, J. (2014). Man's violent destiny and his struggle against the natural universe in McCarthy's Blood Meridian.

Vibbert, J. (2015). Barbershop. *The New York University.*

Williams, S. (2002). *Free as in freedom: Richard Stallman's crusade for free software.* O'Reilly and Associates, Sebastopol.

Zipes, J. (n.d.) The forgotten tales of the Brothers Grimm. *The Public Domain.* Retrieved from https://publicdomainreview.org/2012/12/20/the-forgotten-tales-of-the-brothers-grimm/

This page is intentionally left blank.

PRAXIS® CORE ACADEMIC SKILLS FOR EDUCATORS: WRITING

This page is intentionally left blank.

The writing section of the Praxis® Core Writing subtest exam is divided into two parts:

1. Text Types Purposes and Production – This includes the essay task and some selected response.
2. Language and Research Skills for Writing – This is all selected response.

You will have 100 minutes total to complete the entire writing exam: a 40-minute selected response test and two 30-min essays.

There are two basic parts of the *Praxis*® Core Writing subtest exam:

3. **Grammar and Mechanics** – This part of the exam will test all the basic grammar and mechanics rules. This includes usage, sentence correction, revision in context, and research skills.
4. **Essays** – This part of the exam requires you to write 2 separate essays that are well organized and display proper grammar usage.

Quick Tip!

The essay and grammar are connected. So be sure to use all the grammar and mechanics rules that are outlined in the grammar portion of this book. All of the tips and tricks in the grammar part of the book will help you during the essay task.

For this exam, your essay scores and your selected response scores are combined.

Test at a Glance	
Test Name	Core Academic Skills for Educators: Writing
Test Code	5723
Time	100 minutes
Number of Questions	40 selected-response questions and 2 essays
Format	Selected response questions involving usage, sentence correction, revision in context, and research skills.
Test Delivery	Computer delivered

Content Categories	Approximate number of questions	Approximate percentage of the exam
I. Text Types, Purposes, and Production	6-12 selected response and 2 essays	60%
II. Craft, Structure, and Language Skills	28-34 selected response	40%

This page is intentionally left blank.

Grammatical Relationships - Recognize and Correct:

- Errors in the use of adjectives and adverbs

- Errors in noun-noun agreement

- Errors in pronoun antecedent agreement

- Errors in pronoun case

- Errors in interrogative and relative pronouns

- Errors in the use of intensive pronouns

- Errors in pronoun number and person

- Vague pronouns

- Errors in subject verb agreement

- Inappropriate shifts in verb tense

Adjectives & adverbs

Adjectives modify or describe nouns or pronouns. They are either attributive adjectives (before the noun) or predicate adjectives (after a verb of being):

EXAMPLE: The <u>brave</u> girl rescued her mom from the burning home. She is a hero.

In this case, the adjective—brave—is describing the noun –girl.

EXAMPLE: The girl is so <u>brave</u>. She looks <u>brave</u>, too.

In both cases, the adjective—brave—is describing the noun –girl.

Adverbs modify or describe **verbs**.

EXAMPLE: The girl bravely rescued her mom from the burning home. She acted heroically.

Many times, adding an *ly, ally* or *i + ly t*o an adjective, forms an adverb:

- brave + ly = bravely

    She **bravely walked** into battle.

- beautiful + ly = beautifully

    She **wrote** her name **beautifully** on the paper.

- gentle + ly = gently (drop the e)

    She **pets** the sick dog **gently** on the head.

- easy + i + ly = easily (drop the y and add the i to words that end in y)

    She **worked** through the math problems **easily**.

> **Think About it!**
>
> If you ever want to make an English teacher twitch, ask her to come **quick**, so you can show her something. Instead, ask her to come **quickly**, so you can show her you understand how to use adverbs correctly.

Of course, there are exceptions to the *ly* rule. Some adjectives and adverbs cannot be morphed by adding or taking away endings. Some examples are:

Adjectives	Adverbs
few, fewer	very, hardly
old, seldom	always, never, often, seldom(ly)*
many, much, more, most, less, almost	more, less, almost
no, any, every, all	not, never
good	well

*both forms are acceptable for the adverb

Common adjective-adverb combinations: notice that there are some common exceptions to the "-ly" pattern. Also notice the verb participle forms acting as adjectives.

Adjectives	Adverbs
good, great, fine	well, great, fine ("finely" has a different meaning)
fast, quick	fast, quickly
slow, deliberate, lethargic	slowly, deliberately, lethargically
tired	tiredly
needless	needlessly
sick, sickly	(sickly can be a verb or adj.; never an adverb)
super, superb	superbly
responsible	responsibly
drunk, drunken	drunkenly
near, far	nearly, far

Errors in noun-noun agreement

When looking through answer the grammar section on the *Praxis®* Core writing subtest exam, pay attention to noun-noun agreement. In other words, the number of nouns in the sentence should match throughout the sentence.

Incorrect

- The school counselors are looking over their students' academic **history** while making decisions on class placement.

In this case, there are several school counselors for several students. Those students do not share just one academic history. They each have their own academic history. Therefore, the sentence should read:

Correct

- The school counselors are looking over their students' academic **histories** while making decisions on class placement.

Noun-noun agreement can be tricky because these errors are difficult to spot. For example, the sentence below may seem correct; however, it contains a noun-noun agreement error. Slow down when you see the word **every**. **Every** is singular (we go over this in more detail later in the book).

Incorrect

- Every cat in the kennel had missing tails.
- It seemed like every girl at the party had ponytails.

When you see every cat in the kennel, you are seeing multiple cats with multiple tails. However, the sentence is saying, every one of the cats (singular) had a missing tail (singular). Therefore, the sentence should be corrected.

Correct

- Every cat in the kennel had a missing tail.
- It seemed like every girl at the party had a ponytail.

Sample Question:

Dentists should look over their patient's dental history before making suggestions for braces.

A. Dentists should look over their patient's dental history before making suggestions for braces.
B. Dentists should look over their patients dental history before making suggestions for braces
C. Dentists should look over their patients' dental history before making suggestions for braces.
D. Dentists should look over their patients dental histories before making suggestions for braces.
E. Dentists should look over their patients' dental histories before making suggestions for braces.

> **Take note!**
>
> The words *every*, *each*, and *any* represent a singular noun in the sentence. Every girl at the party is NOT all the girls at the party. Instead, every girl at the party means every single one of the girls at the party.
>
> Slow down when you see *every, each,* or *any* in the subject of a sentence on the test.

The correct answer is **E** for two reasons. First, there are multiple dentists with multiple patients. Therefore, the plural possessive noun—patients'—should be used. Second, the multiple patients have multiple dental histories—plural.

Remember, it always helps to look over your answer choices. When you do, you will see that the choice **histories** is an option. That will help you remember to think about your noun-noun agreement.

Pronoun/antecedent agreement

Just as subjects and verbs must agree, pronouns must agree with the noun they replace or the *antecedent*.

Here are some examples of pronoun antecedent **AGREEMENT**:

- My <u>mother</u> went to the store, and <u>she</u> bought some cookies from the bakery.

  The pronoun is **she,** and the antecedent is **mother**.

- Good <u>bosses</u> make sure <u>their</u> employees get a raise every year.

  The word **bosses** is plural; therefore, the plural pronoun—**their**—is correct.

- The <u>dog</u> barked constantly, so <u>its</u> owner put a shock collar on <u>it</u>.

  The pronoun **it** agrees with the antecedent **dog.** Also, **its** is the correct possessive pronoun to use here.

- The <u>team</u> lost so many of <u>its</u> games, the coach decided to quit.

  Even though there may be 10 people on a **team**, the **team** is *singular*. Therefore, **it** is the correct pronoun here. Beware of collective nouns; they can be tricky on the exam.

- The <u>board members</u> were tired, so <u>they</u> delayed the vote until the next meeting.

  There are multiple **board members**—plural. Therefore, the pronoun **they** is correct.

Here are some examples of pronoun antecedent **DISAGREEMENT**:

- The <u>university</u> had <u>their</u> annual gala to raise funds.

  While there may be thousands of people who are part of the university, university is a singular noun—a collective noun. In this case, the plural pronoun **their** does **NOT** agree with the singular antecedent **university**. **Their** should be replace with **it**.

- <u>Some</u> of the <u>marbles</u> rolled out of <u>its</u> bag.

  Some and marbles indicate this is a plural antecedent. Therefore, the proper pronoun is **their**.

- A <u>student</u> should go to <u>their</u> locker during lunch.

  This is a common error. Often people will use the pronoun **their** in singular situations like the one above. A student is singular. Therefore, a singular pronoun is needed here—**his or her**.

> ### Quick Tip!
>
> On most standardized English grammar exams, pronoun antecedent is assessed when the test taker has to identify the plural pronoun that is being used incorrectly. Because we often use their/they/them incorrectly in our everyday vernacular, sometimes these errors can be difficult to spot. Therefore, whenever you see the pronouns **they, their, or them**, slow down and make sure your subject or antecedent is *plural*. If it is singular, you need to use a singular pronoun.

Correction: <u>A student</u> should go to **his or her** locker during lunch. **His or her** in this case is a singular pronoun.

Better yet, change the subject to match the pronoun **their**. You will most likely have the opportunity to change the subject on the test. See below.

Correction: **Students** should go to **their** lockers before lunch.

*Also, notice the noun-noun agreement here—multiple students have multiple lockers.

Pronoun case

Just like nouns, pronouns have distinctive cases based upon sentence function: the subjective (occurring in the subject of the sentence), the objective (occurring in the predicate or after a prepositional phrase in a sentence), and the possessive (occurring when ownership is happening in the sentence).

Subject Pronouns usually occur in the subject in a sentence	Object Pronouns usually occur in the predicate (after the action verb) in a sentence	Possessive Pronouns show possession in a sentence
I – **I** went to the store. The pronoun **I** is the subject of the sentence.	**me** – Sally went to the store with **me.** The pronoun **me** is an object of the preposition **with**.	**my/mine** – I need to increase **my** grade-point average. That pencil is **mine**. **My/mine** is the possessive form of the noun me/I.
he/she – **She** went to the store. The pronoun **she** is the subject of the sentence. **He** is wearing a coat. The pronoun **he** is wearing a coat.	**him/her** – Sally went to the store for **him**. The pronoun **him** is an object of the preposition **for**. Mom gave **her** all the money. Her is the indirect object of the action verb gave.	**his/her/hers** – Mark needs to increase **his** GPA. The pronoun **his** is possessive for the GPA. **Her** car was parked outside. The pronoun **her** car was parked outside.
We – **We** went to the store. The pronoun **we** is the subject of the sentence.	**us** – Sally went to the store with **us**. The pronoun **us** is in the predicate of the sentence (after the action verb **went**).	**our/ours** – Sally and I need to increase **our** grade-point averages. The pronoun **our** is possessive. That big dog is **ours**. The pronoun **ours** follows the verb is acting a predicate adjective modifying dog.
They – **They** went to the store. The pronoun **they** is the subject of the sentence.	**them** – My brother went to the party with **them.** **Them** is in the predicate of the sentence (after the action verb **went**).	**their/theirs** – The cars in the parking lot are theirs. The pronoun **theirs** is the plural possessive because there are multiple cars belonging to multiple people.

What will it look like on the test?

Here are some common ways in which pronoun case is assessed on the exam. We almost always see examples like these on the test. They can be tricky because people often use pronoun case incorrectly in their everyday vernacular.

Sample Question:

Choose the portion of the sentence that needs to be corrected. If there is no error, choose E.

I was happy when the <u>president</u> of the <u>university</u> came to see my <u>bother</u> and <u>I</u> on Saturday. <u>No error.</u>
               A   B   C   D   E

The answer is **D**. In this case, the pronoun **I** is used incorrectly. **I** is a subject pronoun, and should *not* be used in the predicate like it is above. Instead, the pronoun **me** should be used.

When you see these problems, take out the other person in the sentence and see if the sentence reads correctly.

Correct - The president came to see **me**.

Incorrect - The president came to see **I**.

BE CAREFUL!

Sometimes we use **I** in the predicate even though it is a subjective pronoun. Look at the examples below and determine which one uses the underlined portion correctly.

> **Think about it!**
>
> Lots of people make this mistake in their speech. When we ask students to choose the correct answer in the example above, 9 out of 10 times they will choose *I* because they think that sounds grammatically correct. They will often say, **"Sally went to the store with Kim and I,"** or, **"She didn't want to offend John and I."** However, both are incorrect. *Me* is the correct pronoun because you would say, **"Sally went to the store with me,"** or, **"She didn't want to offend me."**

A. I was disappointed to see that my sister received a higher score on her math exam <u>than me</u>.
B. I was disappointed to see that my sister received a higher score on her math exam <u>than I</u>.

In this case, B is correct. I know what you're thinking. You're thinking me should be the correct answer because me is in the direct object. However, if you take this sentence out all the way, it should read:

√   I was disappointed to see that my sister received a higher score on her math exam <u>than I did</u>.
√   I was disappointed to see that my sister received a higher score on her math exam <u>than I received</u>.

> **Quick Tip!**
>
> When trying to determine what pronouns to use in the examples above, look at the surrounding words. Ask yourself:
>
> - Is this a comparison? Do I see the word **than**? If so, use **I**.
>   **She is taller than I. She is taller than I am.**
> - Is this a prepositional phrase? Do I see the word **to** or **with**? If so use **me**.
>   The president came **to** see my son and **me**.
>   Sally came **with** Kim and **me**.
>
> And of course, you can always take the sentence out fully—taller than I am—or take the extra person out of the sentence—Sally came with **me**.

Intensive & reflexive pronouns

Intensive pronouns are pronouns ending in *self* or *selves* and are used to add emphasis to the subject or antecedent of the sentence. You'll often find the intensive pronoun right after the noun or pronoun it's modifying, but not all the time. Remember this is English, and English doesn't always follow the rules.

Intensive pronouns intensify the noun in the sentence.

Example

• The CEO **herself** came down to work on the factory floor.

The purpose of this sentence is to emphasize the CEO came down to work on the factory floor.
The word *herself* intensifies the *CEO*.

Example

• The teachers themselves were overwhelmed with the education changes.

Again, the term *themselves* intensifies the word *teachers*.

Reflexive pronouns are pronouns ending in *self* or *selves* and reflect back upon the subject of the sentence.

Intensive pronouns are not used to intensive anything. They just refer back to the antecedent of the sentence.

Example

• The CEO believed in <u>herself</u> to make the right decision about the merger.

The purpose of the pronoun is just to refer back to who the sentence is about.

Example

• The teachers needed to prepare <u>themselves</u> for a challenging year ahead.

The purpose of the reflexive pronoun here is to refer back to the teachers.

Quick Tip!

To figure out if the pronoun is intensive or reflexive, remove it from the sentence.
If it still makes sense without it, it is an intensive pronoun.

√   The CEO ~~herself~~ came down to work on the factory floor.
×   The CEO believed in ~~herself~~ to make the right decision about the merger.

Avoid improper use of intensive and reflexive pronouns. You will most likely see it like this on the exam:

If you have any questions, please do not hesitate to <u>contact my colleague or myself</u>.

A.   contact my colleague or myself.

B.   contact my colleague or I.

C.   contact my colleague or my.

D.   contact my colleague or me.

E.   contact my colleague and myself.

Quick Tip!

The correct answer is **D**. Take out the other person, and *myself* does not work.

×   Please do not hesitate to contact myself.

√   Please do not hesitate to contact me.

These are called interrogative pronouns because they are used to ask questions—an interrogative sentence asks a question.

- **Who** is going to the dance?
- With **whom** is she going to the dance?
- **Whoever** thought the dance would be this exciting?

On the exam, this is all about **who vs whom**, and most people do not have a clue as to how to use these pronouns correctly. Most people just use **who** and never even think about using **whom**. Have no fear! We have some quick tricks for you to use, and you will never mess up who vs whom again.

Just like with regular pronouns—he/him/his, she/her/hers, we/us/ours, etc.—who, whom, and whose belong in certain parts of the sentence as well.

Subject Pronouns occur in the subject part of a sentence	**Object Pronouns** occur in the prepositional phrase or in the predicate part of a sentence	**Possessive Pronouns** show possession in a sentence
who/whoever	**whom/whomever**	**whose**
Who went to the store?	**To whom** are you speaking**?**	**Whose** car is this?
The pronoun **who** is the subject of the sentence.	He had a date with **whom?**	This is **whose** car**?**
The winner is **who**?	That is the man **whom** my father gave fifty dollars.	This is the lady **whose** generous funding created this scholarship.
Whoever thought this would happen.	You can go with **whomever** you want.	

The quickest and easiest way to distinguish between who/whoever and whom/whoever is to answer the question and decide whether you are answering with a subject pronoun—he/she—or an objective pronoun—him/her.

Examples

Correct

- Question: **Who** went to the store?
- Answer: **He** went to the store.

Both **he** and **who** are subject pronouns. Therefore, **who** is used correctly here.

Incorrect

- **Whom** went to the store?

You would never say *him went to the store* or *her went to the store*.

Correct

- Question: **Whoever** thought this would happen?
- Answer: **She** thought this would happen.

Incorrect

Whomever thought this would happen?

You would never say *him thought this would happen* or *her thought this would happen*.

Correct

- Question: He went to the dance with **whom**? With **whom** did she go to the dance?
- Answer: He went with **her**. She went with **him**.

Quick Tip!

If you see the words **of** or **with** (**prepositions**) in the sentence, the correct answer is **whom**.

- When we went to the game, I took my friends, all **of whom** are athletes. You took him, her, or them to the game.
- You can go with **whomever** you want. You can go with **him, her,** or **them**.

Also, match the **m's**! Hi*m*, and the*m* go with who*m*.

Pronoun number and person

Pronouns and the number of people in the sentence must agree. This also falls under pronoun antecedent agreement as well.

Correct Example

- Every time a person comes into the restaurant right before closing time, the **cook and bartender** roll **their** eyes.

In this case, the sentence contains have two people—the cook and the bartender. It also contains the pronoun **their**. **Their** is plural. Therefore, the pronoun number and person are correct.

Incorrect Example

- The teacher told the student to bring their permission slip tomorrow.

In this case, the sentence contains one student and one permission slip. It also contains the pronoun **their**. Because the sentence is referring to one student here, **their** will not work. To fix the error, change the pronoun **their** to **his** or **her**. Better yet, change the subject to students and make permission slip plural—permission slips.

Correction

The teacher told the **students** to bring **their** permission **slips** tomorrow.

Vague pronouns

Vague pronouns do not clearly identify a specific subject or antecedent. Usually this happens when the sentence contains more than one person or more than one object and only one pronoun.

For example, read the sentence below.

- My aunt and her sister took our dog to the beach, and on the way, **she** chewed the car seats.

In this case, **she** is the pronoun. Most would assume the dog chewed the seats. However, the way it is written, the pronoun **she** can refer to the aunt, the sister or the dog.

Vague pronouns are a common mistake in writing. Look at the paragraph below and determine which sentences—numbered below—contain vague pronouns.

> (1) Online courses provide students with a variety of ways to access knowledge.
> (2) Students like online courses because they provide flexibility in learning. (3)
> For example, students can access online courses from the comfort of their own
> home, at a coffee shop, or at the university library. (4) Students and teachers
> can use online courses to increase engagement in their lessons.

In the paragraph above, vague pronouns are present in sentence 2 because the pronoun **they** can be referring to the online classes or the students—both plural nouns. A vague pronoun is also present in sentence 4—their lessons. It is not clear if the pronoun is referring to the students or teachers.

Pronoun shift

When writing, it is important to stay with the same voice. However, students often use more than one point of view when they write.

First Person Pronouns	Second Person Pronouns	Third Person Pronouns
I, me, mine, myself, we, us, ours, ourselves	you, yours, yourself, yourselves	he, she, it, him, her, his, hers, its himself, herself, itself, they, them, their, theirs, themselves

Correct Examples

- When I buy new clothes, I have to remember to cut the labels off.

- We were starving after 1st period, but we couldn't get food at our school until lunch.

- She was not sure which road to take, so she ended up getting lost.

Incorrect Examples

- When I buy new clothes, you have to remember to cut the labels off.

- We were starving after 1st period, but you can't get food at our school until lunch.

- She was not sure which road to take, so you ended up getting lost.

Subject/verb agreement

Singular subjects are paired with singular verbs while plural subjects are paired with plural verbs.

Singular

- John is late for work.

- He buys roses for his wife on her birthday.

Plural

- They are late for work.

- The children buy roses for their mother on her birthday.

Simple, right?

What about when two subjects are joined together? You may assume they would take a plural verb. Not always.

When two subjects are joined with **either/or** or **neither/nor**, use a singular verb. Why? If you think about it, only ONE of the subjects is completing the action.

Examples

- Neither Ann nor John is available for a meeting at noon.

- Either Ann or John is available for a meeting at noon.

Then, you have the fun addition of this rule: The verb in a sentence using **neither/nor** or **either/or** with mixed subjects will agree with the noun closest to it.

Examples

- Neither the bikes nor the car fits into the garage.

- Either the car or the bikes fit into the garage.

When two subjects are joined together with **and**, use a plural verb.

Examples

- John and Ann are available for a meeting at noon.
- The bikes and the car fit into the garage.

There are some exceptions. When the subject is a **compound noun**, it is treated as a single subject, even though the two words are connected with **and**.

Examples

- Law and order prevails in the courtroom.
- Room and board is a monthly expense she must include in her budget.

Another exception is money as it is always considered a non-count amount.

Examples

- Fifty dollars has been donated to the charity.
- There is only $1.38 left in the account.

How will it look on the exam?

The way we see this on almost every grammar exam is with collect nouns.

The board of directors are having their meeting today.

A. The board of directors are having their meeting today.

B. The board of directors is having their meeting today.

C. The board of directors are having a meeting today.

D. The board of directors are having its meeting today.

E. The board of directors is having its meeting today.

The correct answer is **E**. There are two errors in the sentence given, and the first error has to do with the fact that the board is a collective noun. Second, the board is the subject. The prepositional phrase is, of directors. Therefore, you should use the board when determining the verb and pronoun in the sentence.

The board **is** having **its** meeting today.

Quick Tip!

Be aware of prepositional phrases when looking for subject verb agreement. Test makers will often squeeze in a prepositional phrase to confuse you.

× The use of cell phones and computers **are** prohibited.

In this case, **the use** is the subject, not cell phones and computers. Therefore, the verb should be in singular form.

√ The use of cell phones and computers **is** prohibited.

Take out the prepositional phrase and you have:

√ The use **is** prohibited.

Inappropriate shift in verb tense

A shift in verb tense occurs when there are two or more instances in a sentence happening within the same time period. Typically, the verb tense in a sentence should remain consistent. However, there are always exceptions to the rule.

Correct

- As I *drove* along the highway, I *saw* two eagles and *thought* of the amazing trip I had.

In this case *drove*, *saw*, *thought*, and *had* are all past-tense verbs. The tense remains consistent throughout the sentence.

Incorrect

- She is **driving** in the car and **went** down the wrong street.

In this case, **driving** is present tense and **went** is past tense.

Shifts in verb tense are usually easy to spot on the selected response part of the exam. Where this can hurt you is during the writing portion of the exam. Therefore, when you proof your writing, pay attention to verb tense.

Structural Relationships - Recognize and Correct:

- Errors in the placement of phrases and clauses within a sentence
- Misplaced and dangling modifiers
- Errors in the use of coordinating and subordinating conjunctions
- Fragments and run-ons
- Errors in the use of correlative conjunctions
- Errors in parallel structure

Errors in the placement of phrases and clauses within a sentence

Errors occur when clauses and phrases are awkwardly placed in a sentence. While not grammatically incorrect, these are errors of usage in modern English that should be avoided.

Incorrect

- He while doing his laundry noticed the missing sock.

Correct

- While doing his laundry, he noticed the missing sock.
- He noticed the missing sock while doing his laundry.

Incorrect

- The man because he couldn't hear did not notice the oncoming bus.

Correct

- Because the man couldn't hear, he did not notice the oncoming bus.

Incorrect

- The team in order to win had to score the next touchdown.

Correct

- In order to win, the team had to score the next touchdown.
- The team had to score the next touchdown in order to win.

> **Quick Tip!**
>
> Yes, you can start a sentence with **because**, as long as it is part of the introductory phrase.
>
> **Because** she was exhausted, she went home early from work.
>
> She went home early from work **because** she was exhausted.

Misplaced and dangling modifiers

A misplaced modifier is a word, phrase, or clause that is improperly separated from the word it modifies or describes. The separation causes an error that makes the sentence confusing.

Incorrect

- Yolanda realized too late that it was a mistake to walk the neighbor's dog in high heels.

The phrase *in high heels* modifies *the neighbor's dog* in this sentence. The dog is not in high heels; Yolanda is.

To correct the sentence, rearrange the sentence so the modifying clause is close to the word it should modify.

Correct

- Yolanda realized too late that she shouldn't have worn high heels while walking the neighbor's dog.

Incorrect

- I saw the magnificent owls skiing down the mountain.

The phrase *skiing down the mountain* is modifying the owls not I.

Correct

- While I was skiing down the mountain, I saw the magnificent owls.

Incorrect

- Sitting in the kennel, I saw the dog.

Correct

- I saw the dog that was sitting in the kennel.

Quick Tip!

Misplaced phrases are often subject or predicate location issues.

By moving the phrase to the other part of the sentence, you can usually correct these easily.

- ✗ The professor returned the exam with a smile. (The exam isn't smiling.)
- √ With a smile, the professor returned the exam to the student.
- ✗ She notified the man in an email that he would be fined. (The man is not in an email.)
- √ In an email, she notified the man that he would be fined.

Coordinating and subordinating conjunction

While conjunctions link words and groups of words, subordinating and coordinating conjunctions connect clauses (a group of words containing a subject and a verb).

Coordinating Conjunctions

These are the seven words that combine two sentences (independent clauses that can stand alone as they state a complete thought) with the addition of a comma. These are the ONLY seven words used to combine two sentences using a comma.

The 7 coordinating conjunctions **(FANBOYS):**

1. for   **F**
2. and   **A**
3. nor   **N**
4. but   **B**
5. or   **O**
6. yet   **Y**
7. so   **S**

> **Quick Tip: FANBOYS**
>
> An acronym to help you remember all the coordinating conjunctions is **FANBOYS—for, and, nor, but, or, yet, so**. Memorizing these seven words takes all the guesswork out of sentence combining with commas. Using this mnemonic device makes it easy to remember.

It is helpful to locate independent clauses and dependent clauses when using subordinate conjunctions.

Remember:

- An **independent clause is a sentence**. It contains a subject and a predicate, and it stands on its own independently.

- A **dependent clause is NOT a sentence**. It only contains a verb phrase or a noun phrase.

Independent clauses and dependent clauses are often joined together with punctuation and subordinating clauses.

IMPORTANT

A conjunction alone can separate an independent clause and a dependent clause.

A comma + a conjunction must be used when separating two independent clauses.

Example - Independent Clause with a Dependent Clause

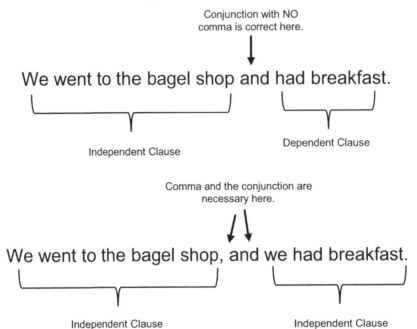

EXAMPLES

The brave girl rescued her mom from the burning home, and now she is a hero.

The town gave a parade, but no one bothered to come.

In both cases, two independent clauses (sentences) are being connected with a comma and a coordinating conjunction (FANBOYS).

Quick Tip!

No, you cannot start sentences with coordinating conjunctions.

- **And** I went to the mall.
- **But** he was taller than I.
- **So** I went home to sleep.
- **Yet** I voted anyway.

While often used to start sentences in informal writing, when writing formally, you should NEVER start a sentence with a Coordinating conjunction.

Subordinating Conjunctions

These are all the other conjunctions used to combine clauses.

These commonly include:

- Since
- Because
- Although
- While
- Due
- Though
- Whenever
- When
- If
- Therefore

Quick Tip!

YES, you can start sentences with subordinating conjunctions.

- **While** I was watching TV, I did my homework.
- **Since** it was cold, I wore a jacket.
- **Whenever** I go to Canada, I stop in Seattle.
- **Because** I was on the committee, I voted on the issue.

*When a subordinating conjunction starts a sentence, a comma will always follow.

Grammatically, there are two patterns for these subordinating conjunctions:

Pattern 1

Independent Clause + Subordinating Conjunction + Clause (independent, dependent, or prepositional)

Example:

The girl rescued her mom from the burning home because she was brave.

Independent Clause | Subordinating Conjunction | Independent Clause

Pattern 2

Subordinating Conjunction + Clause (independent, dependent, or prepositional) + Comma + Independent Clause

Example:

Because she was so brave, the girl rescued her mom from the burning home.

Subordinating Conjunction | Independent Clause | Independent Clause

Here are more examples using complex sentences with multiple clauses that use coordinating and subordinating conjunctions. See if you can locate the clauses, subordinating and coordinating conjunctions, and punctuation.

Correct

When the *Praxis*® Core Writing subtest was scheduled for this week, she had planned on studying every night, but since it was postponed until next week, she decided to watch movies every night this week instead.

- **Dependent Clause**: *When the Praxis® Core Writing subtest was scheduled for this week.*
- **Independent Clause**: *she had planned on studying every night.*
- **Comma** is used correctly to separate the two clauses.
- **Coordinating Conjunction and Comma:** , but
- **Dependent Clause:** since it was postponed until next week
- **Independent Clause:** she decided to watch movies every night this week instead
- **Comma:** Used correctly to separate the clauses.

Here, two complex sentences with subordinating clauses are combined into a compound complex sentence.

Correct

- Since Bob knew the *Praxis*® Core writing was going to be difficult, he had planned on studying with Sheila, but he could not find her in the dorm.
- Donna knew that she had passed the *Praxis*® Core Writing subtest exam, for as she reviewed her grammar, she had memorized the FANBOYS.
- Whenever Dan has to study, he must have a quiet environment, or he won't be able to concentrate.

Incorrect

- If there is a problem he panics, because he gets too excited.

This has two errors. First, the subordinating conjunction, **if**, begins the sentence. Therefore, a comma is needed after the clause, **If there is a problem**. Second, there should not be a comma before **because**.

> **Quick Tip!**
>
> The subordinating conjunction **because** is one of the most commonly tested conjunctions due to the fact that people often mistakenly put a comma with it.
>
> Do **NOT** use a comma before **because**.

Correction

- If there is a problem, he panics because he gets too excited.

Incorrect

- Bob knew the *Praxis*® Core writing would be difficult so he studied with a friend, since she knew the test well.

This has two errors. First, a comma is missing before **so**. Remember, if you have two independent clauses, you must use a **comma + conjunction.** The conjunction alone is not enough to separate 2 independent Clauses. Also, you do not need a comma before since.

Correction

- Bob knew the *Praxis*® Core writing would be difficult, so he studied with a friend since she knew the test well.

Sample Question:

Directions: correct the following sentence by choosing the best option from the answer choices below.

The ranger was dressed properly for the cold and felt confident, due to his weeks of training.

A. The ranger was dressed properly for the cold and felt confident, because of his weeks of training.

B. The ranger was dressed properly for the cold and felt confident, because he had trained for weeks.

C. Because he had trained for weeks, the ranger was dressed properly for the cold, and felt confident.

D. The ranger was dressed properly for the cold and felt confident, because he had trained for weeks.

E. Because he had trained for weeks, the ranger was dressed properly for the cold and felt confident.

The answer is E: This question and its answer set actually test one's knowledge of conjunctions in several ways. Choice A (no error), B and D are incorrect because there is a comma before *because* (just say NO to a comma before *because*). Choice C is incorrect because, although there is a comma used correctly after the subordinating conjunction that introduces the sentence, there is a comma placed incorrectly before *and* at the end of the sentence. Remember, the comma + conjunction is only used to separate two independent clauses. The clause, **felt confident**, is a dependent clause. Therefore, no comma is needed. Only E has the comma used appropriately, after the subordinating conjunction that introduces the sentence.

Fragments and run-ons

Fragments and run-ons are common sentence-level mistakes assessed on the *Praxis®* Core Writing subtest exam.

- **Fragments** are any group of words that do NOT create a complete sentence.

- **Run-ons** are multiple sentences in a row lacking clear grammatical punctuation with periods or commas.

These usually appear on the exam in the form of independent clauses pushed together without the comma + conjunction.

Fragments come in several forms. Other forms of fragments include predicates without a subject, subjects without a predicate, and phrases that are neither a subject nor predicate.

Here are examples of fragments as stand-alone subordinate clauses.

Incorrect

- I suspect he can't read a map. Because he always gets lost.

In this example, because starts the second sentence as a fragment. You can correct this in two ways.

Correction

- I suspect he can't read a map because he always gets lost.

- Because he always gets lost, I suspect he can't read a map.

Incorrect

- Sure, if he calls.

Correction

- Sure, I'll let you know if he calls.

> **Quick Tip!**
>
> **Locate the Independent Clause**
>
> **Independent clauses** are a group of words that contain a **subject** (noun or noun phrase) and a **predicate** (verb or verb phrase). Locating the independent clause in the sentence will help you identify errors in punctuation or conjunctions.

Here, we have **Sure**—the subordinating conjunction—followed by a comma and an independent clause.

Run-ons have subcategories according to the type of mistake, comma splices, and fused sentences. While it is not important to name such derivations, it is important to know that sentence recognition and proper punctuation with sentences is the key to recognizing these grammatical mistakes.

Here are some examples of common run-on mistakes

Incorrect

- He went to the store he maxed out his credit card again and when his dad found out he got in a lot of trouble.

The two clauses, **he went to the store** and **he maxed out his credit cards**, are independent clauses. There is no punctuation or conjunctions here, so this is a run-on. In addition, **when his dad found** out is also an independent clause. Therefore, the conjunction alone is not enough. Finally, there is no punctuation after the subordinating conjunction and clause, **when his dad found out.**

Corrections

- He went to the store and maxed out his credit card again, and when his dad found out, he got in a lot of trouble.

- He went to the store and maxed out his credit card again. When his dad found out, he got in a lot of trouble.

- He went to the store; he maxed out his credit card again. When his dad found out, he got in a lot of trouble.

- He went to the store; he maxed out his credit card again, and when his dad found out, he got in a lot of trouble.

Correlative conjunctions

Correlative conjunctions are multi-word phrases that relate two terms, usually in a **parallel** fashion. These terms are often nouns, but can be verbs, modifiers and even clauses.

Correlative conjunctions	Examples in context
neither/nor	**Neither** the waiter **nor** the customer knew how to open the wine bottle.
either/or	**Either** he leaves, **or** I do.
not only/but also	**Not only** did Jane pass the *Praxis®* exam, **but** she **also** got the job.
rather/than	I would **rather** run **than** get caught.
more/than	Mom gave sis **more** dessert **than** me.
as/as	The giant spider was **as** big **as** a house.
whether/or	**Whether** you like it **or** not, we must go to see your parents.
such/that	She was **such** a success **that** they made her supervisor.
both/and	**Both** the father **and** the son are left-handed.

IMPORTANT: Correlative conjunctions must be used with their counterparts. If there is one, there has to be the other.

- **neither** has to go with **nor**
- **either** has to go with **or**
- **not only** has to go with **but also**
- **rather** has to go with **than**
- **more** has to go with **than**

- **as** has to have another **as**
- **whether** has to go with **or**
- **such** has to go with **that**
- **both** has to go with **and**

Sample Question:

Rewrite the following sentences with the best choice below.

John was out of shape. He was weak and undernourished.

A. Out of shape, John was weak or also undernourished.

B. Out of shape, John was both weak and also undernourished.

C. Out of shape, John was weak but also undernourished.

D. Out of shape, John was not only weak, but he was also undernourished.

E. Out of shape, John was either weak or also undernourished.

The correct answer is **D**. This is the only correlative combination that is fully intact (not only...but also).

> **Quick Tip!**
>
> Test makers usually test correlative conjunction recognition by simply leaving out some or all of the second part. They just want to see if you can recognize the pair in the context of a sentence.
>
> For example, if you see the phrase **not only**, you must have a **but also** in the sentence.

Pronoun Errors with Correlative Conjunctions

On the test, you may be faced with correlative conjunction errors. Most people have a hard time finding these errors because throughout language evolution, people have started to use these incorrectly.

For example, many people may think the sentences below are correct. However, they are incorrect.

Incorrect

- My sister is bigger <u>than me</u>.

- She is not as tall <u>as me</u>.

- Not only is she taller <u>than me</u>, but she is also younger <u>than me</u>.

Corrections

- My sister is bigger than I.

   My sister is bigger <u>than I am</u>.

- She is not as tall as I.

   She is not as tall as <u>I am</u>.

- Not only is she taller <u>than I</u>, but she is also younger <u>than I</u>.

   Not only is she taller <u>than I am</u>, but she is also younger <u>than I am</u>.

Comparatives as subjects	Comparatives as objects	Comparatives as possessives
Dan is not **as tall as** <u>I am.</u> Dan is not **as tall as** <u>I am tall.</u> The comparative pronoun is the subject of a sentence.	Dan gave <u>her</u> **more** attention **than** he gave <u>me</u>. Dan **gave** <u>her</u> more attention than he **gave** <u>me</u> attention. The comparative is the indirect object of the verb. Therefore, we use the objective pronoun, **me**.	**Your** team is <u>better</u> coached <u>than</u> <u>ours</u>. **Your** team is <u>better</u> coached <u>than</u> **our** <u>team is coached</u>. The comparative is the possessive form **ours** acting in this special case as a noun.

Parallel structure

In grammatical terms, parallel structures are used to organize a series or a list in a sentence. They are used with nearly all parts of speech, phrases, and clauses. The key to parallel structures is that all the things in the series must be the same part of speech.

Nouns and pronouns in a series.

- The good one, the bad one, and the ugly one are all in the last scene.
- The last scene contains the good one, the bad one, and the ugly one.

Adjectives in a series.

- The big, red, round beach ball is the one that I want.
- The beach ball that I want is big, red and round.

Adverbs in a series

- I agree with you completely and wholeheartedly.

Predicates in a series

- They danced, laughed, and told stories all night.

Prepositional phrases in a series.

- We looked for your socks in the living room, in the dining room, and in your bedroom.

Participles in a series

- In the evening, she loves jogging on the nature paths, drinking hot chocolate, and warming herself by the fire.

Infinitives in a series

- Yes, I like to jog on nature paths, drink hot chocolate, and warm myself by the fire as well.

*Notice that the infinites **to jog, to drink, and to warm** all share the same **"to"** in the sentence.

Clauses in a series

- The person who has the best resume and who has the best interview will get the job.

Sentences in a series

- Go to your room, turn off the light, and go to sleep.

> **Quick Tip!**
>
> When faced with a test question with a list of nouns, verbs, or phrases, think **MATCHY MATCHY**. Everything in the list must match.
>
> **Example**
>
> While on vacation we **rode** our bikes, **swam** in the ocean, and **visited** with friends.
>
> Here you can see that all the verb tenses match; they are all past-tense verbs.
>
> Also, the past tense verbs are all followed by a prepositional phrase: our bikes, in the ocean, with friends.

Errors in Parallel Structure

Common errors in parallel construction occur when the part of speech is violated. Another parallel construction issue is the form of that part of speech. This is especially true with infinitives and participle forms when they take on the role of nouns:

Incorrect

- She prefers hiking, rowing, and to ski.

Correct

- She prefers hiking, rowing, and to skiing.

Keep all the word forms as consistent as possible.

Incorrect

- We searched everywhere for your wallet: under the beds, in the seat cushions and the clothes hamper.

Correct

- We searched everywhere for your wallet: under the beds, in the seat cushions and inside the clothes hamper.

In parallel construction, once a series is started, that same form of the series should continue.

Incorrect

- My friend is so loving, thinking, and considering.

Correct

- My friend is so loving, thoughtful and considerate.

Here, idiomatic meanings are more important than the form. Thinking is a verb; thoughtful is an adjective. In this sentence **loving, thoughtful** and **considerate** are all adjectives.

Incorrect

- After the accident, the child was upset, crying, and totally beside herself.

Correct

- After the accident, the child was upset, crying, and inconsolable.

Idiomatic phrases often don't work in formal parallel structures as the form varies too much from the other elements.

Sample Question: Choose the best revision of the sentence below. If there is no change necessary, select answer choice A.

After reaching level three, you have three chances to defeat the dragon, finding the treasure chest, and collect the magic sword.

A. After reaching level three, you have three chances to defeat the dragon, finding the treasure chest, and collecting the magic sword.
B. After reaching level three, you have three chances to defeat the dragon, to find the treasure chest, and collect the magic sword.
C. After reaching level three, you have three chances to defeat the dragon, find the treasure chest, and collect the magic sword.
D. After reaching level three, you have three chances to defeating the dragon, finding the treasure chest, and collecting the magic sword.
E. No error.

The correct answer is **C**. Here, the phrase, **you have three chances to,** connects each of the parallel form items: **defeat**, **find**, and **collect**.

> ### Quick Tip: Find the key word
>
> The key to correct usage is to look at the **key word or words** that join with the first entry. You should be able to construct separate sentences with the exact stating of the key words and the parallel entries.
>
> **Mom** <u>tucked me</u> into bed, <u>turned off</u> the light and <u>said</u> good night.
>
> **Mom** is the key word as she is the subject of all three verb phrases.
>
> Mom tucked me into bed.
>
> Mom turned off the lights.
>
> Mom said good night.

Word choice: Errors in the use of idiomatic expressions

Idiomatic expressions exist throughout the language, but for the purpose of standardized testing, usually the idiomatic usage problem centers on verb + phrase usage. These idiomatic questions can be especially difficult for students whose first language is not English. There is no hard-fast rule for idiomatic phrases. Here, if it sounds familiar, then usually it is correct.

Usually the errors in idiomatic phrases happen in the verb + preposition part of a sentence. See the examples below.

Incorrect

- Let's **plan with** it.

Correct

- Let's **plan on** it.

Incorrect

- I'll **meet** you **at the corner of the room**.
- I'll **meet** you **in the corner of Washington and Vine**.

Correct

- I'll **meet** you **in the corner of the room**.
- I'll **meet** you **at the corner of Washington and Vine.**

Incorrect

- Please **write** this **in accordance to** the rules.
- **According with** her, the driver ran the stop sign.

Correct

- Please **write** this **in accordance with** the rules.
- **According to** her, the driver ran the stop sign.

> **Quick Tip!**
>
> Because there is no rule for idiomatic phrases, it is best to go with the answer choice that sounds the best. A sentence with idiomatic errors in it will often sound awkward. We always say, if it sounds awkward, don't choose it.

Errors in the use of frequently confused words

Standardized English tests often include questions that include the following commonly confused words.

accept - to agree to receive or do
except - not including

coarse - rough
course - a direction; a school subject; part of a meal

adverse - unfavorable, harmful
averse - strongly disliking; opposed

complement - an addition that improves
compliment - to praise or express approval; an admiring remark

advice - recommendations about what to do
advise - to recommend something

council - a group of people who manage or advise
counsel - advice; to advise

affect - to change or make a difference to
effect - a result; to bring about a result

elicit - to draw out a reply or reaction
illicit - not allowed by law or rules

aisle - a passage between rows of seats
isle - an island

ensure - to make certain that something will happen
insure - to provide compensation

all together - all in one place, all at once
altogether - completely; on the whole

foreword - an introduction to a book
forward - onwards, ahead

along - moving or extending horizontally on
a long - referring to something of great length

principal - most important; the head of a school
principle - a fundamental rule or belief

aloud - out loud
allowed - permitted

sight - the ability to see
site - a location

altar - a sacred table in a church
alter - to change

stationary - not moving
stationery - writing materials

amoral - not concerned with right or wrong
immoral - not following accepted moral standards

allusion - indirect reference
illusion - false idea

assent - agreement, approval
ascent - the action of rising or climbing up

allude - to make indirect reference to
elude - to avoid

bare - naked; to uncover
bear - to carry; to put up with

capital - major city, wealth, assets
capitol - government building

bated - in phrase *with bated breath*; in great suspense
baited - with bait attached or inserted

conscience - sense of morality
conscious - awake, aware

censure - to criticize strongly
censor - to ban parts of a book or film

eminent - prominent, important
imminent - about to happen

cereal - a breakfast food
serial - happening in a series

everyday - routine, common
every day - each day, all of the day

Wrong word use

Common words are often misused in speech and text. In this case, one usually is misused for the other. Here are some that usually appear on the test.

Word usage	Examples in context
then/than • Then is used to mark time. • Than is used for comparisons.	**Error**: This is farther **then** I thought. **Correct**: This is farther **than** I thought.
between/among • Between involves two things • Among involves three or more things.	**Error**: That matter must be discussed **between** Jeff and his brothers. **Correct**: That matter must be discussed **among** Jeff and his brothers.
number/amount • Number is used for quantifiable nouns (things you can count). • Amount is used for non-quantifiable nouns (things you don't count).	**Error**: There were a large **amount** of people there. **Correct**: There were a large **number** of people there. **Error**: The **amount** of dollars she made was staggering. **Correct**: The **amount** of money she made was staggering. Correct: The **number** of dollars she made was staggering.
many/much • Many is used for count nouns. • Much is used for non-count nouns.	**Error**: **Much** of the people had left. **Correct**: **Many** of the people had left. **Correct**: **Much** of the cake was left over after the party.
less/fewer • Fewer is used for count nouns. • Less is used for non-counts.	**Error**: There are even **less** people here now. **Correct**: There are even **fewer** people here now. **Correct**: The population is **less** this year than last year.
imply/infer • The speaker implies. • The listener infers.	**Error**: The author **inferred** that Ned was the killer. **Correct**: The author **implied** that Ned was the killer.

.

Redundancy

Some words expressions are commonly used in the vernacular that needlessly relate the meaning. These redundancies should be correct in proper English practice.

Reason why, and also, every single, not hardly, double negatives

Word usage	Examples in context
reason why Both are reasons.	**Error**: That is the **reason why** I did it. **Correct**: That is **why** I did it. That is the **reason** I did it.
double negatives Negatives do not repeat in English lest they cancel out the original meaning.	Error: We **can't never** win against them. Correct: We **can never** win against them.
not hardly, hardly never **Hardly** is a negative word, so using it with another negative produces a double negative effect.	**Error**: I **can't hardly** wait. **Correct**: I **can hardly** wait.
and also Both mean additionally.	**Error**: She lacked the stamina to finish **and also** the will. **Correct**: She lacked the stamina to finish, **also** the will.

Here are some other examples of redundancy that may not be as obvious.

Incorrect

- He sat **alone** in **solitude**.

Correct

- He sat **alone**.

- He sat in **solitude**.

Incorrect

- She **quickly sped** up to catch the light.

Correct

- She **sped** up to catch the light.

- She drove **quickly** to catch the light.

Incorrect

- He **scrupulously** wrote **carful** notes.

- He wrote **careful** notes.

- He wrote **scrupulously**

This page is intentionally left blank.

Structural Relationships - Recognize and Correct:

- Errors in capitalization
- Errors in punctuation
  - commas
  - semicolons
  - apostrophes

Capitalization

Capitalization for standard English follows a few basic rules.

Rule One: Always capitalize the first word of a sentence.

The key here is to recognize where the sentences start and stop. For example, semicolons connect two sentences together as one; therefore, they do not need capitalization except at the beginning.

Example:

- Capitalization can be tricky; there are several rules.

Notice that the **C** in capitalization is capitalized, but the **t** in there is not.

Rule Two: Always capitalize proper nouns and their titles as well as the abbreviations of these.

Names of specific people and places are capitalized.

Examples:

- During the Civil War, President Abraham Lincoln was president of the United States.

Civil War is a specific name of a war. President is the title of Abraham Lincoln in the subject. However, president is a common noun in the predicate.

- Today, Congress passed a law banning congressional pay raises even though the Senate had to vote on it three times.

Congress and the Senate are in this case are names.

Rule Three: Capitalize the main words in a multiword title.

Here the emphasis is also on what **not** to capitalize: articles (other than the first word), conjunctions, and prepositions.

Examples:

He works at the Federal Bureau of Investigation in Washington, DC.

Poe's *Tales of Mystery and Imagination* is one of my favorite collections.

Notice that the articles and prepositions—is, in, of, and—are not capitalized in the title.

> **Quick Tip!**
>
> Knowing what **NOT** to capitalize is also important when taking grammar exams. Do not capitalize:
>
> - seasons (winter, spring, summer fall), unless they are used in a title like The New York Fall Festival.
> - general class names (math, science, social science, language arts).
> - general titles of family members (my mom, her uncle, your dad).
> - general titles of officials (the governor, the president, the director)

Punctuation: commas, semicolons, apostrophes

Punctuation is necessary in writing to indicate how the writing should be read. One great activity to drive this home to students is to read a paragraph devoid of punctuation aloud until you just cannot help taking a breath. Better yet, have them read a paragraph without punctuation, telling them they cannot pause until they see a punctuation mark. They will make comments like, "I was about to pass out!" and "I had to take a breath!" They begin to realize that punctuation is not just an English teacher's nitpicky way to take points off; punctuation it is necessary for written communication.

Commas (,)

No other punctuation mark is misused as often as the comma. Its use in items in a series is also hotly debated right now. The traditional Oxford comma separates items in a series of three items or more, including the item before the coordinating conjunction.

Example:

- I went to the store to buy milk, eggs, cheese, and bread.

- I went to the store to buy milk, eggs, cheese and bread.

In the first example, the Oxford comma is used before and in the sentence; in the second example, the Oxford comma is not used before and in the sentence. It is important to understand that you will not be asked on a grammar test to choose between using the Oxford comma and not using the Oxford comma because both are considered correct. The choice is a stylistic one.

Comma Usage Rules

Usage	Example
after an introductory word, phrase, or clause	However, he did not follow the rules.
to separate a dependent clause from an independent clause when the dependent clause comes first	When he turned in his homework a day late, the teacher tossed it in the garbage.
before a coordinating conjunction to separate two independent clauses	I went to my interview today, and I think it went really well.
to separate items in a series of three items or more	The girl went shopping for school supplies such as notebooks, pens, pencils, highlighters, and binders.
to separate two consecutive adjectives	The tall, muscular girl was the star of the basketball team.
on both sides of nonessential words, phrases, or clauses	The teacher, who had little experience, assigned reading from a banned book.
to set off someone's name or title	Excuse me, Alyssa, but I need to take this call.
to separate the day, month, and year in a date (and after the year if it is part of a sentence)	June 14, 1969, is my birthdate.
to separate a city from a state	I am from Dunedin, Florida.
to introduce or separate a quote	She screamed, "I hate you!" "Why," I asked, "do you hate me?"
before the end quotation mark if the quote is followed by an attribution such as he said	"I can't stand it anymore," he said.
to separate contrasting parts of a sentence	That is my drink, not yours.

Semicolons (;)

Semicolons join two independent clauses that are related and are alternatives to a period or comma with conjunction.

Examples:

- I needed to go to the store; I was almost out of milk, egg, cheese, and bread.

- He knew he would be punished for skipping school; he did it anyway.

In both examples above, there are two independent clauses joined by the semicolon. This is the only way to use a semicolon.

Quick Tip!

Never use a **coordinating** conjunction (FANBOYS) after a semicolon because you cannot start a sentence with a coordinating conjunction.

However, you can use a **subordinating** conjunction after a semicolon because subordinating conjunctions can start a sentence.

Incorrect

- I was exhausted after work; but I still went to the party.

Correct

- I was exhausted after work; however, I still went to the party.

You would not start a sentence with but; however, you can start a sentence with **however**.

If you do use a subordinating conjunction after the semicolon, you MUST use the comma after the subordinating conjunction (...; however,)

Colons (:)

Colons are used to separate and independent clause and a list. Colons can also be used to separate an independent clause and an independent clause or dependent clause that elaborates, restates, explains, or defines.

Example:

- I brought all the necessities to the campsite: tent, food, fishing pole, and wine.

Notice that the clause, **I brought all the necessities to the campsite**, is a sentence—an independent clause. Therefore, the colon is used correctly.

Examples:

- We decided to focus on the most important thing: increasing student achievement.

Notice that the independent clause is **We decided to focus on the most important thing.** The dependent clause (verb phrase only) that defines what the most important this is **increasing student achievement.**

- I had lunch with the president of the university: Dr. Cunningham.

Here you have an independent clause followed by the name of the person mentioned in the first clause. Therefore, the colon is appropriate.

Apostrophes (')

There are two main reasons to use apostrophes:

1. To form a contraction such as do + not = don't. In this case, the apostrophe replaces or stands in for the letter that is taken out when the words are combined.

2. To show possession. When the noun is singular or plural but does not end in **s**, add **'s** to show possession. When the noun is singular or plural but does end in **s**, add the apostrophe **after the s** to show possession.

Below are some examples for using the apostrophe to show possession.

Correct Apostrophe Usage Examples:

- Please bring **Lisa's** book when you come to class tomorrow.

Lisa is a singular proper noun (there is only one Lisa here); therefore, the **'s** is appropriate.

- We will be going to the **women's** soccer tournament on Wednesday.

Women is a plural noun that does NOT end in s; therefore the **'s** is appropriate.

- Please bring all the **girls'** books when you come to class tomorrow.

Girls is a plural noun that ends in s; therefore, the **s'** is appropriate.

- We will be going to the **ladies'** luncheon on Friday.

Ladies is plural and ends in s, and the ladies own the luncheon. Therefore, the **s'** is appropriate.

> ### Quick Tip!
>
> Make sure you use possessive nouns and the apostrophe when talking about events or things that happen at a certain time. People often miss these necessary apostrophes when writing and taking grammar exams. We often see these on grammar assessments of all kinds!
>
> **Incorrect**
>
> - **Yesterdays** faculty meeting was a waste of time.
> - Do you think anyone when to last **nights** event?
>
> **Correct**
>
> - **Yesterday's** faulty meeting was a waste of time.
> - Do you think anyone went to last **night's** party?

- Assess the credibility and relevance of sources.

- Recognize the different elements of a citation.

- Recognize effective research strategies.

- Recognize information relevant to a particular research task.

Assess the credibility and relevance of sources

Evaluating Sources

It is important to evaluate source information for relevancy, validity, and reliability, but this is especially important with internet sources. There is a lot of false information out there. Understanding credibility in resources is essential for scoring well on the *Praxis®* Core Writing subtest exam.

- **Peer-reviewed journals/articles.** These academic sources of materials are found on a database and can be considered credible. These are great to use when you need very specific research information on a topic but are not very helpful for general background information.

- **Websites.** Websites are great for a general audience, for background information, to evaluate different perspectives on a topic, and for current news evets. **This cannot be emphasized enough: Anyone can post information on a website, so it is very important to evaluate the site carefully!** Things like ads and heavy political or controversial opinion statements are red flags that the site is biased and unreliable.

- **Print sources (books, newspapers, magazines).** Books can be a good place to start for historical information or context, and magazines and newspapers will be useful for current events in an easy-to-understand format.

	Humanities	Sciences
Primary Sources	• Diaries, journals, and letters • Interviews with people who lived during a particular time (e.g., survivors of genocide in Rwanda or the Holocaust) • Songs, plays, novels, stories • Paintings, drawings, and sculptures • Autobiographies	• Published results of research studies • Published results of scientific experiments • Published results of clinical trials • Proceedings of conferences and meetings
Secondary Sources	• Biographies • Histories • Literary criticism • Book, art, and theater reviews • Newspaper articles that interpret	• Publications about the significance of research or experiments • Analysis of a clinical trial • Review of the results of several experiments or trials

These questions assess the critical thinking skills relating to sources of information. Credibility relates to the ability of the source to honestly provide information that is authoritative and objective. Relevance means that the data relates directly to the question of the research.

Sample Questions

1. A car commercial boasts that its brand is the most reliable brands based upon research. Which of the following types of information collection would be the most relevant and credible:
    A. Survey of Chevrolet owners.

    B. Survey of car dealership mechanics from 2002 to 2012.

    C. Report of mechanical repairs by all Chevrolet dealerships.

    D. Report of mechanical repairs by Toyota, Honda, and Chevrolet dealerships.

    E. Report of mechanical repairs made on all types of cars by independent repair shops over the last five years.

There are bias and relevance issues with all answers except **E**. A relates only one brand, not all. Owners of a product are likely to be biased as well. C and D have similar issues. B looks more credible in that its lists general car dealerships and has a data range date. However, car dealership mechanics could have a bias, and they mostly see their brand of cars. The key concepts that make E valid are a report of statistics (instead of a survey, which could be opinion), the independence of the source (with no obvious bias towards one brand) and a time period for data collection.

2. Identify the primary resources below. Check all that apply.

    ❑   A biography on Dr. Martin Luther King's life.

    ❑   Dr. Martin Luther King's *I have a Dream* Speech.

    ❑   Letters Dr. Martin Luther King wrote to his wife during the Civil Rights Protest.

    ❑   A publication about the significance of the work of Dr. Martin Luther King.

    ❑   An interview with an expert in Dr. Martin Luther King's work.

Refer to the chart on the previous page and you will see that the 2nd and third option (Dr. Martin Luther King's speech and letters) are the only examples of primary sources in the list of sources provided. All the other options are secondary resources.

On the *Praxis®* Core Writing subtest exam, you will be asked to distinguish between Modern Language Association (MLA) citations and the American Psychological Association (APA) citations. These are the main associations that govern the way we cite relevant research. It seems complicated at first glance; however, the two have distinct elements that make it easy to answer these questions correctly.

Where should citations occur?

Citations should occur within the body of the document. These are called in-text citations or parenthetical citations. See the example paragraphs below.

Citations should also be included on a **works cited page** (MLA) or **reference page** (APA) at the end of the document.

IMPORTANT: Citations should always occur in the document (in-text) **AND** at the end of the document in a list. They should be in **BOTH** places.

Works Cited MLA

In MLA, citations are organized on a **works cited** page that is placed at the end of the document. This lists all the references used in the paper. They are in alphabetical order according to author last name.

Example – Book (MLA)

- Last Name, First Name. *Title of Book*. Additional Contributors. City of Publication, Publisher, Publication Date.

*Notice the punctuation. Periods and commas matter in a citation.

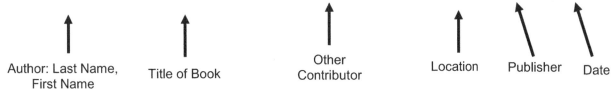

Tolstoy, Leo. *War and Peace*. Translated by Anthony Briggs, Moscow, Viking, 1968,

| Author: Last Name, First Name | Title of Book | Other Contributor | Location | Publisher | Date |

Reference List APA

The works cited page comes at the end of the document and lists all the references you used when writing the paper. They are in alphabetical order according to author last name. Citations on the work cited page are organized according to the example below.

Example: **Book (APA)**

- Author, (Year of publication). *Title of work: Capital letter also for subtitle*. Location: Publisher.

*Notice the punctuation. Periods and commas matter in a citation. Also, in APA, only the first letter of the title is capitalized. The rest of the title, unless it is a proper noun or occurs after a colon, is lowercased.

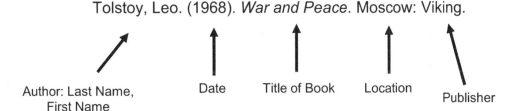

Tolstoy, Leo. (1968). *War and Peace*. Moscow: Viking.

| Author: Last Name, First Name | Date | Title of Book | Location | Publisher |

Example: **Journal Article (MLA)**

- Author(s). "Title." *Container.* Version (edition), Number (vol. and/or no.), Publisher, Publisher Date, Page Number(s) (pp.).

Burgess, Anthony. "Politics in the Novels of Graham Greene." *Literature and Society,* special issue of *Journal of Contemporary History,* vol. 2, no. 2, 1967, pp. 93-99.

Example: **Journal Article (APA)**

- Author(s). (Date). Title. *Journal Name*, *Volume*, Page number(s).

Wegener, D. T., & Petty, R. E. (1994). Mood management across affective states: The hedonic contingency hypothesis. *Journal of Personality and Social Psychology, 66*, 1034-1048.

> **Quick Tip!**
>
> Not every citation will have every element of the citation. For example, some publications do not have an edition number or volume number. The main thing to look for when determining whether the citation is MLA or APA is where the date is located in the citation.
> - **MLA** – The date is located towards the end of the citation.
> - **APA** – The date is located at the front of the citation.

*Notice the hanging indent for both the MLA and APA citation.

In-Text Citations

Citations should also occur in the body of the research paper. As the writer is communicating information and supporting that information with research, the writer must cite as he or she writes the paper.

In-Text Example: **(MLA)**

> **Smith** asserted that third-grade students, who used technology in math class, increased their math learning gains by 72% **(223).** In addition, students who were given time to use that technology at home also increased their math gains. Teachers also saw an increase in student engagement when technology was used **(Smith 223).**

*IMPORTANT: You will **not** bold the in-text citation in your own writing. We do here because we want it to stand out.

In the above example, there are two correct MLA citations.

1. The author's last name in the beginning of the first sentence, and the page of publication in parentheses at the end of the sentence.

2. The author's last name and page number at the end of the sentence. Notice the period comes **AFTER** the citation. The citation is part of the sentence.

In-Text Example: **(APA)**

> According to **Smith (2018)**, third-grade students, who used technology in math class, increased their math learning gains by 72%. In addition, students who were given time to use that technology at home also increased their math gains. Teachers also saw an increase in student engagement when technology was used **(Smith, 2018)**.

*****IMPORTANT**: You will **not** bold the in-text citation in your own writing. We do here because we want it to stand out.

In the above example, there are two correct APA citations.

1. In the beginning of the paragraph with the author's last name followed by the date of publication in parentheses.

2. At the end of the sentence with the author's last name, a comma, and date. Notice the period comes **AFTER** the citation. The citation is part of the sentence.

Sample Citation Test Questions

Which of the following citations is in APA format? Check all that apply

❑ Romantic poetry is characterized by the "spontaneous overflow of powerful feelings" (Wordsworth 263).

❑ Wordsworth stated that Romantic poetry was marked by a "spontaneous overflow of powerful feelings" (263).

❑ Wordsworth extensively explored the role of emotion in the creative process (263).

❑ According to Wordsworth (2012), extensively explored the role of emotion in the creative process.

❑ Romantic poetry is characterized by the spontaneous overflow of powerful feelings (Wordsworth, 2012).

> **Quick Tip!**
>
> To quickly determine if the citation is MLA or APA, look for whether or not the in-text citation has a date or a page number.
>
> - **APA** is author and date.
> - **MLA** is author and page number.
>
> You don't even have to get bogged down with all the information in the citations. Just look for page numbers or dates to determine the type of citation.

The last two options are the APA options. These are the only options containing a date. The other three have page numbers, which is indicative of MLA.

Recognize effective research strategies

Certain research strategies, especially related to texts, are tested on the *Praxis®* Core writing subtest in the research section of the exam. The emphasis will be on recognizing common best practices in conducting research.

Example:

You just completed multiple database searches for an education research topic and found three academic references from peer reviewed journals. Your assignment requires a fourth peer reviewed article. What would be an effective strategy to find additional source? Choose all that apply.

- ❑ Expand your search with a search engine like Google.
- ❑ Contact the reference librarian at the local university for research assistance.
- ❑ Do searches on the authors of the articles that you already have since scholars are known to do multiple studies on related topics.
- ❑ Look through the reference list of the articles that you found for related studies.
- ❑ Use a database to search through newspaper archives on your topic.

Box 2, 3 & 4. Anything that mentions a non-academic source like Google or Wiki would not be satisfactory for academic purposes. While newspapers can be good secondary sources, they do not fulfill the peer reviewed requirement. The reference librarian, box 2, is a tremendous resource when trying to find peer-reviewed relevant research. He or She is an expert in this area. Researchers often write multiple papers and studies on one topic, box 3. Reference lists, box 4 have relevant authors and works related to the topic you are studying. Box 2, 3, and 4 are all strategies that researchers use for gathering their literature review.

Recognize information relevant to a particular research task

Evaluating research sources requires an understanding of the purpose of the research, the relevance of the sources to the purpose of the research, and the credibility of those sources. The ability to distinguish primary from secondary sources can be a key to the credibility questions. The questions are usually written with multiple acceptable answers and one that is not acceptable.

Example questions of resource relevance:

1. You are researching the hardships endured by the people, both combatants and civilians, during the battle for Okinawa in WWII. Which of the following would NOT be a good source for the study?
   A. A memoir of a Japanese soldier who fought in the battle.
   B. Photographs of devastated villages made by a US Army journalist stationed with a fighting unit.
   C. A biography of an Okinawan citizen who endured the battle.
   D. Declassified field reports of the US military campaign of Okinawa.
   E. Army intelligence reports of troop strengths and locations in the planning of the invasion.

E. While all of these pertain to Okinawa and the battle, E does not relate to the purpose of the study because it is only about the US troops. Everything else could show the hardships endured by the people.

2. Which of the following would be the best primary source for understanding how Japanese soldiers felt about the battle?
   A. An autobiography of a Japanese soldier who fought in the battle.
   B. Japanese newspaper accounts written in Tokyo.
   C. A Stars and Stripes article written during the Korean conflict.
   D. A 1953 aerial photograph of the island.
   E. A biography of the Japanese fleet commander.

A. The key phrase here is *primary source*. Therefore, A is the best answer because B, C, and E are secondary sources. While a photograph is a primary source, it does little to show how a Japanese soldier felt about the war.

This page is intentionally left blank.

Sentence Correction

Directions: In each of the following sentences, some part of the sentence or the entire sentence is underlined. Beneath each sentence, you will find five ways of writing the underlined part. The first answer choice (A) repeats the original, but the other four choices are different. If you think the original sentence is better than any of the suggested changes, you should select the first answer choice (A); otherwise, you should select one of the other answer choices.

This is a test of correctness and effectiveness of expression. In choosing answers, follow the requirement of standard written English; i.e. pay attention to acceptable usage and grammar, diction (choice of words), sentence construction and punctuation. Choose the answer that expresses most effectively what is presented in the original sentence; this answer should be clear and exact, without awkwardness, ambiguity, or redundancy.

1. For people escaping war, the most difficult part of leaving home is not leaving behind sacred possessions, <u>but rather, lost memories of a life long ago.</u>

    A. but rather, lost memories of a life long ago.

    B. but rather, losing memories of a life long ago.

    C. but rather also losing memories of a life long ago.

    D. but additionally, losing memories of a life long ago.

    E. however, losing memories of a life long ago.

2. His name is <u>synonymously aligned to that of a warrior</u>, so much so that his name has been appropriated for a wide range of military.

    A. synonymously aligned to that of a warrior

    B. synonymously and continuously aligned to that of a warrior

    C. synonymous to that of a warrior

    D. synonymous as warrior

    E. synonymous with warrior

3. She didn't know <u>which was worst: traveling</u> without credentials or sleeping in the subway.

    A. which was worst: traveling

    B. which was worst; traveling

    C. which was worse: traveling

    D. which was worse; traveling

    E. which was worst, traveling

4. The university decided to reduce the number of academic <u>programs because they could no longer monitor them.</u>

    A. programs, because they could no longer monitor them.

    B. programs because it could no longer monitor them.

    C. programs because they essentially could no longer monitor them.

    D. programs, because they could no longer monitor and observer them.

    E. programs because they could essentially no longer monitor them.

5. As a student at this university, one can accept the status quo, or we can reject it, but we cannot pretend it is not happening.

    A. As a student at this university, one can

    B. As a student at this university, we can

    C. Either the students accept

    D. Either us students accept

    E. As students at this university, we can

6. The actress, using a disguise, passing through the market without being detected by no one.

    A. The actress, using a disguise, passing through the market without being detected by no one.

    B. The actress, who used a disguise, passed through the market without being detected by no one.

    C. The actress, who used a disguise, is passing through the market without being detected by no one.

    D. The actress, using a disguise, passed through the market without being detected by anyone.

    E. The actress, who using a disguise, passed through the market without being detected by anyone.

7. Even though she seemed unaffected, the senator spoke passionately about the tragedy.

    A. the senator spoke passionately about the tragedy.

    B. the senator did spoke passionately about the tragedy.

    C. the senator did actually speak passionate about the tragedy.

    D. the senator spoke passionate about the tragedy.

    E. The senator had spoken passionately about the tragedy.

8. In the voting area, the use of cellphones and computers are prohibited.

    A. In the voting area, the use of cellphones and computers are prohibited.

    B. In the voting area the use of cellphones and computers are prohibited.

    C. In the voting area; the use of cellphones and computers are prohibited.

    D. In the voting area, the use of cellphones and computers is prohibited.

    E. In the area where voting will take place, the use of cellphones and computers is prohibited.

9. When asked about the accident, the witness was confused as to whom the driver was.

    A. the witness was confused as to whom the driver was.

    B. the witness was confused as to who the driver was.

    C. the witness was confused as to whom the driver is.

    D. the witness was confused as to whomever the driver was.

    E. the witness was confused as to whoever the driver was.

10. Why is it that every time a student comes to my office, they want something?

    A. every time a student comes to my office,

    B. every time a student coming to my office,

    C. when a student comes to my office,

    D. every time each student comes to my office,

    E. every time students come to my office,

Usage

Directions: Each question consists if a sentence that contains four underlined portions. Read each sentence and decide whether any of the underlined portions contains a grammatical construction, a word use, or an instance of incorrect or omitted punctuation or capitalization that would be inappropriate in carefully written English. If so, select the underlined portion that must be revised to produce a correct sentence. If there are no errors in the sentence as written, select **no error** (E). No sentence has more than one error.

11. She forgot her list when <u>she</u> went to the grocery <u>store;</u> this oversight <u>caused</u> her to forget many of the
           A   B   C

    <u>items</u> she needed. <u>No error.</u>
     D   E

12. The <u>doctor's</u> assistant mistakenly overbooked the <u>schedule,</u> <u>causing frustration</u> on the part of the
       A   B   C

    doctor and the <u>patients</u>. <u>No error.</u>
         D   E

13. For <u>this weeks</u> <u>meeting, I</u> would like to <u>not only focus</u> on attendance, <u>but also</u> on academic
       A   B   C   D

    engagement. <u>No error.</u>
         E

14. When the university went through <u>its</u> academic programs, <u>they</u> saw students, who were never on
               A   B

    campus, were more likely to drop out during <u>their</u> second year <u>than</u> those who were on campus all the
                   C   D

    time. <u>No error.</u>
       E

15. <u>Everyone was</u> excited to get <u>started</u> on their projects that they trampled over each other as they <u>dashed</u>
     A   B   C

    over to the <u>supplies</u> table. <u>No error.</u>
        D   E

16. As scientists discover galaxies far away, <u>one has</u> to decide if <u>they</u> are going to publish every idea or
                 A   B

    <u>only</u> expand on theories that have been <u>substantiated</u>. <u>No error.</u>
     C   D   E

17. Every <u>Fall,</u> tourists come from far and wide to <u>bear</u> witness to the leaves <u>changing</u> colors as the season
       A   B   C

    <u>progresses</u>. <u>No error.</u>
      D   E

18. As we move forward with <u>new</u> <u>employees,</u> we must be sure to train them <u>properly,</u> inspire them
                                A   B   C

    regularly, <u>and ask them appropriate questions.</u> <u>No error.</u>
                         D   E

19. I not only want you to <u>succeed,</u> <u>and</u> I <u>also</u> want you <u>to be happy.</u> <u>No error.</u>
                             A   B   C   D   E

20. She only understood three <u>things about that</u> time <u>period:</u> <u>being hungry,</u> grace<u>, and acceptance</u>.
                                   A   B   C   D

    <u>No error.</u>
      E

Directions: The following passage is a draft of an essay. Some parts of the passage need to be strengthened through editing and revision. Read the passage and choose the best answers for the questions that follow. Some questions ask you to improve particular sentences or portions of sentences. In some cases, the indicated portion of the passage will be most effective as it is already expressed and thus will require no changes. In choosing answers, consider development, organization, word choice, style and ton, and follow the requirements of standard written English.

Adapted from *Geronimo: The Warrior* by Edward Rielly. Retrieved from the Public Domain[1].

(1) Most people do not know who Geronimo really is, other than the famous phrase yelled out when jumping off of a high place. (2) But he is one of the most famous figures in the history of the American Indian resistance effort. (3) His name is synonymous to warrior, so much so that his name has been appropriated for a wide range of military (or simply adventuresome) endeavors. (4) Geronimo's reputation is well deserved, for his very name excited fear in settlers both North and South of the U.S. – Mexican border.

(5) Geronimo lacked the social and political leadership skills to propel a movement forward with the U.S. Government. (6) Geronimo's fighting skills set him apart from all others. (7) His lasting led American paratroopers in World War II to call out the name "Geronimo" before plunging from their planes. (8) Schoolchildren, for decades after Geronimo's death, would similarly yell his name before undertaking a real or imagined feat of bravery, such as leaping from a swing into a river. (9) A much more recent, and highly controversial, use of Geronimo's name was its employment by the U.S. military as a code name linked to the 2011 operation that resulted in the death of Osama bin Laden.

21. What would be the best way to combine and rewrite sentences 1 and 2 (reproduced below)?

Most people do not know who Geronimo really is, other than the famous phrase yelled out when jumping off of a high place. But he is one of the most famous figures in the history of the American Indian resistance effort.

A. (As it is now)

B. Even though most people today only know Geronimo as the word people yell when jumping off of something high in the air, Geronimo was one of the most famous figures in the history of the American Indian resistance effort.

C. Even though most people today do not know who Geronimo really is, he is essentially one of the most famously well-known figures in the history of the American Indian resistance effort.

D. The fact that most people today do not know who Geronimo is, he is one of the most famous figures in the history of the American Indian resistance effort.

E. Can you believe people today do not know who Geronimo is, even though he is one of the most famous figures in the history of the American Indian resistance effort?

22. The word employment, as highlighted below, means:

A much more recent, and highly controversial, use of Geronimo's name was its employment by the U.S. military as a code name linked to the 2011 operation that resulted in the death of Osama bin Laden.

A. service

B. salary

C. occupation

D. work

E. application

[1] https://publicdomainreview.org/2011/08/29/geronimo-the-warrior/

23. What revision would be the most appropriate for sentenced 4 (reproduced below)?

Geronimo's reputation is well-deserved, for his very name excited fear in settlers both North and South of the U.S-Mexican border.

A. Take the apostrophe off "Geronimo's"

B. Change the *N* in "North" and the *S* in "South" to lowercase letters.

C. Change the comma before "for" to a period, and capitalize the *f* in "for"

D. Change the hyphen in "U.S. – Mexican border" to a slash (/).

E. Change the comma to a semicolon.

24. The word *feat*, as highlighted below, means:

Schoolchildren, for decades after Geronimo's death, would similarly yell his name before undertaking a real or imagined feat of bravery, such as leaping from a swing into a river.

A. fear

B. excitement

C. enthusiasm

D. act

E. spare

25. Which of the following sentences can be eliminated from the passage without sacrificing meaning or detail?

A. 1

B. 3

C. 5

D. 7

E. 8

Directions: The following passage is a draft of an essay. Some parts of the passage need to be strengthened through editing and revision. Read the passage and choose the best answers for the questions that follow. Some questions ask you to improve particular sentences or portions of sentences. In some cases, the indicated portion of the passage will be most effective as it is already expressed and thus will require no changes. In choosing answers, consider development, organization, word choice, style and ton, and follow the requirements of standard written English.

(1) In today's modern world of technology people prefer to get information from the Internet instead of books. (2) Now, the creation of internet and other devices helped people to find information very easy and quick. (3) Everyday people rely on the internet for their routines.

(4) The internet is so responsive that in just a few seconds people can find the most recent information about current events and politics, latest products and services, and to get updates from all around the world. (5) Too often however, the internet provides unreliable information, and we fail to notice. (6) People have to research beyond one or two websites to find trustworthy websites.

(7) Modern technology has many positive uses. (8) Nowadays, people are using technology in their daily lives. (9) Internet users need to learn how to find and use reliable sources of information.

26. In context, which revision of sentence 3 (reproduced below) is most appropriate?

Every day people rely on the internet for their routines.

A. Every-day people rely on the internet for their routines.

B. Every day, people rely on the internet for their routines.

C. Everyday people rely on the internet for their routines.

D. Everyday people rely on the internet for their routines.

E. Every day people rely on the internet for one's routines.

27. If the author wanted to draw attention to specific ways in which people use the internet in their daily lives, what sentence can be added to the first paragraph to support that idea?

A. (As it is now)

B. People wake up every morning, and the first thing they do is look at their phones.

C. People going for a morning jog might search the web for upbeat music, while people headed to work might use an app to check the weather.

D. In other words, the internet is everywhere and used for so many things.

E. People are so addicted to the internet, they can't stop looking at their phones.

28. Which revision uses parallel structure to revise sentence 4 (reproduced below)?

The internet is so responsive that in just a few seconds people can find the most up-to-date information about current events and politics, latest products and services, and to get updates from all around the world.

A. (As it is now)

B. The internet is so responsive that in just a few seconds people can find the most up-to-date information about current events and politics, latest products and services, and updates from all around the world.

C. The internet is so responsive that in just a few seconds people can find the most up-to-date information about current events and politics, latest products and services, and real-time updates from around the world.

D. The internet is so responsive that in just a few seconds people can find the most up-to-date information about current events and politics and latest products and services, and to get updates from all around the world.

E. The internet is so responsive that in just a few seconds people can find the most up-to-date information from around the world on current events, politics, products, and services.

29. In context, what would be the best way to combine and revise sentences 7 & 8 (reproduced below) so the author can introduce the conclusion and support the main idea of the essay?

Modern technology has many positive uses. Nowadays, people are using technology in their daily lives.

   A. (As it is now)

   B. Today, the internet has had a positive impact on people's daily lives.

   C. Too many people use the internet without understanding how to get reliable information.

   D. In conclusion, people must understand the internet can only produce what a person is searching for.

   E. Even though the internet is convenient, it has a long way to go before it is truly reliable.

30. What error did the author make in sentence 5 (reproduced below)?

Too often, however, the internet provides unreliable information, and we fail to notice.

   A. The author shifts from 3rd person to 1st person.

   B. The author uses too many commas in the sentence.

   C. The author uses the transitional word "however" incorrectly.

   D. The author should put the word **unreliable** in quotations because it's the author's opinion.

   E. There are no errors in sentence 5.

Directions: The following passage is a draft of an essay. Some parts of the passage need to be strengthened through editing and revision. Read the passage and choose the best answers for the questions that follow. Some questions ask you to improve particular sentences or portions of sentences. In some cases, the indicated portion of the passage will be most effective as it is already expressed and thus will require no changes. In choosing answers, consider development, organization, word choice, style and ton, and follow the requirements of standard written English.

(1) The subject of whether or not Shakespeare should be studied in high school English classes has caused much debate. (2) On the one side, you have the diehard traditionalists who insist that learning to appreciate Shakespearean language is the crux of a well-rounded education. (3) However, others will argue that the archaic language used in Shakespeare's works is a source of confusion for students. (4) They also argue that todays students need more practice reading and interpreting the type of text they will be exposed to in a professional setting. (5) With valid arguments on both sides, this debate will most likely not be settled any time soon.

31. What is the best placement for the sentence below?

    They also point out that because many modern-day sayings have roots in his works, studying Shakespeare will help students grasp the history of our language.

    A. after sentence 4
    B. after sentence 2
    C. after sentence 5
    D. after sentence 1

32. In sentence 2 (reproduced below) what is the most appropriate definition of the word *crux* as it pertains to the meaning in this passage?

    On the one side, you have the diehard traditionalists who insist that learning to appreciate Shakespearean language is the crux of a well-rounded education.

    A. intersection
    B. piece
    C. effect
    D. foundation
    E. portion

33. Which of the following statements would best enhance the author's position that Shakespeare's work can often be confusing to students?

    A. Most universities want to see that students took at least some Shakespeare in high school.
    B. Students can strengthen their reading skills by reading Shakespeare.
    C. Shakespeare often used a language and dialect in his plays that many students have not been exposed to.
    D. Watching movies based on Shakespearean plays can help students relate to the scenes in Shakespearean plays.
    E. Traditionalists will always want students to stretch beyond their comfort zones and read Shakespeare.

34. How should sentence 4 (reproduced below) be revised so it is grammatically correct.

    They also argue that todays students need more practice reading and interpreting the type of text they will be exposed to in a professional setting.

    A. (As it is now)
    B. They also argue that today's students need more practice reading and interpreting the type of text they will be exposed to in a professional setting.
    C. They also argue that todays students needed more practice reading and interpreting the type of text one will be exposed to in a professional setting.
    D. They also argue, that todays students actually need more practice reading and interpreting the type of text students will be exposed to in a professional setting.
    E. They also argue that todays students need more practice by reading and interpreting the type of text they will be exposed to in a professional setting.

35. What is the main purpose of reviewing the references in a research article in an academic paper?

   A. To check that the authors only used primary source documents

   B. To identify additional relevant resources on the topic

   C. To observe how to write citations correctly

   D. To verify the authors did not cite themselves

   E. To avoid plagiarism of the research article

36. What is the main purpose of a style guide?

   A. To find multiple meanings of words.

   B. To find synonyms of words.

   C. To research formatting guidelines and citation requirements in a document.

   D. To identify databases where academic articles can be found.

   E. To reference grammar and mechanics best practices.

37. Which of the following citations is written in correct APA formatting?

   A. Wordsworth, W. *Lyrical Ballads*. Oxford UP, 1967.

   B. William Wordsworth. *Lyrical Ballads*. Oxford UP, 1967.

   C. Wordsworth, W (1967). *Lyrical Ballads*. Oxford UP.

   D. *Lyrical Ballads* by Wordsworth, William. Oxford UP, 1967.

   E. *Lyrical Ballads* (1967) by Wordsworth, William. Oxford UP.

38. Which of the following is NOT included in the citation below?

Whitehurst, G., & Lonigan, C. (1998). Child Development and Emergent Literacy. *Child Development, 69*(3)

   A. authors

   B. date

   C. name of publication

   D. volume number

   E. page number

39. A student is using a ***direct quote*** from a paper on student behavior. What would be the correct way to cite the direct quote (reproduced below) using MLA formatting?

James Rodriguez says, students are social beings, and teachers must encourage students to engage in cooperative learning activities.

   A. According Rodriguez, "students are social beings, and teachers must encourage students to engage in cooperative learning activities."

   B. According Rodriguez (1979), "students are social beings, and teachers must encourage students to engage in cooperative learning activities."

   C. According the author James Rodriguez, "students are social beings, and teachers must encourage students to engage in cooperative learning activities" (direct quote).

   D. Direct quote from Rodriguez: Students are social beings, and teachers must encourage students to engage in cooperative learning activities.

   E. "Students are social beings, and teachers must encourage students to engage in cooperative learning activities" (Rodriguez 45).

40. Where is the best place for students to find scholarly information when writing a research paper?

   A. database for academic journals

   B. government website

   C. Internet search engine

   D. school website

   E. blog

Number	Answer	Content Category	Explanation
1.	B	II	By changing the word *lost* to *losing* the sentence maintains parallel structure between the two clauses. Both *leaving* and "losing" end in *ing*.
2.	E	II	The word *synonymous* means the *same as*. In this case the adverb *synonymously* is used to modify "aligned." Also, answer E contains the most succinct version of the sentence. When in doubt, always go for the shortest answer on a grammar test. The shortest answer is usually the correct answer.
3.	C	II	In this case, two items are compared. Thus, one would be worse than the other. The word *worst* is used in a comparison of three or more.
4.	B	II	In the original sentence the pronoun *they* is used to mean the university. The correct pronoun for an impersonal, non-gender specific item is the pronoun *it*.
5.	E	II	In order to maintain pronoun antecedent agreement throughout the sentence, the word *student* becomes *students* and the word *one* becomes *we*.
6.	D	II	This sentence fragment contains 3 problems. First, it is a fragment as it is lacking a complete thought. Second, *no one* should be changed to *anyone* to avoid a double negative. Finally, *passing* should be changed to *passed* to avoid a shift in verb tense.
7.	A	II	No change is needed. The word *passionately* is an adverb and should modify the verb spoke.
8.	D	II	Often subject verb agreement becomes a problem when a prepositional phrase such as *of cellphones and computers* is placed between the subject and verb. By reading the sentence without the phrase, the subject *use* and the verb *are* clearly do not agree. The verb should be *is*. Finally, the comma is the correct punctuation here because it separates the dependent clause from the independent clause. The semicolon in answer choice C is incorrect because a semicolon is used to separate 2 independent clauses. This sentence has a dependent clause with an independent clause.
9.	B	II	When determining whether to use *who* or *who*, remember who is the subject of the sentence or phrase, while whom is the object of the verb or preposition. (Tip: often times *who* can be replaced by he/she and *whom* can be replaced by him/her). In this case, if I asked, "Who was the driver?" You would respond, "He is the driver," or "She is the driver." You would not say, "Him is the driver," or "Her is the driver." **He** and **she** are subject pronouns. **Who** is also a subject pronoun.

Number	Answer	Content Category	Explanation
10.	E	II	The plural pronoun "they" is used to rename student, which is a singular noun. In order to maintain pronoun antecedent agreement, change student to students.
11.	E	II	No error. The semicolon is used correctly here in that it is used to separate two independent clauses.
12.	E	II	No error. The possessive form of the word *doctor* is correct. The comma is also correct because it separates a dependent clause from an independent clause.
13.	A	II	An apostrophe is needed in the word *week's*. The meeting referred to in the sentence is exclusive to that particular week, allowing for the word *week's* to show possession. Other examples of this would be *last night's class* or *tomorrow's conference call*.
14.	B	II	The pronoun *they* should be changed to the impersonal pronoun *its* to maintain pronoun antecedent agreement. In addition, the university may have many people who attend and work there; however, the university is a collective singular noun and should have a singular pronoun—it.
15.	A	II	The pronoun *everyone* is a singular indefinite pronoun which means its antecedent, the word *their*, needs to be singular as well. Because you do not have the option to correct *their*, you must change the subject *everyone* to *the students*. This will make the subject plural, and it will match the pronoun *their* and *they*.
16.	A	II	Change the word *one* to *they* to maintain pronoun antecedent agreement.
17.	A	II	The names of the season are not capitalized unless referring to a specific time such as the Fall of 2018. Remember, summer, fall, winter, and spring are all lowercase in a sentence, unless they are part of a proper noun.
18.	D	II	Items or action in a list should have parallel structure. By changing *ask them appropriate questions* to *question them appropriately*, all items follow the same parallel structure.
19.	B	II	The word *and* is used incorrectly here. Remember, if you have a *not only* in the intro clause, you must have a *but also* in the proceeding clause. The correct revision would be ***I not only** want you to succeed, **but I also** want you to be happy*.
20.	C	II	Change *hungry* to *hunger* to maintain parallel structure in the list of items.

Number	Answer	Content Category	Explanation
21.	B	I	Using an introductory dependent clause followed by an independent clause is an effective way to not only join two statements without losing meaning, but also to create sentence variety within a passage. C is incorrect because it contains redundancy …*but he is also the most famously well-known*… Answer D contains an error—*the fact that*—In the intro clause. Answer E is not the best choice because it begins by asking the reader a question. B is the most effective choice here.
22.	E	I	The US military used Geronimo's name as stated in the line above the word employment. To employ can mean to hire, but here employ means to apply or the application of the name by the US Military for the military operation. Also, if you substituted all the words in for employment, application makes the most sense.
23.	B	I	Compass directional words (north, south, east, west) are never capitalized when offering directions. However, the directional words are capitalized when referring to a definite geographical region. (Example: *She goes to **South** Florida for the winter*).
24.	D	I	The word **feat** means *an achievement that requires great courage, skill, or strength* making it the best choice. Also, if *feat* is replaced with the words in the answer choices, *act* makes the most sense.
25.	C	I	Sentence 5 could be removed without changing the main idea of the passage. The article is primarily focusing on Geronimo's physical skills. Sentence 5 refers to mental skills that he was lacking.
26.	B	II	First, there needs to be a comma after every day because that is the intro clause. Second, the word *everyday* should be changed to *every day*. As is, the word *everyday* is acting as an adjective describing the type of people (everyday people). However, the author is intending for it to mean that people use the internet every single day; therefore, it should be changed to *every day*.
27.	C	I	The question stem is asking what could make the statement most specific. Answer C provides the most specific examples—morning jog, upbeat music, weather app—to back up the author's claim.
28.	E	I	By creating a list of all nouns, the author is able to maintain parallel structure when describing the type of information found on the internet.
29.	E	I	This sentence combines the two statements effectively while restating the main idea: the internet is convenient, but the internet can be unreliable. By recapping these two concepts addressed in the passage, the author is recapping the main idea.

Number	Answer	Content Category	Explanation
30.	A	I	Throughout the passage the author is using 3rd person by using words such as *people* and *they*. In sentence 5, the author switches to the 1st person by using the pronoun *we*.
31.	B	I	This sentence would best fit after sentence 2 in the paragraph as it supports the use of Shakespearean works in schools. In addition, this sentence starts with "They also…" This makes it easy to place the sentence appropriately. Sentence 3 begins the opposed side of the argument, so "They also…" would not work. Putting "They also…" at the end of the paragraph here does not work either. The best place for this line is after sentence 2.
32.	D	I	The word *crux* means the decisive or most important point at issue. In this case, the author is stating that Shakespearean language is most important or foundational for a well-rounded education. Also, out of all the answer choices, *foundation* makes the most sense when it is substituted for the word *crux*.
33.	C	I	Choices A, B, D, E all argue the case to keep Shakespearean works in the high school curriculum. Choice C argues against it by stating that students are not familiar with the language. Thus, they will be confused.
34.	B	I	The sentence contains an apostrophe error. Change *todays* to *today's* because the author is referring to students that belong to today.
35.	B	I	Reviewing the reference page provides a wealth of additional and creditable sources on the same topic.
36.	C	II	Style Guides provide information on formatting and citing requirements.
37.	C	II	For APA reference page citations, information is listed in the order of author last name, author's first initial, year, title, publication, publisher, volume, issue, page number(s).
38.	E	II	The page number is missing from this particular citation. See APA on page _____.
39.	E	II	For MLA a direct quote will include quotation marks around quoted material followed by author and page number in parentheses.
40.	A	II	Databases for academic journals are created to house scholarly, academic information for research purposes.

Sentence Correction

Directions: In each of the following sentences, some part of the sentence or the entire sentence is underlined. Beneath each sentence, you will find five ways of writing the underlined part. The first answer choice (A) repeats the original, but the other four choices are different. If you think the original sentence is better than any of the suggested changes, you should select the first answer choice (A); otherwise, you should select one of the other answer choices.

This is a test of correctness and effectiveness of expression. In choosing answers, follow the requirement of standard written English; i.e. pay attention to acceptable usage and grammar, diction (choice of words), sentence construction and punctuation. Choose the answer that expresses most effectively what is presented in the original sentence; this answer should be clear and exact, without awkwardness, ambiguity, or redundancy.

1. Last Saturday evening, we arrived early for the movie, yet we were able to choose the best seats in the theater.

   A. movie, yet we were able to choose the best seats in the theater.

   B. movie, we were able to choose the best seats in the theater.

   C. movie, so we were able to choose the best seats in the theater.

   D. movie and, yet, we choose the best seats in the theater.

   E. movie yet we had chosen the best seats in the theater.

2. When the computer store checked their records, it realized the company was improving in product sales, customer service, and customer satisfaction.

   A. When the computer store checked their records,

   B. When the computer store checked on their records,

   C. When the computer store, checking on their records,

   D. When the computer store looked at it's records,

   E. When the computer store checked its records,

3. After driving all over the neighborhood, my cat was found casually wandering around a vacant lot.

   A. my cat was found casually wandering around a vacant lot.

   B. casually wandering around the vacant lot, my cat was found.

   C. I found my cat casually wondering around a vacant lot.

   D. in a vacant lot my cat was found by me casually walking around.

   E. my cat was found by me casually walking around a vacant lot.

4. I was not sure who I should ask for help with the calculus problem, so I called my third-grade teacher.

   A. who I should ask for help with the calculus problem

   B. whom I should ask for help with the calculus problem

   C. whoever I should ask for help with the calculus problem

   D. as to who I should ask for help with the calculus problem

   E. as to whoever I should ask to help me with the calculus problem

5. Although the new café is located in a neglected section of town, <u>it is nicely decorated, has great lighting, and comfortably arranged.</u>

    A. it is nicely decorated, has great lighting, and comfortably arranged.

    B. it is nicely decorated, lit well, and comfortably arranged.

    C. it is nicely decorated, well lit, and comfortably arranged.

    D. it is nicely decorated, lit with bright lights, and comfortably arranged.

    E. it is nicely decorated, has been well lit, and comfortably arranged.

6. <u>Before doctors make a diagnosis, they should review their patients' medical history.</u>

    A. Before doctors make a diagnosis, they should review their patients' medical history.

    B. Before doctors make a diagnosis they should review their patients' medical history.

    C. Before doctors make a diagnosis, he should review their patients' medical history.

    D. Before doctors make a diagnosis, they should review their patients' medical histories.

    E. Before doctors make a diagnosis they should review their patients' medical histories.

7. <u>Its mandatory at the university for every student to attend orientation before scheduling their classes.</u>

    A. Its mandatory at the university for every student to attend orientation before scheduling their classes.

    B. It's mandatory at the university for students to attend orientation before scheduling their classes.

    C. For every student at the university its mandatory to attend orientation before scheduling their classes.

    D. It's mandatory for every university student to attend orientation before scheduling their classes.

    E. As a student at the university, its mandatory to attend orientation before scheduling their classes.

8. <u>If every student could write as neat as Jamie,</u> I would not have to spend so much time grading papers.

    A. If every student could write as neat as Jamie,

    B. If every student could write neat like Jamie,

    C. If every student could write as neatly as Jamie,

    D. If every student could neatly write as Jamie,

    E. If every student could write neat like Jamie,

9. Although often thought to be shy animals, <u>the elephants in the large enclosure seems to show off for the crowds</u> visiting at the zoo.

    A. the elephants in the large enclosure seems to show off for the crowds

    B. the elephants in the large enclosure shows off seemingly for the crowds

    C. the elephants in the large enclosure seemingly shows off for the crowds

    D. the elephants in the large enclosure seem to show off for the crowds

    E. in the large enclosure, the elephants seems to show off the crowds

10. <u>My dad, who loves westerns,</u> has always wanted to travel to a ghost town near the Grand Canyon.

    A.   My dad, who loves westerns,

    B.   My dad who loves westerns

    C.   My dad a western lover

    D.   My dad, whom loves westerns,

    E.   My dad always loving westerns,

11. After visiting Disneyland and Disney World last year, both <u>parks seem to be one in the same to me.</u>

    A.   parks seem to be one in the same to me.

    B.   parks seem to be all in the same to me.

    C.   parks seem to be one and the same to me.

    D.   parks are basically one in the same to me.

    E.   parks are one in the same to me.

12. After years of searching, <u>the money was found casually walking in the woods</u> on a long winter's hike.

    A.   the money was found casually walking in the woods

    B.   casually walking in the woods the money was found

    C.   the money in the woods was found casually walking in the woods

    D.   I found the money as I was casually walking in the woods

    E.   I found the money casually walking in the woods

13. Each day, after a cruise ship docks nearby, <u>a busload of tourists arrives</u> to visit the ancient city of Tulum and admire the Caribbean ocean views.

    A.   a busload of tourists arrives

    B.   the tourists arrives by the busload

    C.   a busload of tourists arrive

    D.   a busload with tourists arrive

    E.   tourists by the busload arrives

14. Jessica, realizing something was amiss, <u>entered the dark room then she screamed at the top of her lungs</u> when she saw a figure appear from the shadows.

    A.   entered the dark room then she screamed at the top of her lungs

    B.   then entered the dark room and she screamed at the top of her lungs

    C.   entered the dark room then screaming at the top of her lungs

    D.   entering the dark room, then screaming at the top of her lungs

    E.   entered the dark room, and then she screamed at the top of her lungs

Usage

Directions: Each question consists if a sentence that contains four underlined portions. Read each sentence and decide whether any of the underlined portions contains a grammatical construction, a word use, or an instance of incorrect or omitted punctuation or capitalization that would be inappropriate in carefully written English. If so, select the underlined portion that must be revised to produce a correct sentence. If there are no errors in the sentence as written, select **no error** (E). No sentence has more than one error.

15. Each female participant in the <u>race</u> received <u>their</u> own t-shirt with the company <u>emblem</u> on the <u>back</u>.
                               A   B   C   D

    <u>No error.</u>
    E

16. The mall was crowded with <u>holiday</u> <u>shoppers,</u> <u>therefore,</u> we decided to <u>shop</u> online this year. <u>No error.</u>
                                   A   B   C   D   E

17. After the waiter <u>made</u> a mistake on the <u>bill,</u> the angry customer <u>refused</u> to <u>except</u> an apology from the
                      A   B   C   D

    manager. <u>No error.</u>
           E

18. Each of <u>these</u> books <u>are</u> meant to help young people deal with difficult situations and to encourage
             A   B

    <u>them</u> to seek additional help <u>when</u> necessary. <u>No error</u>.
     C   D   E

19. Greg <u>enjoys</u> several outdoor <u>activities:</u> hiking in the woods, <u>swimming</u> in the lake, and
       A   B   C

    <u>to camp</u> out overnight. <u>No error.</u>
     D   E

20. <u>Due</u> to the heavy <u>rainfall,</u> the river was higher <u>than</u> usual and <u>floods</u> the roadway. <u>No error.</u>
 A   B   C   D   E

21. My favorite season <u>used</u> to be <u>summer, but</u> now I <u>prefer</u> the cooler temperatures of the <u>other</u> seasons.
                    A   B   C   D

    <u>No error.</u>
    E

22. Although he is <u>older,</u> my brother is <u>shorter</u> <u>than</u> <u>me</u>. <u>No error.</u>
                  A   B   C D   E

23. <u>Because</u> last <u>months</u> schedule <u>was</u> filled with meetings and presentations, I <u>was</u> constantly working
   A   B   C   D

    late. <u>No error</u>.
        E

24. <u>Irregardless</u> of the <u>winter</u> storm, <u>several</u> people attended the high school <u>play and</u> stayed for the
        A   B   C   D

    reception last night. <u>No error.</u>
                             E

Directions: The following passage is a draft of an essay. Some parts of the passage need to be strengthened through editing and revision. Read the passage and choose the best answers for the questions that follow. Some questions ask you to improve particular sentences or portions of sentences. In some cases, the indicated portion of the passage will be most effective as it is already expressed and thus will require no changes. In choosing answers, consider development, organization, word choice, style and ton, and follow the requirements of standard written English.

Adapted from *Kittens and Cats: A First Reader (1911)- Cats and Captions before the Internet Age*, Retrieved from the Public Domain.

(1) Before LOLCat, Grumpy Cat, Longcat, Nyan Cat and all the other famed kitties of the internet age, there were the felines featured in *Kittens and Cats: A First Reader* (1911). (2) If this delightful yet also slightly creepy book is anything to go by, then taking photos of cats and brandishing them with an amusing caption was far from being a phenomenon born with the internet. (3) Within its pages we meet "Queen Cat", "Dunce Cat", "Party Cat", and perhaps our favorite "Hero Cat", amongst others. (4) The book is attributed to the American children's author Eulalie Osgood Grover, who uses the pictures to tell the tale of the Queen's party and all the kitty characters attending. (5) As for the photographs themselves, the book credits them courtesy of the Rotograph Company, a popular postcard manufacturer, which implies they are almost certainly an early example of the work of Harry Whittier Frees, their staff animal photographer. (6) A few years later Frees would become associated with a whole host of similar pictures under his own name such as *The Little Folks of Animal Land*. (7) Several other publications of photograph collections followed until he ended his own life in 1953. (8) How did Frees get his cats to pose for such photographs? (9) Even before the days of super quick shutter speeds? (10) Although he denied the use of dead or taxidermized animals and asserted only humane methods were used, you can't help but wonder if this is really true, especially in the case of his later work which involved more elaborate scenes than displayed in this book.

25. What would be the best way to combine and rewrite sentences 8 and 9 (reproduced below)?

    How did Frees get his cats to pose for such photographs? Even before the days of super quick shutter speeds?

    A. (As it is now)

    B. Even before the days of super quick shutter speeds, so how did Frees get his cats to pose for such photographs?

    C. How did Frees get his cats to pose for such photographs even before the days of super quick shutter speeds?

    D. How did Frees get his cats to pose for such photographs, yet even before the days of super quick shutter speeds.

    E. Although without super quick shutter speeds available back then, how did Frees get his cats to pose for such photographs?

26. Which of the following sentences can be eliminated from the passage without sacrificing meaning?

    A. 1

    B. 2

    C. 3

    D. 5

    E. 10

27. What revision would be most appropriate for sentence 2 (reproduced below)?

    If this delightful yet also slightly creepy book is anything to go by, then taking photos of cats and brandishing them with an amusing caption was far from being a phenomenon born with the internet.

    A. Add commas before and after the phrase "yet also slightly creepy."

    B. Add an apostrophe to the word *cats.*

    C. Capitalize the word *internet.*

    D. Add a comma after *delightful.*

    E. Add a comma after the word *caption.*

28. The word *brandishing* as highlighted below, means:

   If this delightful yet also slightly creepy book is anything to go by, then taking photos of cats and brandishing them with an amusing caption was far from being a phenomenon born with the internet.

   A. beating

   B. shaming

   C. alarming

   D. displaying

   E. correcting

29. What error did the author make in sentence 10 (reproduced below)? Choose all that apply.

   Although he denied the use of dead or taxidermized animals and asserted only humane methods were used, you can't help but wonder if this is really true, especially in the case of his later work which involved more elaborate scenes than displayed in this book.

   ❑ The author used too many commas in the sentence.

   ❑ The author switched from 3rd person to 2nd person.

   ❑ The author should delete the word *taxidermized* as it means the same as the word *dead*.

   ❑ The author used the subordinating conjunction *although* incorrectly.

   ❑ The author should use a question mark at the end because he is questioning the situation.

30. Which of the following statements would be an appropriate conclusion for this passage?

   A. Clearly, the photographer was photographing deceased cats.

   B. In conclusion, by looking closely at photographs from the early 1900's, we can see that the cats were posed in comical positions.

   C. All in all, the art of cat photography has been around a long time.

   D. In the end, however, the photographer committed suicide before he could answer more questions about his work.

   E. Either way, Americans were amused with humorously captioned cat photographs long before silly cat memes posted online.

Directions: The following passage is a draft of an essay. Some parts of the passage need to be strengthened through editing and revision. Read the passage and choose the best answers for the questions that follow. Some questions ask you to improve particular sentences or portions of sentences. In some cases, the indicated portion of the passage will be most effective as it is already expressed and thus will require no changes. In choosing answers, consider development, organization, word choice, style and ton, and follow the requirements of standard written English.

Adapted from *The Dancing Plague of 1518*, Retrieved from the Public Domain Review.

(1) On a hastily built stage before the busy horse market of Strasbourg, scores of people dance to pipes, drums, and horns. (2) The July sun beats down upon them as they hop from leg to leg, spin in circles and whooped loudly into the crowd. (3) From a distance they might be carnival celebrators. (4) But closer inspection reveals a more disquieting scene. (5) Their arms are flailing and their bodies are convulsing spasmodically. (6) Ragged clothes and pinched faces are saturated in sweat. (7) Their eyes are glassy, distant. (8) Blood seeps from swollen feet into leather boots and wooden clogs. (9) These are not revelers but "choreomaniacs", entirely possessed by the mania of the dance.

(10) In full view of the public, this is the summit of the choreomania that tormented Strasbourg for a midsummer month in 1518. (11) Also known as the "dancing plague", it was the most fatal and best documented of the more than ten such contagions which had broken out along the Rhine and Moselle rivers since 1374. (12) Once thought to be caused from a mold that grew on cornstalks and even believed to be caused by demonic possessions. (13) Numerous accounts of the bizarre events that unfolded that summer can be found scattered across various contemporary documents and chronicles compiled in the subsequent decades and centuries.

31. Which revision uses parallel structure to revise Sentence 2 (reproduced below)?

    The July sun beats down upon them as they hop from leg to leg, spin in circles and whooped loudly into the crowd.

    A. (As is now)

    B. The July sun beats down upon them as they hop from leg to leg, spin wildly, and whooped loudly into the crowd.

    C. The July sun beats down upon them as they hop around, spin in circles and whooped loudly into the crowd.

    D. The July sun beats down upon them as they hop from leg to leg, spin in circles and whoop into the crowd.

    E. The July sun beats down upon them as they hop crazily from leg to leg, spin wildly in circles and whooped loudly into the crowd.

32. What is the best placement for the sentence below?

    Even though they are obviously suffering physically, they continued this trance-like dance for hours with no apparent intention of pausing anytime soon.

    A. After sentence 3

    B. After sentence 8

    C. After sentence 9

    D. After sentence 10

    E. After sentence 12

33. How should sentence 12 (reproduced below) be revised so it is grammatically correct?

Once thought to be caused from a mold that grew on cornstalks and even believed to be caused by demonic possessions

A. (As is now)

B. Once thought to be caused from a mold that grew on cornstalks, and even believed to be caused by demonic possessions.

C. Even once thought to be caused from a mold that grew on cornstalks and even believed to be caused by demonic possession

D. The dancing plague was once thought to be caused from a mold that grew on cornstalks and even believed to be caused by demonic possessions.

E. Once, the dancing plague, thought to be caused from a mold that grew on cornstalks and even believed to be caused by demonic possession.

34. In sentence 4 (reproduced below) what is the most appropriate definition of the word *disquieting* as it pertains to the passage?

But closer inspection reveals a more disquieting scene.

A. disturbing

B. loud

C. messy

D. sorrowful

E. annoying

35. Which of the following is not considered a credible source?

A. The Journal of Infectious Diseases

B. a peer reviewed academic paper

C. www.science.gov

D. America Cancer Society Newsletter

E. social media outlet

36. Which of the following is a primary source?

A. The Biography of John Smith

B. The Autobiography of John Smith

C. An article titled How John Smith Lived his Life

D. An unauthorized book written by John Smith's brother.

E. None of the above.

37. Which of the following citations is written in correct APA formatting?

A. Smith, Sarah. Journal of Medicine. "A Cure on the Horizon" 2018. New York, New York.

B. Smith, S. "A Cure on the Horizon" Retrieved from the Journal of Medicine, Issue 6. PG 10-12. (2018)

C. Smith, Sarah. (2018). A Cure on the Horizon. *Journal of Medicine*, 6, 10-12.

D. Journal of Medicine, "A Cure on the Horizon by Sarah Smith" 6, 10-12. 2018.

E. A Cure on the Horizon. Smith, Sarah. *Journal of Medicine.6,10-12. 2018*

38. In both MLA and APA formatting styles, citations must be:

A. Cited only on the reference page.

B. Cited only after a direct quotation in the body of the paper.

C. Cited only if the information is from a journal article.

D. Cited within the paper as well as the reference page.

E. As long as a citation is included, it does not matter where it is cited in either style.

39. Which of the following cited from pg. 5 of *The Success Principles* by Jack Canfield written in 2015 is in correct MLA style when using a direct quote.

    A. In his book, author Jack Canfield states that "you are the one person responsible for the quality of life that you live."

    B. In his book, the author suggests "you are the one person responsible for the quality of life that you live."

    C. In his book, author Jack Canfield states that "you are the one person responsible for the quality of life that you live." (2015).

    D. In his book, author Jack Canfield (5) states that "you are the one person responsible for the quality of life that you live."

    E. In his book, author Jack Canfield states that, "you are the one person responsible for the quality of life that you live" (5).

40. It is important to cite references within a research paper to

    A. Credit the author(s) of the original material.

    B. Avoid plagiarism,

    C. To add creditability to the points made within the paper.

    D. To offer additional resources for interested readers.

    E. All the above.

Number	Answer	Content Category	Explanation
1.	C	II	In the original sentence, the coordinating conjunction *yet* does not show the correct relationship between the two events. A better conjunction choice would be the word *so*, meaning as a result of arriving early. Also, a comma is needed before a conjunction when the conjunction is separating two independent clauses.
2.	E	II	The possessive pronoun *their,* is referring to the company. However, the correct pronoun for an impersonal, non-gender specific item is the possessive pronoun *it*.
3.	C	II	When using a modifying phrase such as "After driving all over the neighborhood," the next noun after the phrase should always be the noun that the phrase is describing. In the case above, if left as is, the next noun after the phrase is "cat." Therefore, the phrase is suggesting that the cat was driving all over the neighborhood. This is known as a misplaced modifier. By placing the correct noun right after the modifying phrase, it is clear that the phrase is describing "I" instead of the cat.
4.	B	II	When deciding to use *who* or *whom*, determine if it is being used in the phrase or sentence as a subject (who) or an object of the verb (whom). In this case, *whom* should be used because it is not the subject, but rather the object or person receiving the action. Another way to determine which to use is by replacing *who* with *he* or *whom* with *him*.
5.	C	II	Items in a list should have parallel structure. By changing *has good lighting* to *well lit*, all items used to describe the restaurant have the same parallel structure of adverb followed by an adjective.
6.	D	II	First, the intro clause in the beginning—*Before making a diagnosis*—should be followed by a comma because it is a dependent clause followed by an independent clause. Because the word *doctors* is plural, all pronouns related to doctors should be plural as well. Therefore, the pronoun *they* is correct. Also, the word patients should be plural possessive—*patients'*. If there are multiple doctors, there are multiple patients. If those patients own the records, it should be *patients'*. Finally, for noun noun agreement and noun and number agreement, *history* should be plural—*histories*—because there are multiple patients with multiple *histories*.
7.	B	II	The word *its* is used as a contraction to mean *it is* in this sentence. Therefore, an apostrophe is needed to form the contraction word, *it's*. *Its* without an apostrophe is used as a possessive pronoun. Also, every student is singular; therefore, the plural pronoun *their* is incorrect. The words *every student* should be changed to *students*. That way, the pronoun—*their*—and the antecedent—*students*—agree.

Number	Answer	Content Category	Explanation
8.	C	II	Because the word *neat* is used to describe how Jamie writes, it should be changed to the adverb form, *neatly*. Adverbs are used to modify verbs, adjectives, and other adverbs. While answer D does have the adverb *neatly*, it is placed before the verb. This this is often referred to as a split infinitive and makes the sentence read awkwardly. It is best to put the adverb *neatly* after the verb *write*.
9.	D	II	Subject verb agreement can become tricky when a prepositional phrase such as *"in the large enclosure"* comes between the subject and verb. By reading the sentence without the prepositional phrase, the subject, *elephants* and verb, *seems* do not agree. Thus, change *seems* to *seem* to maintain subject verb agreement.
10.	A	II	This sentence is correct as is. The commas around the phrase are used to set off nonessential information. In other words, the phrase could be removed without changing the meaning of the sentence. Choice B, C, and E could be corrected by adding commas around the nonessential phrases. For example, choice B should be changed to *My dad, who loves westerns,*
11.	C	II	The idiomatic phrase "*one in the same*" is often used instead of the correct phrase "*one and the same*" to describe two similar items. However, the phrase "one in the same" or "all in the same" would mean that one item is actually inside of a nearly identical item.
12.	D	II	This sentence contains a dangling modifier, or a modifying phrase without a nearby noun to modify. In this case, it is not apparent who was searching for years, who found the money, or who was walking in the woods. Without correction, it appears that that after years of searching the money itself was walking in the woods. Answer D correctly places the modifier in the sentence, so it is clear who is walking through the woods and who found the money.
13.	A	II	The subject and verb agree in this sentence. The prepositional phrase *of tourists* may cause some confusion in this case. However, the word *busload* is the subject and is actually a singular noun which would require a singular verb.
14.	E	II	Left as is, this sentence is a run-on because two independent clauses are inappropriately joined by the word *then*. To correct, a comma and a conjunction can be added to join the clauses. Choice B is wrong because there is not a comma before the conjunction, and choice D is wrong because there is not a conjunction after the comma.
15.	B	II	The plural pronoun *their* is used incorrectly to refer to each singular female participant. To maintain pronoun number agreement, the word "her" should be used as each individual female received a t-shirt.

October 2019

Number	Answer	Content Category	Explanation
16.	B	II	A semi-colon is needed before the adverbial conjunction, therefore. In this case two independent clauses are combined with a semi-colon and conjunction. The correct punctuation is independent clause; adverbial conjunction, independent clause.
17.	D	II	The word *except* means "not including," and it is commonly confused with the word *accept*. The word accept means "to receive" and should be used in this sentence as the man refused to receive an apology.
18.	B	II	The verb *are* should be changed to the verb *is* to maintain subject verb agreement. The word *each* is a collective pronoun that requires a singular verb. Also, notice the prepositional phrase (of these books) in between the subject *each* and the verb. Try reading the sentence without the phrase "of these books" to check for subject verb agreement.
19.	D	II	Change the word phrase *to camp* to *camping* in order to continue parallel structure throughout the sentence. Notice that *hiking* and *swimming* both end in *ing* as should the word camp. Also, the colon is used correctly here because it separates an independent clause and a list.
20.	D	II	To avoid a shift in verb tense, the verb *floods* needs to be changed to *was flooded* because both events occurred in the past; the water became high and the roadway was flooded.
21.	E	II	No error. The word *summer*, as with all seasons, should not be capitalized, unless referring to a specific time such as the *Summer of 2000* or part of a proper noun such as *Ohio's Summer Festival*. In addition, *used to* is correct because the sentence is referring to something in the past that no longer happens.
22.	D	II	Choosing the correct pronoun in a comparison can be determined by finishing the sentence with an understood verb. For example, the sentence could read "Although he is younger, my brother is two inches taller than I *am*." The word *me* could not be interchanged with *I* when the understood verb is added making it clear as to which pronoun to choose.
23.	B	II	The word *months* requires an apostrophe. The schedule referred to is exclusive to a particular month, allowing the word *month's* to show possession of that schedule. Other example of this would be *yesterday's meeting* or *last year's concert*.
24.	A	II	The word *irregardless* is often mistakenly used in place of *regardless*, meaning in spite of. The word *irregardless* is not an actual word and should never be used.

Number	Answer	Content Category	Explanation
25.	C	II	Left as is, sentence 9 is considered a fragment as it is a dependent clause without a complete thought. Joining a dependent clause such as *How did Frees get his cats to pose for such photographs* with the depended clause *even before the days of super quick shutter speeds* is an effective way two join two clauses with losing meaning as well as correcting a fragment.
26.	C	I	Although the information in sentence 3 adds interesting information to the passage, it can be removed with changing the main idea. Sentence 1 and 2 contain pertinent information, creating the main idea of the passage. Sentence 10 may seem like extra information as well; however, it cannot be removed as it answers the question before it.
27.	A	II	The phrase *yet also slightly creepy* is a nonessential information, or information that can be removed without changing the meaning of a sentence. Nonessential information is set off with a comma before and after.
28.	D	I	To *brandish* means to show or to make a display of. The author of the book *displayed* a caption with each picture. Also, out of all the other choices *displaying* makes the most sense when it is substituted for *brandishing*.
29.	Choices 2 and 3	I	In sentence 10, the author mistakenly switches from the 3rd person point of view used throughout the passage, by using the word *you* which is in the 2nd. A better choice would be to use the word *one* or *people* here to avoid a shift a person. Also, an animal cannot be taxidermized if it is not already dead. Therefore, the author should eliminate either the word **dead** or **taxidermized** to avoid redundancy.
30.	E	I	This statement is the best choice as it sums up the overall main idea of the passage. Choice A, B, C, D all mention just one of the supporting details in the text without mention of the main idea which is that cats' pictures with funny captions were around before the internet age.
31.	D	II	To maintain parallel structure in this sentence the three actions mentioned must be grammatically the same. Thus, the first two actions are written with a present tense verb followed by a preposition. Thus, the third action, *whooped into the crowd*, must follow the same pattern, by changing *whooped* to its present tense, *whoop*.
32.	B	I	The best place for this additional sentence would be after sentence 8 as sentences 5-8 mention the dancers' apparent physical exhaustion. It would not follow sentence 9 as it is a concluding sentence for the first paragraph. Likewise, it would not fit anywhere in the second paragraph because it is discussing the general history of the disease.

Number	Answer	Content Category	Explanation
33.	D	I	If left as is, sentence 12 is a fragment. It is lacking a subject and complete thought. Therefore, the subject, The Dancing Plague, should be added. All other choices presented are fragments as well.
34.	A	I	The word *disquieting* means disturbing or alarming. In this case, the author is describing something that is *disturbing*, as the crowd described is in a trance-like state. Also, out of all the other choices, the word *disturbing* makes the most sense when substituted for the word *disquieting*.
35.	E	II	Social media sites are not considered credible sources as participants are able to post any information without documented research. All the other choices listed would provide citations and references both within the piece and at the end.
36.	B	I	A primary source is a document that provides firsthand information from the subject. An autobiography is written about the author by the author—a firsthand account. A biography, an article, and a study are all written about John Smith by other people—secondhand accounts.
37.	C	I	APA citations use the following format for journal articles: Last, First name. Year published. Article Title. *Journal Title*, Volume/Issue, Page numbers.
38.	D	I	In both APA and MLA citations must be provided within the text as in-text citations and on the final page of the document.
39.	E	I	When using a direct quote in MLA formatting both the authors name and page number(s) must be presented. All the other choices are missing at least one of those elements. Also, the page number comes before the period in the sentence.
40.	E	I	Citing material is mandatory to avoid cases of plagiarism and to give the author credit. Offering additional resources and credibility are important in producing an effective research paper as well.

This page is intentionally left blank.

PRAXIS® CORE WRITING TEXT TYPES, PURPOSES, AND PRODUCTION: (TWO 30-MINUTE ESSAYS)

This page is intentionally left blank.

In this section we will discuss what will be asked of you on each part of the essay test as well as develop a strategy designed to cover all aspects of the rubric.

On test day, you will be presented with two essay prompts: one argumentative and one source-based (informative). You will have just 60 minutes to write both essays—30 minutes to write essay number one and 30 minutes to write essay number two. It's important to understand that—due to the short time frame—your essay is going to be significantly less developed than a typical academic essay, so it's very important to be well-organized and succinct in your responses. The readers who score your essay will be looking for cohesive and specific responses that are organized in a way that is easy to understand. The key aspects to your essay will be organization and specificity; creativity and flowery language are not your friends in regard to the *Praxis®* Core essay.

An important point to note is that these are meant to be single subject essays. This means that you must avoid diverging into tangents and unnecessary digressions that could pull the reader away from the main idea.

Essay Number 1 – The argumentative essay task will require you to offer an opinion on a topic with which you either agree or disagree. Once you take a position on the issue, you must provide your opinion and specific examples to support your argument. It's very important that your argument is supported by relevant and sufficient evidence that is clearly and coherently written. Your argument and its supporting evidence have to be organized and developed logically. To be sure that the readers completely understand your argument, it is crucial that you write without ambiguity. Most importantly you should provide clear and concise details with concrete examples to support each idea. The rubric also requires that your essay be grammatically correct and show a use of sentence variety and structures.

Text Production: Writing Arguments

Test Specifications

1-Produce an argumentative essay to support a claim using relevant and specific evidence

2- Write clearly and coherently

a. Address the task appropriately for an audience of educated adults
b. Organize and develop ideas logically, making coherent connections between them
c. Provide and sustain a clear focus or thesis
d. Use supporting reasons, examples, and details to develop clearly and logically the ideas presented
e. Demonstrate a facility in the use of language and the ability to use a variety of sentence structures
f. Construct effective sentences that are generally free of errors in standard written English

Essay Number 2 – The explanatory or informational essay task will require you to evaluate a pair of passages, each outlining a different opinion on a particular issue. The most important aspect of the source-based essay is that you adequately summarize the individual passages (author's opinions/arguments). You will be asked to identify each author's opinion on the issue presented in the assignment, as well as, the arguments and supporting details provided by each author. To achieve a high score, an essay must address each text and provide citations from each. **For the explanatory essay, it is important to understand that you are not supporting any particular side, but rather summarizing both sides of each author presented in the prompt.**

Text Production: Writing Informative/Explanatory Texts

Test Specifications

1- Produce an informative/explanatory essay to examine and convey complex ideas and information clearly and accurately through the effective selection, organization, and analysis of content

a. Write clearly and coherently
b. Address the assigned task appropriately for an audience of educated adults
c. Draw evidence from informational texts to support analysis
d. Organize and develop ideas logically, making coherent connections between them
e. Synthesize information from multiple sources on the subject
f. Integrate and attribute information from multiple sources on the subject, avoiding plagiarism
g. Provide and sustain a clear and focused thesis
h. Demonstrate facility in the use of language and the ability to use a variety of sentence structures
i. Construct effective sentences that are generally free of errors in standard written English

Scoring

Both of the Core Writing essays are scored holistically. Holistic scoring is based on an essay's overall quality, not the individual aspects of the piece. The argumentative essay will be scored by one human reader and the *ETS e-rater* computer scoring program. The sourced-based essay will be evaluated by two human readers, each scoring the essay on the 1-6 scale. In the event that the readers' scores are greater than one point apart, a third reader will be brought in to evaluate the essay on the same scale. The 6-point scale—as shown in the rubric—will determine how well you unify a variety of writing elements— organization, sentence variety, thesis, etc.

For the purposes of this book, we will focus on what it takes to obtain a score of 4 on the argumentative essay and a score of 4 on the informative essay. According to ETS, a score of 4 demonstrates competence. That is all you have to do: write an essay that demonstrates you have the fundamental skills to communicate effectively in writing. Below is an infographic explaining the way both essays are graded.

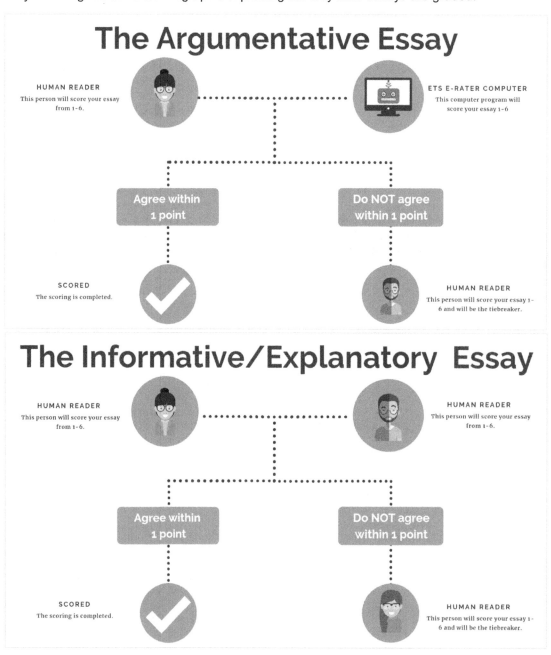

The Argumentative Essay

HUMAN READER
This person will score your essay from 1-6.

ETS E-RATER COMPUTER
This computer program will score your essay 1-6

Agree within 1 point

Do NOT agree within 1 point

SCORED
The scoring is completed.

HUMAN READER
This person will score your essay 1-6 and will be the tiebreaker.

The Informative/Explanatory Essay

HUMAN READER
This person will score your essay from 1-6.

HUMAN READER
This person will score your essay from 1-6.

Agree within 1 point

Do NOT agree within 1 point

SCORED
The scoring is completed.

HUMAN READER
This person will score your essay 1-6 and will be the tiebreaker.

For this task, you must show competence in your ability to:

- Produce an argumentative essay to support a claim using relevant and sufficient evidence.
- Write clearly and coherently.
- Address the assigned task appropriately for an audience of educated adults.
- Organize and develop ideas logically, making coherent connections between them.
- Provide and sustain a clear focus or thesis.
- Use supporting reasons, examples, and details to develop clearly and logically the ideas presented.
- Demonstrate facility in the use of language and the ability to use a variety of sentence structures.
- Construct effective sentences that are generally free of errors in standard written English.

You will be tasked with writing an argumentative essay that responds directly to a prompt. The prompt will offer an opinion on an issue that is commonly the subject of public debate; you will **either agree or disagree** with the prompt, and then support your opinion with specific examples.

> **Here is what the writing prompt will look like:**
>
> *"The only important criterion by which to judge a prospective teacher is his or her ability to get along with the widest possible variety of students."*
>
> Discuss the extent to which you agree or disagree with this opinion. Support your views with specific reasons and opinions from your own experiences, observations, or reading.

Scoring

The essay is scored 1-6. We recommend you strive to write an essay that scores a 4 or above. A score of 4 shows competence or proficiency and is a sufficient score on the writing exam.

Score	Criteria
6 - demonstrates a high degree of competence in response to the assignment but may have a few minor errors.	• Author provides a clear and declarative thesis statement • Organizes and develops ideas logically, providing cogent details and supporting examples that connect to the thesis • Clearly explains key details, supporting them with tangible examples • Demonstrates and successfully applies varied sentence structures • Clearly displays facility in the use of language • Displays a thorough command of grammar, usage, and mechanics
5 - demonstrates clear competence in response to the assignment but may have minor errors.	• States or clearly implies the writer's position or thesis • Organizes and develops ideas clearly, making connections between them • Explains key ideas, supporting them with relevant reasons, concrete examples, and specific details • Displays some sentence variety • Displays facility in the use of language • Is virtually free from errors in grammar, usage, and mechanics
4 - demonstrates competence in response to the assignment.	• States or implies the writer's position or thesis • Shows control in the organization and development of ideas • Offers some key ideas, details and examples, but lacks specificity • Displays adequate use of language • Shows control of grammar, usage, and mechanics, but may contain errors

IMPORTANT: You will **NOT** write this essay in order—introduction, details, conclusion. Instead, you will write the detail paragraphs first. Writing the details first helps to generate ideas and makes writing the intro and conclusion easier than if you tried to write the introduction paragraph first.

Steps to writing the argumentative essay

Step 1: Read and analyze the prompt and develop an opinion. **(1 min)**	Read the prompt.
	Analyze what it says.
	Take a *definitive* positon - EITHER agree OR disagree.
	Type your thesis.
Step 2: Map your essay **(5 mins)**	Build the argument.
	On your scratch paper, organize your main ideas and specific details.
	Organize the examples the way they will appear in your essay.
Step 3: Type your detail paragraphs. **(17 mins)**	Write your detail paragraphs first.
	Be direct.
	Use the specific details mapped in your essay.
	PROOF your detail paragraphs. Watch for grammatical errors and confusing or poorly developed ideas.
Step 4: Type your introduction and conclusion. **(5 mins)**	Type the introduction.
	Type the conclusion.
	Do NOT add any additional information in either the introduction or conclusion.
Step 5: Put it all together and proofread the entire passage. **(2 min)**	Put everything together - intro, detail 1 & 2, and conclusion.
	Check for any glaring errors in the essay.
	DO NOT add anything new. This is the time to quickly proofread, not rewrite the essay.

Let's practice!

We will use the example prompt to model an effective writing strategy for this exam.

We will write a 4-paragraph essay:

Paragraph 1 – Introduction which includes the thesis

Paragraph 2 – Detail 1

Paragraph 3 – Detail 2

Paragraph 4 - Conclusion

"The only important criterion by which to judge a prospective teacher is his or her ability to get along with the widest possible variety of students."

Discuss the extent to which you agree or disagree with this opinion. Support your views with specific reasons and opinions from your own experiences, observations, or reading.

Step 1: Develop an Opinion (2 minutes)

- Read the prompt.

- Analyze the issue.

- **Pick a side:** I disagree. There are other qualities by which we should judge teachers.

Step 2: Building Your Argument (5 minutes)

- **Write the thesis:** There are a several important factors to consider when judging a teacher's effectiveness in the classroom.

- Map the essay on scratch paper, quickly organizing your main points and specific examples. See example essay map graphic.

- Organize examples like they will appear in the essay.

Step 3: Write your detail paragraphs (15-20 minutes)

Example Essay Map	
Detail Paragraph 1	Detail Paragraph 2
Popularity is not the most important attribute of a teacher.	I had an English teacher who was unpopular. Content area expert.
• Content area knowledge is key.	• In college I was more prepared than other students.
✴Biology and English teachers need to be experts.	✴The assignments I hated prepared me for college English.
• Teachers should prepare students for college/future	• Unpopular teacher was effective because of content knowledge.
✴Specific Details - Necessary for a score of 4.	

Detail Paragraph 1

There are factors that should be considered when evaluating a perspective teacher that are more important than a teacher's ability to simply get along with people *(intro sentence)*. It is important that teachers are experts in the content in they teach *(main idea)*. For example, a biology teacher must have a detailed understanding of topics like cell division, osmosis, photosynthesis, etc. *(specific detail 1)*. Similarly, English teachers must have a thorough academic understanding of grammar, usage, structure, composition, and literature *(specific detail 2)*. It takes an immense amount of knowledge to disseminate information and develop skills students will need to be successful in education and beyond *(closing sentence)*.

Detail Paragraph 2

In high school, I had an English teacher who was notorious for being difficult to deal with *(personal experience which is also the intro sentence)*. I, along with others, found him abrasive and stuffy; he certainly wasn't getting along with most of his students at the time *(main idea)*. We found his teaching style to be outdated and boring; he demanded us to diagram sentences, rewrite paragraphs over and over, and proofread constantly *(specific detail 1)*. However, during my freshman year of college I quickly realized that, because of my English teacher's approach, my knowledge of grammar, punctuation, and structure was far beyond my classmates' skills and understanding *(specific detail 2)*. It turns out, my English teacher had prepared me to be a successful college writer, even though he was easily the least popular teacher I'd ever had.

Step 4: Write the Introduction and Conclusions

Introduction

I disagree with the idea that prospective teachers should be judged solely on his or her ability to get along with the widest possible variety of students *(clear position—disagree)*. I do not feel that popularity alone is an accurate way to determine how effective an educator is. Prospective teachers should be judged on more important and substantial factors, such as being able to deliver important information clearly and preparing students for the next step in their academic career *(building the argument)*. There are a variety of important factors involved in judging prospective teachers *(thesis)*.

> **Quick Tip!**
>
> State your position right away. Do not let the reader get 2-3 sentences in without knowing exactly how you feel. This is not the time to take a middle-of-the-road approach. Be direct and state your opinion in the very first sentence.

Conclusion

I do not agree with the claim that the only criterion on which a prospective teacher should be judged is his or her ability to connect with a wide variety of students *(repetition of the prompt)*. Being an effective teacher is not a popularity contest *(your position)*. Teachers must be experts in their fields to be able to give students the information they need to be successful. Although it is helpful for a teacher to be well-liked, that is not the only quality that makes a teacher effective.

Putting the essay together

I disagree with the idea that prospective teachers should be judged solely on his or her ability to get along with the widest possible variety of students. I do not feel that popularity is an accurate way to determine how effective an educator is. Prospective teachers should be judged on more important and substantial factors such as being able to deliver important information clearly and preparing students for the next step in their academic career. There are a variety of important factors involved in judging prospective teachers.

There are factors that should be considered when evaluating a perspective teacher that are more important than a teacher's ability to simply get along with people. It is important that teachers are experts in the content in they teach. For example, a biology teacher must have a detailed understanding of topics like cell division, osmosis, and photosynthesis. Similarly, English teachers must have a thorough academic understanding of grammar, usage, structure, composition, and literature. It takes an immense amount of knowledge to disseminate information and develop skills students will need to be successful in education and beyond.

In high school, I had an English teacher who was notorious for being difficult to deal with. I, along with others, found him abrasive and stuffy; he certainly wasn't getting along with most of his students at the time. We found his teaching style to be outdated and boring; he demanded us to diagram sentences, rewrite paragraphs over and over, and proofread constantly. However, during my freshman year of college I quickly realized that, because of my English teacher's approach, my knowledge of grammar, punctuation, and structure was far beyond my classmates' skills and understanding. It turns out, my English teacher had prepared me to be a successful college writer, even though he was easily the least popular teacher I'd ever had.

I do not agree with the claim that the only criterion on which a prospective teacher should be judged is his or her ability to connect with a wide variety of students. Being an effective teacher is not a popularity contest. Teachers must be experts in their fields to be able to give students the information they need to be successful. Although it is helpful for a teacher to be well-liked, that is not the only quality that makes a teacher effective.

Things to consider

Thesis

Immediately after reading and organizing your notes you should write your thesis. Your thesis statement should be clear and explain to the reader what the essay is about. There is no need to elaborate on any ideas or details in the thesis. The goal of your thesis is to state the purpose of the essay without ambiguity. You don't want your readers—the *Praxis*® Core essay subtest scorers—to have any doubts about your position on the issue.

Creating a Clear and Coherent Argument

Now that you have a clearly stated thesis, use your scratch-paper to construct your argument. At this point, you will identify specific details and relevant examples to support your argument.

When coming up with supporting details and examples, it's important to use ideas that you can discuss with some confidence. These ideas usually come from three sources:

- Personal experience

- History

- Literature

> **IMPORTANT**
>
> The instructions in the prompt say, "...Support your views with specific reasons and opinions from your own experiences, observations, or reading." Because you are instructed to do so, you can use first-person narrative (I, we, me, our, us).

According to the rubric, achieving a passing score will require you to strategically arrange the supporting details of your thesis. Choose evidence that supports your argument completely. Also, make sure all of your key ideas and supporting evidence unfold logically. Your ideas should appear in an order that's easy to understand, with smooth transitions from one idea to the next.

How to organize the details

Paragraph structure

It's important to have a plan when building your detail paragraphs. In order to convey your ideas clearly and accurately you must understand the order and purpose for each of your sentences. An easy strategy to create effective paragraphs is the P.I.T. method.

The P.I.T. Method of Paragraph Structure

P-*Purpose*- (sentence 1) You should think of your purpose sentence like the thesis of you paragraph. It is a simple introduction to what you are about to tell the reader. For your argumentative essay that might include your opinion and/or a main argument which you will elaborate on in the following sentences.

I-*Information*- (sentences 2-?) This is the "body" of the paragraph. It is in these sentences that you will arrange your argument in detail with specific examples to support your argument. All the information in this part of the paragraph will support the purpose; in the case of the argumentative essay, the information used will support your opinion on the topic provided in the prompt.

T-*Transition*- (final sentence) A sentence that closes out the information in passage one. Do not offer a final detail without a supporting example. All ideas must be closed-out before moving on to the next paragraph.

Let's break down the P.I.T. Structure of our detail paragraph. Think to yourself as we go: Why are the sentences arranged this way?

Detail Paragraph One:

Purpose (sentence 1) There are factors that should be considered when evaluating a perspective teacher that are more important than a teacher's ability to simply get along with people. *(The author immediately states what the rest of the paragraph will be discussing. The purpose sentence is a general argument that the rest of the sentences in the paragraph will specifically support. In this example, the author is introducing the argument that, when hiring a teacher, there are more important factors to consider than popularity.)*

Information (sentences 2-4) It is important that teachers are experts in the content they teach. For example, a biology teacher must have a detailed understanding of topics like cell division, osmosis, and photosynthesis. Similarly, English teachers must have a thorough academic understanding of grammar, usage, structure, composition, and literature. *(In the informational sentences the author provides specific supporting evidence to support the claim made in the purpose sentence. The author uses a biology teacher and an English teacher along with the different aspects of teaching each class.)*

Transition (final sentence) It takes an immense amount of knowledge to disseminate information and develop skills students will need to be successful in education and beyond. *(The transition sentence closes out the main idea of the paragraph.*

Things to avoid

While proofreading your essay, you will want to look for a variety of things in your writing:

- clichés
- awkward wording
- poor parallel structure
- misplaced/dangling modifiers
- slang or informal language
- improper grammar—see the English grammar section of this book for more details.
- shifting point of view—always stay in the first person for the argument essay.
- who vs that—people are always *who*, things are always *that.*
    - **Correct Example:**

      Students *who* brought their permission slips in will be able to attend the field trip.

      The school *that* is right around the corner is East Hampton High School
    - **Incorrect Example:**

      The students *that* brought their permission slips in will be able to attend the field trip.

Now you practice!

Follow the steps previously outlined and write an essay. Strive for a score of 4. Use the steps to guide your process.

Argumentative Essay- 30 minutes

Use this area to map your essay.

Sample Prompt

"Advanced degrees have limited usefulness in the job market. Employers seldom require more than a bachelor's degree. Most jobs that do require a master's degree or a doctorate are so highly competitive that getting an advanced degree does not guarantee employment."

Discuss the extent to which you agree or disagree with this opinion. Support your views with specific reasons and opinions from your own experiences, observations, or reading.

Sample essay

Position: I disagree.

Thesis: Having an advanced degree is beneficial to one's career.

Sample Response: *Score of 4*

I disagree with the statement "Advanced degrees have limited usefulness in the job market." In today's job market there are many careers in which an advance degree would be useful or necessary. Due to their specialized nature, jobs that require an advanced degree are often extremely competitive. However, an advanced degree is almost always seen as a positive addition to ones resume and can open doors to many opportunities peripheral to that degree. Having an advanced degree is beneficial to one's career.

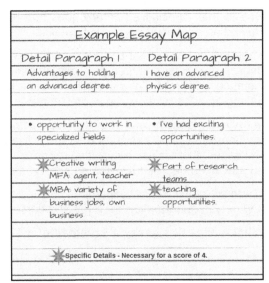

Though the job market can be competitive, there are a variety of advantages to earning an advanced degree. A master's degree provides graduate students with the opportunity to work in specialized fields. For instance, an individual with a master of fine arts (MFA) in Creative Writing could accept a variety of positions that go beyond being a writer. Having an advanced understanding of writing would open up potential positions in teaching, a literary agency, or a publishing house. Similarly, having an MBA would make someone qualified for a variety of business and management positions. Not only is having an advanced degree useful, in many cases it is a great asset.

In my experience, having an advanced degree has been extremely useful throughout my career. I was able to be part of several exciting research teams because of my advanced degree. I also had the opportunity to be part of an interdisciplinary team that studied connections between my two passions: astrophysics and Science Fiction. Because I earned an advanced degree, I was able to obtain a teaching position. I feel that most people who have chosen to pursue an advanced degree have some level of passion for the field and can find a job they enjoy within that field.

While some may say that advanced degrees have limited usefulness and that employers rarely require more than a bachelor's degree, there are clear advantages to having an advanced degree. These degrees provide an opportunity to work in a variety of specialized fields. Those who pursue advanced degrees are passionate about the subject area they have studied. That passion can be applied to a variety of opportunities for a fulfilling career.

This essay would receive a score of 4 because it:

- states or implies the writer's position or thesis.

- shows control in the organization and development of ideas.

- offers some key ideas, details and examples, but lacks specificity.

- displays adequate use of language.

- shows control of grammar, usage, and mechanics.

Sample Response: *Score of 3*

In today's job market there are many careers in which an advance degree would be useful or necessary. Due to their specialized nature, jobs that require an advanced degree are often extremely competitive. Having an advanced degree is beneficial to one's career.

Though the job market can be competitive, there are a variety of advantages to earning an advanced degree. A master's degree provides students with the opportunity to work in more specialized fields. For instance, with an MFA you could accept a bunch of positions that go beyond being a writer. Not only is having an advanced degree useful, in many cases it is a great asset.

In my experience having an advanced degree has been extremely useful throughout my career. Thanks to my degree I will be exploring my newly discovered passion for teaching. Though my degree has obvious limitations, there is flexibility within my chosen specialty. I feel that most people who have chosen to pursue an advanced degree have some level of passion for the field and can find a job they enjoy within that field.

There are some clear advantages to having an advanced degree. Holding an advanced degree can provide a variety of opportunities for a fulfilling career.

What makes this essay a 3 instead of a 4?

You can see the author committed the following errors that contributed to a failing score of 3:

- The writer does not clearly and immediately state his/her opinion on the topic.
- There is a lack of fully formed ideas.
- The essay does not have specific examples to sufficiently support the argument.
- The essay jumps between all three points of view as if interchangeable.
- Ideas are started but never finished.

For this task, you must show competence in your ability to:

- Write clearly and coherently
- Address the assigned task appropriately for educated audiences
- Draw evidence from informational texts to support analysis
- Organize and develop ideas logically, making coherent connections between them
- Synthesize information from multiple sources on the subject
- Integrate and attribute information from multiple sources on the subject, avoiding plagiarism
- Provide and sustain a clear focus or thesis
- Demonstrate facility in the use of language and the ability to use a variety of sentence structures
- Construct effective sentences that are generally free of errors in standard written English

Source-Based Essay Rubric

Score	Criteria
6 - Demonstrates a high degree of competence in response to the assignment but may have a few minor errors.	• Insightfully explains why the concerns are important, supporting the explanation with effective links between the two sources and well-chosen reasons, examples, or details • Incorporates relevant information from both sources to identify and elaborate on important concerns discussed in the sources • Organizes and develops ideas logically • Displays effective sentence variety • Clearly displays facility in the use of language • Is free from errors in grammar, usage, and mechanics • Cites both sources when paraphrasing or quoting
5 - Demonstrates clear competence in response to the assignment but may have minor errors.	• Clearly explains why the concerns are important, supporting the explanation with clear links between the two sources and relevant reasons, examples, or details • Incorporates information from both sources to identify and explain important concerns regarding the issue discussed in the sources • Organizes and develops ideas clearly • Displays some sentence variety • Displays facility in the use of language • Is generally free from errors in grammar, usage, and mechanics • Cites both sources when paraphrasing or quoting
4 - Demonstrates competence in response to the assignment.	• Adequately explains why the concerns are important, supporting the explanation with some links between the two sources and adequate reasons, examples or details • Incorporates information from both sources to identify and explain important concerns regarding the issue discussed in the sources • Shows control in the organization and development of ideas • Displays adequate use of language • Shows control of grammar, usage, and mechanics, but may display errors • Cites both sources when paraphrasing or quoting

Because a score of 4 is considered proficient or competent, you should focus on that specific criteria when writing your essay and then try to improve on that score.

Text Production: Writing Informative/Explanatory Texts (Source-Based Essay) - 30 minutes

Source-Based Essay: Your goal is to write an informative essay that summarizes the arguments of two different authors with opposing viewpoints.

You will be presented with an assignment—an overview of an issue. The issue will be a somewhat controversial social issue like prison reform, education reform, or voting rights. You will also be presented with two passages written by two different authors, each offering a different opinion on the issue. Your task is to summarize the two differing opinions. You will **NOT** include your own opinion. Your essay is meant to be strictly informative. You are to analyze the issue in the assignment, and then summarize the two opinions outlined in the sources.

What can you expect on test day?

The directions for the source-based writing task on the *Praxis®* Core essay subtest will look just like the following page. Pay attention to the task and how the sources are structured.

Directions: In the following section you will have 30 minutes to read two short passages on a topic and then plan and write an essay on that topic. The essay will be an informative essay based on the two sources that are provided.

Read the topic and the sources carefully. You will probably find it best to spend a little time considering the topic and organizing your thoughts before you begin writing. DO NOT WRITE ON A TOPIC OTHER THAN THE ONE SPECIFIED. Essays on topics of your own choice will not be acceptable. In order for your test to be scored, your response must be in English.

The essay questions are included in this test to demonstrate how well you can write. You should, therefore, write clearly and effectively, using specific examples where appropriate. Remember, that how well you write is more important than how much you write, but to cover topics adequately, you will probably have to write more than one paragraph.

Assignment: In recent years, the push to revise laws pertaining to a felon's right to vote has grown substantially. Many Americans feel that convicted felons should be able to regain their right to vote after they are released from prison. However, others feel that voting is a privilege, and once people are convicted of a serious crime, they should lose that privilege. Both of the following sources address whether or not these felons deserve to have their voting rights re-established and the positive or negative effect the revised law could have on the country.

Read the two passages carefully and write an essay in which you identify the most important concerns regarding the issue and explain why they are important. Your essay must draw on information from BOTH of the sources. In addition, you may draw on your own experiences, observations or reading. Be sure to CITE the sources whether you are paraphrasing or directly quoting.

Source 1

Adapted from: Yaffe, Gideon. "Give Felons and Prisoners the Right to Vote." *The Washington Post*. July 26, 2016. https://www.washingtonpost.com/opinions/let-felons-and-prisoners-vote/2016/07/26.

Most felons—whether in prison, on probation or parole, or entirely free of state supervision—are citizens. They should be afforded the right to decide who represents them and the laws by which they will be governed. By taking away their right to vote, you risk further alienating these individuals; in some cases that alienated feeling was the catalyst for their crimes in the first place.

The vast majority of felons are American citizens; therefore, they have no other geographic home. Taking away their right to vote removes any sense of citizenship they may still have after incarceration.

Even if one considers voting to be purely symbolic, it is a symbol with great psychological power. An increasing body of research in social psychology shows that those who feel a sense of ownership in their government are less likely to commit crimes. Re-establishing felons' voting rights is a potential source of criminal control—granting the vote to felons can discourage recidivism. Furthermore, research has proven that with this sense of ownership, ex-felons enjoy a quality of life that would be impossible without the freedoms that are re-established after their release.

In democracy, felon voting rights should not be a partisan issue. Both political parties must see the importance of re-establishing felon's voting right as a way to not only positively influence the ex-prisoners, but also as a way to protect their citizens by reducing crime. WE should give the vote to citizens, in or out of prison, whom we wish to hold responsible for violating laws that are not just ours but also theirs.

Source 2

Adapted from: von Spakovsky, Hans A. "Ex-cons Should Prove They Deserve the Right to Vote." *The Heritage Foundation*. March 15th, 2013. www.heritage.org/election-integrity/commentary/ex-cons-should-prove-they-deserve-the-right-to-vote.

The proposal to automatically restore felons' right to vote as soon as they have completed their sentence is shortsighted and bad public policy. When presented as a measure of compassion and justice, it is also hypocritical, as automatic restoration is not in the best interest of felons or the general public.

An April 2012 report from the Florida Department of Corrections showed that the recidivism rate of felons ranged from 31% to 34% on average over a five-year period. Recidivism among those convicted of robbery, burglary and sex offenses reached or exceeded 50%, while the overall recidivism rate of felons committing nonviolent offenses also approached 50%. Therefore, to restore voting rights to felons as soon as they leave prison is irresponsible.

Advocates of automatic restoration also seem reluctant to mention that voting rights aren't the only rights people lose when convicted of a felony. In Florida, as in most states, felons also lose their right to own a gun, hold public office, sit on a jury, and obtain certain types of professional and occupational licenses. Many such rights can never be restored without a full pardon.

Felons have, by definition, knowingly and intentionally violated the laws of society. A five-or-seven-year waiting period before restoring their voting rights gives felons the opportunity and an incentive to prove they are deserving of exercising their right to vote.

IMPORTANT: You will *NOT* write this essay in order—introduction, details, conclusion. Instead, you will write the detail paragraphs first. Writing the details first helps to generate ideas and makes writing the intro and conclusion easier than if you tried to write the introduction paragraph first.

Steps to Writing the Informative/Explanatory Essay

Step 1: Read and analyze the prompt and develop a clear thesis. **(1 min)**	Read the assignment part of the prompt. Understand the issue that the following source material (the two differing opinions) will be referring to.
	Read source 1. Determine the position source 1 outlines. Focus on a few key details source one uses to develop the position.
	Read source 2. Determine the position source 1 outlines. Focus on a few key details source one uses to develop the position.
Step 2: Map your essay. **(5 mins)**	Map out the opinion and supporting examples presented by each author on your scratch paper.
	Arrange the authors opinion, argument, and supporting examples in the order in which you want them to appear in your essay.
Step 3: Type your detail paragraphs. **(17 mins)**	Structure the paragraphs based on source notes.
	Keep these paragraphs organized and clear.
	PROOF your detail paragraphs. Watch for grammatical errors and confusing or poorly developed ideas.
Step 4: Type your introduction and conclusion. **(5 mins)**	Use the assigment part of the prompt to guide you in writing the intro and conclusion.
	Rewrite the general ideas in the assignment and use them in your intro and conclusion.
Step 5: Proofread the entire passage. **(2 min)**	Check for any glaring errors in the essay.
	DO NOT add anything new. This is the time to quickly proofread, not rewrite the essay.

Assignment: In recent years, the push to revise laws pertaining to a felon's right to vote has grown substantially. Many Americans feel that convicted felons should be able to regain their right to vote after they are released from prison. However, others feel that voting is a privilege, and once you are convicted of a serious crime you lose that privilege. Both of the following sources address whether or not these felons deserve to have their voting rights re-established and the positive or negative effect the revised law could have on the country.

Read the two passages carefully and then write an essay in which you identify the most important concerns regarding the issue and explain why they are important. Your essay must draw on information from BOTH of the sources. In addition, you may draw on your own experiences, observations, or reading. Be sure to CITE the sources whether you are paraphrasing or directly quoting.

Source 1

Adapted from: Yaffe, Gideon. "Give Felons and Prisoners the Right to Vote." *The Washington Post*. July 26, 2016.
https://www.washingtonpost.com/opinions/let-felons-and-prisoners-vote/2016/07/26.

Most felons—whether in prison, on probation or parole, or entirely free of state supervision—are citizens. They should be afforded the right to decide who represents them and the laws by which they will be governed. By taking away their right to vote, you risk further alienating these individuals; in some cases that alienated feeling was the catalyst for their crimes in the first place.

The vast majority of felons are American citizens; therefore, they have no other geographic home. Taking away their right to vote removes any sense of citizenship they may still have after incarceration.

Even if one considers voting to be purely symbolic, it is a symbol with great psychological power. An increasing body of research in social psychology shows that those who feel a sense of ownership in their government are less likely to commit crimes. Re-establishing felons' voting rights is a potential source of criminal control— granting the vote to felons can discourage recidivism. Furthermore, research has proven that with this sense of ownership, ex-felons enjoy a quality of life that would be impossible without the freedoms that are re-established after their release.

In democracy, felon voting rights should not be a partisan issue. Both political parties must see the importance of re-establishing felon's voting right as a way to not only positively influence the ex-prisoners, but also as a way to protect their citizens by reducing crime. WE should give the vote to citizens, in or out of prison, whom we wish to hold responsible for violating laws that are not just ours but also theirs.

Source 2

Adapted from: von Spakovsky, Hans A. "Ex-cons Should Prove They Deserve the Right to Vote." *The Heritage Foundation*. March 15th, 2013.
www.heritage.org/election-integrity/commentary/ex-cons-should-prove-they-deserve-the-right-to-vote.

The proposal to automatically restore felons' right to vote as soon as they have completed their sentence is shortsighted and bad public policy. When presented as a measure of compassion and justice, it is also hypocritical, as automatic restoration is not in the best interest of felons or the general public.

An April 2012 report from the Florida Department of Corrections showed that the recidivism rate of felons ranged from 31% to 34% on average over a five-year period. Recidivism among those convicted of robbery, burglary and sex offenses reached or exceeded 50%, while the overall recidivism rate of felons committing nonviolent offenses also approached 50%. Therefore, to restore voting rights to felons as soon as they leave prison is irresponsible.

Advocates of automatic restoration also seem reluctant to mention that voting rights aren't the only rights people lose when convicted of a felony. In Florida, as in most states, felons also lose their right to own a gun, hold public office, sit on a jury, and obtain certain types of professional and occupational licenses. Many such rights can never be restored without a full pardon.

Felons have, by definition, knowingly and intentionally violated the laws of society. A five-or-seven-year waiting period before restoring their voting rights gives felons the opportunity and an incentive to prove they are deserving of exercising their right to vote.

Detailed steps to writing the informative/explanatory essay

This is a FOUR paragraph essay that will follow the same basic structure as your argumentative essay.

We will write a 4-paragraph essay:

Paragraph 1 – Intro which includes the thesis

Paragraph 2 – Detail 1

Paragraph 3 – Detail 2

Paragraph 4 - Conclusion

IMPORTANT: You will **NOT** write this essay in order—intro, details, conclusion. Instead, you will write the detail paragraphs first. Writing the details first helps to generate ideas and makes writing the intro and conclusion easier than if you tried to write the introduction paragraph first.

*The important difference between this essay and the argumentative essay is that you will be summarizing the opinions of two different authors, not your own.

Step 1 – Read and analyze the prompt and develop a clear thesis.

THESIS- For the source-based essay, you should be able to write your thesis immediately after reading the prompt. Your thesis statement simply and declaratively tells the reader what the essay is about. There is no need to elaborate on any ideas or details. The goal of your thesis is to state the purpose of the essay without ambiguity. In the thesis you will state the argument. Make sure it's THE argument and not YOUR argument. The argument is chosen for you—in the Assignment portion of the directions—so you will simply restate it in your thesis. It is important that you keep your thesis simple and declarative. State the argument, and then tell the reader that it is important and/or publicly debated.

Important notes regarding your thesis:

- Thesis must be written clearly and directly address the prompt.

- Keep your thesis at the top of your notes page so you can refer to it as needed.

- Your thesis will be the first part of the essay you write.

- Don't forget, anything you include in your thesis must be addressed in the detail paragraph.

Example Thesis:

Re-establishing felon's voting rights is an important topic of national concern.

- The thesis statement is short and declarative. An argument is stated and identified as an important and debated issue.

Step 2 – Map your essay.

Doing a little bit of work on the front end may take some time. However, this action will save you time in the long-run and allow you to stay organized throughout the task.

Carefully read the assignment to understand the issue at hand. Then, read each source and identify the authors' opinion on the issue, and the details the authors present in support of their opinion. For EACH source, use your scratch-paper to break down the authors' arguments:

Important notes regarding your prewriting and mapping:

- Always make your notes in the order in which they appear in the passage and the order you intend to write them in your essay.
- Include both direct quotes and paraphrase.
- Quickly jot down the citation in this format: *(Author's Last name, Year)*

- Identify the author's stated opinion on the issue stated in the prompt

- Find each argument the author uses to support his opinion

- Identify the specific examples the author uses to support arguments

- Select specific quotes you wish to use in your summary of the author's piece

- Organize the information that you find most important from each source in the order in which they will appear in your essay.

This is the reading comprehension portion of the essay test. Since we always write an informative essay in chronological order, you will summarize passage one, followed by passage two.

Be sure you can quickly identify a source-based detail you will use to cite in your essay. You only need one. See the example below. The shaded area is the detail we will summarize and cite in the details paragraph.

Think about it!

Though the rest of the piece contains good information that should be included in the summary, the highlighted sentences include specific information that support the authors' claims. The shaded portion contains specific information you can use to cite in your summary.

Assignment: In recent years, the push to revise laws pertaining to a felon's right to vote has grown substantially. Many Americans feel that convicted felons should be able to regain their right to vote after they are released from prison. However, others feel that voting is a privilege, and once you are convicted of a serious crime you lose that privilege. Both of the following sources address whether or not these felons deserve to have their voting rights re-established and the positive or negative effect the revised law could have on the country.

Source 1

Adapted from: Yaffe, Gideon. "Give Felons and Prisoners the Right to Vote." *The Washington Post*. July 26, 2016. https://www.washingtonpost.com/opinions/let-felons-and-prisoners-vote/2016/07/26.

Most felons—whether in prison, on probation or parole, or entirely free of state supervision—are citizens. They should be afforded the right to decide who represents them and the laws by which they will be governed. By taking away their right to vote, you risk further alienating these individuals; in some cases that alienated feeling was the catalyst for their crimes in the first place.

The vast majority of felons are American citizens; therefore, they have no other geographic home. Taking away their right to vote removes any sense of citizenship they may still have after incarceration.

Even if one considers voting to be purely symbolic, it is a symbol with great psychological power. An increasing body of research in social psychology shows that those who feel a sense of ownership in their government are less likely to commit crimes. Re-establishing felons' voting rights is a potential source of criminal control—granting the vote to felons can discourage recidivism. Furthermore, research has proven that with this sense of ownership, ex-felons enjoy a quality of life that would be impossible without the freedoms that are re-established after their release.

In democracy, felon voting rights should not be a partisan issue. Both political parties must see the importance of re-establishing felon's voting right as a way to not only positively influence the ex-prisoners, but also as a way to protect their citizens by reducing crime. WE should give the vote to citizens, in or out of prison, whom we wish to hold responsible for violating laws that are not just ours but also theirs.

Source 2

Adapted from: von Spakovsky, Hans A. "Ex-cons Should Prove They Deserve the Right to Vote." *The Heritage Foundation*. March 15th, 2013. www.heritage.org/election-integrity/commentary/ex-cons-should-prove-they-deserve-the-right-to-vote.

The proposal to automatically restore felons' right to vote as soon as they have completed their sentence is shortsighted and bad public policy. When presented as a measure of compassion and justice, it is also hypocritical, as automatic restoration is not in the best interest of felons or the general public.

An April 2012 report from the Florida Department of Corrections showed that the recidivism rate of felons ranged from 31% to 34% on average over a five-year period. Recidivism among those convicted of robbery, burglary and sex offenses reached or exceeded 50%, while the overall recidivism rate of felons committing nonviolent offenses also approached 50%. Therefore, to restore voting rights to felons as soon as they leave prison is irresponsible.

Advocates of automatic restoration also seem reluctant to mention that voting rights aren't the only rights people lose when convicted of a felony. In Florida, as in most states, felons also lose their right to own a gun, hold public office, sit on a jury, and obtain certain types of professional and occupational licenses. Many such rights can never be restored without a full pardon.

Felons have, by definition, knowingly and intentionally violated the laws of society. A five-or-seven-year waiting period before restoring their voting rights gives felons the opportunity and an incentive to prove they are deserving of exercising their right to vote.

Source-Based Essay Sample Map

Thesis- Re-establishing felon's voting rights is an important topic of national concern.

Source 1- Detail Paragraph 1

Purpose - *Give Felons and Prisoners the Right to Vote* by Yaffe

- Re-establish the right to vote for felons
- Positive impact on felons and community

Detail 1 comes from the shaded region in the source where we identified a specific detail we will cite in our essay.

An increasing body of research in social psychology shows that those who feel a sense of ownership in their government are less likely to commit crimes.

Example 1 – It is important felons feel they have a say in passing laws and representation

Example 2 – Lack of voting rights causes alienation, and alienation causes more crime. "Re-establishing felon's voting rights is a potential source of criminal control—granting the vote to felons can discourage recidivism."

Source 2 – Detail Paragraph 2

Purpose- *Ex-cons Should Prove They Deserve the Right to Vote* by Hans von Spakovsky

- Re-instatement of felons voting rights
- Poses issues for both the offender and the general public.

Detail 2 comes from the shaded region in the source where we identified a specific detail we will cite in our essay.

Recidivism among those convicted of robbery, burglary, and sex offenses reached or exceeded 50%, while the overall recidivism rate of felons committing nonviolent offenses also approached 50%. Therefore, to restore voting rights to felons as soon as they leave prison is irresponsible

Example 1 – Gun, jury, public office, or obtain licenses, voting rights is another way for the government to protect its citizens

Example 2 – Florida may be the best avenue for a positive outcome, "a five-or-seven-year waiting period gives felons the opportunity--and an incentive--to prove they are deserving of exercising their right to vote."

Example Essay Map

Detail Paragraph 1	Detail Paragraph 2
Source 1	Source 2
• Voting rights should be restored to felons	• Voting rights should not be restored to felons
✳ Felons deserve a say in how they are represented	✳ Several rights are taken away from felons: gun, jury, public office, or obtain licenses, voting right
✳ without rights they will feel alienated	✳ recidivism rates
✳ without rights they will reoffend	✳ FL has the best system - 5-7 year waiting period
◆ (Yaffe, 2016)	◆ (von Spakovsky, 2013)

✳ Specific Details - Necessary for a score of 4.
◆ Citation - Necessary for a score of 4.

Step 3: Type your detail paragraphs.

Organizing your detail paragraphs is perhaps the single most important aspect of your essay. Again, you're summarizing two sides of an argument; while doing so you are being very careful not to include your own opinion on the issue or feelings about the opinion of the source authors. With that in mind, you're adding the authors' details that she used to support her argument by using direct text-based information: you're quoting the details or paraphrasing the authors ideas. The development of each detail paragraph should follow a specific formula which will allow for a logical progression of ideas and specific examples to support each idea. By following the formula, you eliminate the possibility of creating confusion on the part of the reader(s) scoring your essay. Each paragraph should summarize the argument of each author. When summarizing, use specific text-based evidence to support the authors' arguments.

Important notes regarding your detail paragraphs:

- Remember, the *Praxis®* Core writing subtest doesn't focus on style or creativity. Keep your goal in mind: *write an informative essay that summarizes the arguments of two different authors with opposing viewpoints.*
- Write clearly, and do not use vocabulary or punctuation you are not comfortable with.
- Always write in chronological order.
- Cite quotes and any information taken directly from the text. For example, "Organizing your detail paragraphs is perhaps the single most important aspect of your essay" (Vibbert, 2018).

Example Detail Paragraph 1 (Source 1):

In his piece "Give Felons and Prisoners the Right to Vote," published in *The Washington Post*, Gideon Yaffe suggests that giving felons and prisoners the right to vote has a positive impact on the lives of the offenders, and a positive impact on the community. In passage one, Yaffe writes "An increasing body of research in social psychology shows that those who feel a sense of ownership in their government are less likely to commit crimes." This sense of ownership allows convicted felons to feel they have some control over their destiny. The passage also suggests that when basic rights, like voting, are stripped, criminals feel alienated and disenfranchised; once this mentality is instilled in the criminal, they are far more likely to commit further crimes (Yaffe, 2016).

Example Detail Paragraph 2 (Source 2):

However, as outlined by Hans von Spakovsky in passage two, "Ex-cons Should Prove They Deserve the Right to Vote," the immediate re-instatement of felons voting rights poses issues for both the offender and the general public. Studies have shown that, in more than 50 percent of the cases, criminals who commit violent crimes will end up back in prison for similar crimes. In the same way a felon loses the right to own a gun, sit on a jury, run for public office, or obtain certain licenses, a felon losing his or her voting right is simply another way for the government to protect its citizens. The author states that a national system similar to the one used by the state of Florida may be the best avenue for a positive outcome, "a five-or-seven-year waiting period gives felons the opportunity—and an incentive—to prove they are deserving of exercising their right to vote" (von Spakovsky, 2013).

Proof your detail paragraphs.

Because the bulk of your grade will come from the detail paragraphs, you will want to proof these right after you write them. Make sure your grammar is correct and that your ideas are clear. Do not add any more information. This is the time to refine punctuation, spelling, and grammar only.

Make sure you keep this in mind when you are proofing your details.

- Make sure you have identified a specific detail to support each author's position.
- Cite the quote(s) properly. You can use any in-text citation method—APA, MLA, or Chicago. However, we recommend **APA in-text citation** style because it is easy to use. For APA citations, use the author's last name and the year of publication: **(Smith, 2005).**

Step 4: Type the introduction and conclusion.

The introduction and conclusion will be the final things you write. Writing your introduction at the end of the assignment may seem counter intuitive; however, by doing so, you will be able to include information from the detail paragraphs without sacrificing continuity. If you write your introduction first and then change your ideas midway through the detail paragraphs, you must go back and correct the introduction. In the event that you run out of time before you're able to correct the introduction, you will be left with a confusing essay because your introduction does not match your detail paragraphs. Your conclusion should be a summary of what you just wrote. You should restate the thesis, each authors argument, and add a closing sentence.

> **Quick Tip!**
>
> Use the *assignment* part of the prompt to help you with the intro and conclusion. There is a TON of good information in there you can use. Revise what is said in the *assignment* and apply it to the first and last paragraph of your essay.

*Remember to use the assignment when you write your introduction and conclusion.

In recent years, the push to revise laws pertaining to a felon's right to vote has grown substantially. Many Americans feel that convicted felons should be able to regain their right to vote after they are released from prison. However, others feel that voting is a privilege, and once you are convicted of a serious crime you lose that privilege. Both of the following sources address whether or not these felons deserve to have their voting rights re-established and the positive or negative effect the revised law could have on the country.

Example Introduction:

The immediate re-instatement of felons voting rights continues to be a point of contention among American citizens and politicians. Some people feel that if one has committed a major crime, that individual has given-up the right to decide representation and policy changes. However, others feel that all American citizens--regardless of whether they have committed been convicted of a felony or not--have the right to choose who represents them and can vote on local and national policy. Re-establishing felon's voting rights is an important topic of national concern.

Example Conclusion:

The decision whether to give felons the right to vote or continue to take away that right as a form of punishment, will continue to be debated. The importance of every American citizen feeling as though he or she is being represented in government cannot be over stated. Yet, it is the government's responsibility to protect its citizens. Both sides will have to make some concessions if a definitive solution is to be reached.

Step 5: Proofread the entire essay

Now read your essay from beginning to end, fixing any errors in spelling, punctuation, or grammar. Again, this is not the time to add any new information. This is simply an opportunity to ensure your essay is clear, concise, and grammatically correct.

Things to consider

Final Notes:

- Use your scratch-paper board to identify exactly which ideas you plan to include in your essay.

- Do not waste time worrying about minor grammatical errors as they do not count as major flaws.

- Focus on delivering the information in an organized and informative way that makes the authors' arguments easy to understand.

When writing your argumentative essay, avoid using:

- Clichés

- Awkward wording

- Poor parallel structure

- Misplaced/dangling modifiers

- Slang or informal language

- Improper grammar

Directions: In the following section you will have 30 mins to read two short passages on a topic and then plan and write an essay on that topic. The essay will be an informative essay based on the two sources that are provided.

Read the topic and the sources carefully. You will probably find it best to spend a little time considering the topic and organizing your thoughts before you begin writing. DO NOT WRITE ON A TOPIC OTHER THAN THE ONE SPECIFIED. Essays on topics of your own choice will not be acceptable. In order for your test to be scored, your response must be in English.

The essay questions are included in this test to demonstrate how well you can write. You should, therefore, take care to write clearly and effectively, using specific examples where appropriate. Remember that how well you write is more important than how much you write, but to cover topics adequately, you will probably have to write more than one paragraph.

Assignment: In recent years, the push to revise laws pertaining to a felon's right to vote has grown substantially. Many Americans feel that convicted felons should be able to regain their right to vote after they are released from prison. However, others feel that voting is a privilege, and once you are convicted of a serious crime you lose that privilege. Both of the following sources address whether or not these felons deserve to have their voting rights re-established and the positive or negative effect the revised law could have on the country.

Read the two passages carefully and then write an essay in which you identify the most important concerns regarding the issue and explain why they are important. Your essay must draw on information from BOTH of the sources. In addition, you may draw on your own experiences, observations, or reading. Be sure to CITE the sources whether you are paraphrasing or directly quoting.

Source 1

Adapted from: Yaffe, Gideon. "Give Felons and Prisoners the Right to Vote." *The Washington Post*. July 26, 2016. https://www.washingtonpost.com/opinions/let-felons-and-prisoners-vote/2016/07/26.

Most felons—whether in prison, on probation or parole, or entirely free of state supervision—are citizens. They should be afforded the right to decide who represents them and the laws by which they will be governed. By taking away their right to vote, you risk further alienating these individuals; in some cases that alienated feeling was the catalyst for their crimes in the first place.

The vast majority of felons are American citizens; therefore, they have no other geographic home. Taking away their right to vote removes any sense of citizenship they may still have after incarceration.

Even if one considers voting to be purely symbolic, it is a symbol with great psychological power. An increasing body of research in social psychology shows that those who feel a sense of ownership in their government are less likely to commit crimes. Re-establishing felons' voting rights is a potential source of criminal control—granting the vote to felons can discourage recidivism. Furthermore, research has proven that with this sense of ownership, ex-felons enjoy a quality of life that would be impossible without the freedoms that are re-established after their release.

In democracy, felon voting rights should not be a partisan issue. Both political parties must see the importance of re-establishing felon's voting right as a way to not only positively influence the ex-prisoners, but also as a way to protect their citizens by reducing crime. WE should give the vote to citizens, in or out of prison, whom we wish to hold responsible for violating laws that are not just ours but also theirs.

Source 2

Adapted from: von Spakovsky, Hans A. "Ex-cons Should Prove They Deserve the Right to Vote." *The Heritage Foundation*. March 15th, 2013. www.heritage.org/election-integrity/commentary/ex-cons-should-prove-they-deserve-the-right-to-vote.

The proposal to automatically restore felons' right to vote as soon as they have completed their sentence is shortsighted and bad public policy. When presented as a measure of compassion and justice, it is also hypocritical, as automatic restoration is not in the best interest of felons or the general public.

An April 2012 report from the Florida Department of Corrections showed that the recidivism rate of felons ranged from 31% to 34% on average over a five-year period. Recidivism among those convicted of robbery, burglary and sex offenses reached or exceeded 50%, while the overall recidivism rate of felons committing nonviolent offenses also approached 50%. Therefore, to restore voting rights to felons as soon as they leave prison is irresponsible.

Advocates of automatic restoration also seem reluctant to mention that voting rights aren't the only rights people lose when convicted of a felony. In Florida, as in most states, felons also lose their right to own a gun, hold public office, sit on a jury, and obtain certain types of professional and occupational licenses. Many such rights can never be restored without a full pardon.

Felons have, by definition, knowingly and intentionally violated the laws of society. A five-or-seven-year waiting period before restoring their voting rights gives felons the opportunity and an incentive to prove they are deserving of exercising their right to vote.

Sample Essay – Score of 4

The immediate re-instatement of felons voting rights continues to be a point of contention among American citizens and politicians. Some people feel that if one has committed a major crime, that individual has given-up the right to decide representation and policy changes. However, others feel that all American citizens--regardless of whether they have committed been convicted of a felony or not--have the right to choose who represents them and can vote on local and national policy. Re-establishing felon's voting rights is an important topic of national concern.

In his piece "Give Felons and Prisoners the Right to Vote," published in *The Washington Post*, Gideon Yaffe suggest that giving felons and prisoners the right to vote has a positive impact on the lives of the offenders, and a positive impact on the community. In passage one, Yaffe writes "An increasing body of research in social psychology shows that those who feel a sense of ownership in their government are less likely to commit crimes." This sense of ownership allows convicts and ex- convicts to feel that they have some control over the laws that they are breaking and the punishments they could receive for breaking those laws. The passage suggests that, when these basic rights are stripped of them, criminals feel alienated and disenfranchised; once this mentality is instilled in the criminal, they are far more likely to commit further crimes (Yaffe, 2016).

However, as outlined by Hans von Spakovsky in passage two, "Ex-cons Should Prove They Deserve the Right to Vote," the immediate re-instatement of felons voting rights poses issues for both the offender and the general public. Studies have shown that, in more than 50 percent of the cases, criminals who commit violent crimes will end up back in prison for similar crimes. In the same way a felon loses the right to own a gun, sit on a jury, run for public office, or obtain certain licenses, a felon losing his or her voting right is simply another way for the government to protect its citizens. The author states that a national system similar to the one used by the state of Florida may be the best avenue for a positive outcome, "a five-or-seven-year waiting period gives felons the opportunity--and an incentive--to prove they are deserving of exercising their right to vote" (von Spakovsky, 2013).

The decision whether to give felons the right to vote or continue to take away that right as a form of punishment, will continue to be debated. The importance of every American citizen feeling as though he or she is being represented in government cannot be over stated. Yet, it is the government's responsibility to protect its citizens. Both sides will have to make some concessions if a definitive solution is to be reached.

Let's refer to the rubric to see why this essay earned a score of 4:

Score of 4 (passing)

A 4 essay demonstrates competence in response to the assignment

An essay in this category:

- Adequately explains why the concerns are important, supporting the explanation with some links between the two sources and adequate reasons, examples, or details

  o *The author immediately states the issue presented in the assignment. There is no doubt what the issue is and that it is an important topic that should be discussed.*

  o *The author presents the source authors' arguments and their supporting examples.*

- Incorporates information from both sources to identify and explain important concerns regarding the issue discussed in the sources

  o *The author effectively summarizes the original sources.*

- Shows control in the organization and development of ideas

  o *The essay is well developed and organized. The summaries effectively explain each authors opinion, arguments, and examples.*

- Displays adequate use of language

  o *The author displays proficiency in vocabulary and sentence variety.*

- Shows control of grammar, usage, and mechanics, but may display errors
  - *The author uses proper grammar and shows proficiency in usage and mechanics.*
- Cites both sources when paraphrasing or quoting
  - *The author correctly uses APA format to cite both source passages.*

Sample Essay – Score of 3

Some people feel that if one has committed a major crime, that individual has given-up the right to decide representation and policy changes. Others feel that all American citizens have the right to choose who represents them and can vote on local and national policy. Re-establishing felon's voting rights is an important topic of national concern.

In source one the author suggests that giving felons and prisoners the right to vote has a positive impact on the lives of the offenders, and a positive impact on the community. In passage one, the author says "An increasing body of research in social psychology shows that those who feel a sense of ownership in their government are less likely to commit crimes." This sense of ownership allows convicts and ex- convicts to feel that they have some control over the laws that they are breaking and the punishments they could receive for breaking those laws. The passage suggests that, when these basic rights are stripped of them, criminals feel alienated and disenfranchised, once this mentality is instilled in the criminal, they are far more likely to commit further crimes.

Hans von Spakovsky disagrees with the author of source one. Studies have shown that, in more than 50 percent of the cases, criminals who commit violent crimes will end up back in prison for similar crimes. The author states that a national system similar to the one used by some states already may be the best avenue for a positive outcome, a five-or-seven-year waiting period gives felons the opportunity to prove they are deserving of their right to vote.

The decision whether to give felons the right to vote or continue to take away that right as a form of punishment, will continue to be debated. The importance of every American citizen feeling as though he or she is being represented in government cannot be over stated. Yet, it is the government's responsibility to protect its citizens. Both sides will have to will have to make some concessions if a definitive solution is to be reached.

When we refer to the rubric of 4, we can clearly see this essay fails to meet the passing criteria:

Fails to meet the score of 4:

- Adequately explains why the concerns are important, supporting the explanation with some links between the two sources and adequate reasons, examples, or details
    - *The author fails to immediately identify the issue being discussed*
    - *Paragraph 2 lacks specific details*
- Incorporates information from both sources to identify and explain important concerns regarding the issue discussed in the sources
    - *Paragraph one is missing the author and title*
- Shows control in the organization and development of ideas
- Displays adequate use of language
- Shows control of grammar, usage, and mechanics, but may display errors
- Cites both sources when paraphrasing or quoting
    - *The author fails to cite source material in both detail paragraphs.*
    - *Paragraph one is missing the author and title*

Paragraph structure

It's important to have a plan when building your detail paragraphs. In order to convey your ideas clearly and accurately you must understand the order and purpose for each of your sentences. An easy strategy to create effective paragraphs is the **P.I.T.** method.

The P.I.T. Method of Paragraph Structure

Purpose (sentence 1) You should think of you purpose sentence like the thesis of you paragraph. It is a simple introduction to what you are about to tell the reader. For your source-based essay that might include the author and title of the passage you're going to summarize.

Information (sentences 2-?) This is the "body" of the paragraph. In these sentences you will discuss the details and specific examples to support the author's argument. It is in these sentences that you will provide your direct information from the text as well as in-text citations. All the information in this part of the paragraph will support the purpose; in the case of the source-based essay, the information used will support the argument of the author you are summarizing.

Transition- (final sentence) A sentence that closes out the information in passage one. Do not offer a final detail without a supporting example. All ideas must be closed-out before moving on to the next paragraph.

Detail Paragraph One: Source One

In each detail paragraph, you must first identify what the paragraph will be informing the reader of. This is where we use the purpose sentence. You should think of this sentence as the main idea of your paragraph: everything you write in the paragraph must support this statement. You will want to make this sentence as clear and declarative as possible.

Let's break down the P.I.T. Structure of our detail paragraph. Think to yourself as we go: Why are the sentences arranged this way? Keep in mind that we are not writing the essay in order. The following example will display the proper organization of your essay and the order in which the piece should be written.

> **Quick Tip!**
>
> In the source-based essay, you are writing informatively, so you will avoid discussing your personal opinion and instead focus on specific, text-driven, properly cited information. It is also important that you write only in the third person. Avoid using 1st person pronouns *I, we, me, and us*. Avoid using 2nd person pronouns **you** and **your**.

In his piece published in *The Washington Post*, Gideon Yaffe suggest that giving felons and prisoners the right to vote has a positive impact on the lives of the offenders, and a positive impact on the community. In passage one, Yaffe writes "An increasing body of research in social psychology shows that those who feel a sense of ownership in their government are less likely to commit crimes." This sense of ownership allows convicts and ex- convicts to feel that they have some control over the laws that they are breaking and the punishments they could receive for breaking those laws. The passage suggests that, when these basic rights are stripped of them, criminals feel alienated and disenfranchised; once this mentality is instilled in the criminal, they are far more likely to commit further crimes (Yaffe).

Purpose (sentence 1): In his piece "Give Felons and Prisoners the Right to Vote," published in *The Washington Post*, Gideon Yaffe suggests that giving felons and prisoners the right to vote has a positive impact on the lives of the offenders, and a positive impact on the community. (*Here the writer identified the author, title, and the purpose of our paragraph. The reader is now aware that the following sentences will identify Yaffe's feelings: the vote will improve the lives of criminals and citizens.*)

Information (sentences 2-4): In passage one, Yaffe writes "An increasing body of research in social psychology shows that those who feel a sense of ownership in their government are less likely to commit crimes." This sense of ownership allows convicts and ex- convicts to feel that they have some control over the laws that they are breaking and the punishments they could receive for breaking those laws. The passage suggests that, when these basic rights are stripped of them, criminals feel alienated and disenfranchised; once this mentality is instilled in the criminal, they are far more likely to commit further crimes (Yaffe). (*These sentences provide the details, specific examples, and quotes that will best present the authors argument. Paraphrasing and quotations are cited accordingly. The writer of the essay took "An* increasing body of research in social psychology shows that those who feel a sense of ownership in their government are less likely to commit crimes" *as a direct quote from the text as an example of how Yaffe research to support his argument. Keep in mind that the writer is neither agreeing or disagreeing with Yaffee and his assertions about felons voting, but simply explaining Yaffe's opinion on the subject.)*

Detail Paragraph Two: Source Two

However, as outlined by Hans von Spakovsky in passage two, "Ex-cons Should Prove They Deserve the Right to Vote," the immediate re-instatement of felons voting rights poses issues for both the offender and the general public. Studies have shown that, in more than 50 percent of the cases, criminals who commit violent crimes will end up back in prison for similar crimes (von Spakovsky). In the same way a felon loses the right to own a gun, sit on a jury, run for public office, or obtain certain licenses, a felon losing his or her voting right is simply another way for the government to protect its citizens (von Spakovsky). The author states that a national system similar to the one used by the state of Florida may be the best avenue for a positive outcome, "a five-or-seven-year waiting period gives felons the opportunity--and an incentive--to prove they are deserving of exercising their right to vote."

Purpose (sentence 1): However, as outlined by Hans von Spakovsky in passage two, "Ex-cons Should Prove They Deserve the Right to Vote," the immediate re-instatement of felons voting rights also poses issues for both the offender and the general public. *(In this purpose sentence the view—the opposing view—of author number two is being summarized. The author uses the transition word* However *to indicate that the opposing view is going to be discussed in this paragraph.)*

Information (sentences 2-4): Studies have shown that, in more than 50 percent of the cases, criminals who commit violent crimes will end up back in prison for similar crimes (von Spakovsky). In the same way a felon loses the right to own a gun, sit on a jury, run for public office, or obtain certain licenses, a felon losing his or her voting right is simply another way for the government to protect its citizens (von Spakovsky). The author states that a national system similar to the one used by the state of Florida may be the best avenue for a positive outcome, "a five-or-seven-year waiting period gives felons the opportunity- and an incentive- to prove they are deserving of exercising their right to vote." *(The information sentences summarize the argument of author number two. The writer provides specific examples and quotes from the original text. Notice how the writer paraphrases von Spakovsky:* In the same way a felon loses the right to own a gun, sit on a jury, run for public office, or obtain certain licenses, a felon losing his or her voting right is simply another way for the government to protect its citizens (von Spakovsky). *Paraphrasing the author is often just as effective as a direct quote as long as the in-text citation is done correctly.)*

Introduction:

The immediate re-instatement of felons voting rights continues to be a point of contention among American citizens and politicians. Some people feel that if one has committed a major crime, that individual has given-up the right to decide representation and policy changes. However, others feel that all American citizens--regardless of whether they have committed been convicted of a felony or not--have the right to choose who represents them and can vote on local and national policy. Re-establishing felon's voting rights is an important topic of national concern. *(It is important to remember to write the introduction after you have written your detail paragraphs. Notice that the author immediately states the issue presented in the assignment; presenting the topic immediately leaves no doubt in the reader's mind what it is you are writing about. The second and third sentences briefly mention each side of the argument that will be further outlined in the essay. The last sentence is the thesis which re-emphasizes the importance of the issue.)*

Conclusion:

The decision whether to give felons the right to vote or continue to take away that right as a form of punishment, will continue to be debated. The importance of every American citizen feeling as though he or she is being represented in government cannot be over stated. Yet, it is the government's responsibility to protect its citizens. Both sides will have to will have to make some concessions if a definitive solution is to be reached. *(The conclusion will be the last thing you write and is a summary of what you have just written. It is important that you restate the issue and restate the opinions of each author. It is also important that you NEVER ADD NEW INFORMATION in your conclusion. Finally, the conclusion is wrapped up with a closing sentence that completes the essay.)*

Directions: In the following section you will have 30 minutes to read two short passages on a topic and then plan and write an essay on that topic. The essay will be an informative essay based on the two sources that are provided.

Read the topic and the sources carefully. You will probably find it best to spend a little time considering the topic and organizing your thoughts before you begin writing. DO NOT WRITE ON A TOPIC OTHER THAN THE ONE SPECIFIED. Essays on topics of your own choice will not be acceptable. In order for your test to be scored, your response must be in English.

The essay questions are included in this test to demonstrate how well you can write. You should, therefore, take care to write clearly and effectively, using specific examples where appropriate. Remember that how well you write is more important than how much you write, but to cover topics adequately, you will probably have to write more than one paragraph.

Assignment: In the state of Florida, third grade students are required to achieve a "passing" score on statewide standardized tests in order to advance to the next grade. Because of these tests, student retention has grown significantly. Many parents and teachers feel that the mandated retention has a profoundly negative effect on these students. However, others feel that students who are retained show improved academic performance. The following sources address whether or not the mandated retention of third graders has a positive or negative effect on the students.

Read the two passages carefully and then write an essay in which you identify the most important concerns regarding the issue and explain why they are important. Your essay must draw on information from BOTH sources. In addition, you may draw on your own experiences, observations, and reading. Be sure to CITE the sources whether you are paraphrasing or directly quoting the author.

Source 1

Jasper, Kathleen (2016). *The effects of mandated third grade retention on graduation rates and student outcomes: A policy analysis of Florida's a+ plan.*

Florida's mandated retention of third graders who do not meet standardized testing requirements, creates enormous and unnecessary stress on children. In a study of first, third, and sixth graders, researchers asked students to rate a list of 20 stressful life events based on level. Researchers found students, across grade levels, rated the top three stressful life events in this order: losing a parent, going blind, and being retained in school. Sixth grade students rated grade retention as the most stressful life event, rating retention more stressful than losing a parent or going blind. Students who were retained faced difficulty in catching up to their peers, achieving academically, and obtaining a high school diploma. However, hundreds of thousands of students are retained in America.

The decision to retain so many students is not only costly, 589 million in FL alone over the last 10 years, but it is also detrimental students' success. In recent studies, 17% of students who were retained did not graduate high school. In addition, many students who were retained never increased their reading levels. Despite all the retentions, reading and math scores have not improved significantly over the last 10 years.

Source 2

Millbarge, Sharon L., Fitz-Hume, Claudia L. (2013) *Retention: Historical perspectives and new research.* Journal of School Psychology, 51*(3)* 229-232

Retention in third grade had large positive effects on reading and math achievement in the short run. Although these initial benefits faded over time, students who had been held back entered high school performing at a higher level relative to their grade level than similar students who'd been promoted. They needed less remediation, and they earned higher grades while enrolled. Being retained had no effect on students' chances of graduating.

In addition, test-based retention in third grade improved student performance. Students retained in third grade under Florida's test-based promotion policy experienced substantial short-term gains in both math and reading achievement. They were less likely to be retained in a later grade and better prepared when they entered high school. Being retained in third grade led students to take fewer remedial courses in high school and improved their grade point averages. There was no negative impact on graduation. Being held back did delay students' graduation from high school by 0.63 years but being older for their grade did not reduce their probability of graduating or receiving a regular diploma

Score of 4

In the state of Florida, there is significant debate on the effect mandated retention has on students. Some believe the mandate hurts students academically and psychologically. While others argue that retaining students while they're young has a positive academic effect. The effect of Florida's third grade retention mandate is an important, publicly debated issue.

In her piece, *The effect of mandated third grade retention on graduation rates and student outcomes: A policy analysis of Florida's a+ plan,* Kathleen Jasper argues that mandated third grade retention has a negative psychological impact on students, while providing little academic improvement. Students feel an incredible amount of stress when faced with the possibility of being held back from their classmates. A recent study showed that many students considered retention to be their most stress-inducing fear, "…students rated grade retention as the most stressful life event, rating retention more stressful than losing a parent or going blind." The traumatic experience of student retention has proven to have little positive academic impact on the students affected. Jasper claims, "Despite all the retentions, reading and math scores have not improved significantly over the last 10 years." It appears that there are some significant flaws in mandated standardized-test-based third grade retention (Jasper, 2016).

However, in their work *Retention: Historical perspectives and new research,* Sharon L. Millbarge and Claudia L. Fitz-Hume, outline the positive academic effects of test-based retention. The authors claim that students who were held back at a young age performed "at a higher level relative to their grade level than similar students who'd been promoted." The authors' research showed that students who were held back in third grade showed improved academic performance and were less likely to be held back in the future. Retained students took an extra .63 years to graduate from high school, however, the author states that "…being older for their grade did not reduce their probability of graduating or receiving a regular diploma" (Millbarge/Fitz-Hume, 2013).

The effect of test-based retention on Florida's third graders is an important issue that is subject to public debate. Many parents and teachers feel that the threat of retention places unnecessary stress on students. However, others feel that the positive academic outcome is worth holding students back a year. Until there is a resolution that benefits kids academically and reduces harmful stress, student retention will continue to be a highly debated issue.

Let's refer to the rubric to see why this essay earned a score of 4:

Score of 4 (passing)

A 4 essay demonstrates competence in response to the assignment

An essay in this category:

- Adequately explains why the concerns are important, supporting the explanation with some links between the two sources and adequate reasons, examples, or details
  - *The author immediately states the issue presented in the assignment. There is no doubt what the issue is and that it is an important topic that should be discussed.*
  - *The author presents the source authors' arguments and their supporting examples.*
- Incorporates information from both sources to identify and explain important concerns regarding the issue discussed in the sources
  - *The author effectively summarizes the original sources.*
- Shows control in the organization and development of ideas
  - *The essay is well developed and organized. The summaries effectively explain each authors opinion, arguments, and examples.*
- Displays adequate use of language
  - *The author displays proficiency in vocabulary and sentence variety.*
- Shows control of grammar, usage, and mechanics, but may display errors.
  - *The author uses proper grammar and shows proficiency in usage and mechanics.*
- Cites both sources when paraphrasing or quoting
  - *The author correctly uses APA format to cite both source passages.*

Sample Essay - Score of 3

Some believe the mandate hurts students. While others argue that retaining students while they're young has a positive academic effect. The effect of Florida's third grade retention mandate is an important, publicly debated issue.

Author one argues that mandated third grade retention has a negative psychological impact on students, while providing little academic improvement. Students feel an incredible amount of stress when faced with the possibility of being held back from their classmates. A recent study showed that many students considered retention to be their most stress-inducing fear. Students rated grade retention as the most stressful life event, rating retention more stressful than losing a parent or going blind. The traumatic experience of student retention has proven to have little positive academic impact on the students effected. There are some significant flaws in mandated standardized-test-based third grade retention.

Sharon L. Millbarge and Claudia L. Fitz-Hume, show the positive academic effect of test-based retention. The authors claim that students who were held back at a young age performed "at a higher level relative to their grade level than similar students who'd been promoted." The authors' research showed that students who were held back in third grade showed improved academic performance and were less likely to be held back in the future. Retained students only took a little more time to graduate from high school.

The effect of test-based retention on Florida's third graders is an important issue that is subject to public debate. Until there is a resolution that benefits kids academically and reduces harmful stress, student retention will continue to be a highly debated issue.

When we refer to the rubric of 4, we can clearly see this essay fails to meet the passing criteria.

Fails to meet the score of 4:

- Adequately explains why the concerns are important, supporting the explanation with some links between the two sources and adequate reasons, examples, or details
  - *The author fails to immediately identify the issue being discussed*
  - *Paragraph 2 lacks specific details*

- Incorporates information from both sources to identify and explain important concerns regarding the issue discussed in the sources
  - *Paragraph one is missing the author and title*

- Shows control in the organization and development of ideas

- Displays adequate use of language

- Shows control of grammar, usage, and mechanics, but may display errors
  - *Author fails to use quotation marks when directly quoting author one in detail paragraph one.*

- Cites both sources when paraphrasing or quoting
  - *The author fails to cite source material in both detail paragraphs.*
  - *Paragraph one is missing the author and title*

This page is intentionally left blank.

PRAXIS® CORE ACADEMIC SKILLS FOR EDUCATORS: MATH

This page is intentionally left blank.

The *Praxis®* Core Mathematics Subtest is comprised of a variety of math skills over a broad range of math categories. The following guide is designed to highlight specific skills and strategies needed to maximize time and efficiency when taking the *Praxis®* Core mathematics subtest.

Test at a Glance	
Test Name	Core Academic Skills for Educators: Mathematics
Test Code	5733
Time	90 minutes
Number of Questions	56
Format	Selected response questions – select one answer choice Selected response questions – select one or more answer choices Numeric entry questions On-screen calculator available
Test Delivery	Computer delivered

	Content Categories	Approximate Number of Questions	Approximate Percentage of the Exam
	I. Number and Quantity	20	36%
	II. Data Interpretation and Representation, Statistics, and Probability	18	32%
	III. Algebra and Geometry	18	32%

The items on this test are meant to test your knowledge of data analysis and application of number sense as well as basic algebraic and geometric concepts in real-world applications. The questions do not follow a particular course or grade level.

This page is intentionally left blank.

For questions in the number and quantity competency, you will be asked to solve problems using basic math operations to represent quantities in various numerical forms. The problems associated with this component focus on how to manipulate values in the number system, work with math operations, and use logic to critically analyze scenarios. In addition, questions from this content category will include several real-life word problems that require an application of knowledge of ratios, proportions, and rates.

Solve problems involving integers, decimals, and fractions

A fraction is another way to write a division problem. For example, $\frac{1}{4}$ is the same as $1 \div 4 = 0.25$. To find the decimal equivalent of a fraction, divide the numerator (top number) by the denominator (bottom number). Writing all decimal numbers out to three decimal places is suggested when working with and comparing decimal values. When a fraction converts to a "messy" decimal such as, $\frac{2}{3}$, which is equal to $0.66666\ldots$, make it easier to deal with by rounding to 0.667.

With a calculator available on the exam, use it to convert any fraction to a decimal.

Quick Tip!

It helps to memorize quarters and thirds. This will cut down on time spent using the calculator.

$\frac{1}{4} = 0.25$	$\frac{1}{9} = 0.\overline{11}$
$\frac{1}{2} = 0.5$	$\frac{1}{3} = 0.\overline{33}$
$\frac{3}{4} = 0.75$	$\frac{2}{3} = 0.\overline{66}$

Fraction Multiplication and Division

When dividing fractions, you will ultimately be performing multiplication instead of division. For testing purposes, know that when dividing fractions, change the operation to multiplication and flip the <u>second</u> fraction. The following problem will illustrate this.

Example:

1) Solve for x. $\frac{2}{3}x = \frac{1}{2}$

    A. $\frac{2}{6}$

    B. $\frac{4}{3}$

    C. $\frac{3}{4}$

    D. $\frac{3}{2}$

    E. $\frac{1}{6}$

Solution: C

There are two ways to solve this problem.

Method 1:

Divide both sides by $\frac{2}{3}$ to isolate the variable.

When dividing fractions, the number you are dividing by is flipped and then multiplied. (The mathematical term for the "flip" of a fraction is reciprocal.)

$$\frac{\frac{2}{3}x}{\frac{2}{3}} = \frac{\frac{1}{2}}{\frac{2}{3}}$$

$$x = \frac{1}{2} \cdot \frac{3}{2}$$

$$x = \frac{3}{4}$$

Method 2:

When in doubt, convert fractions to decimals and use your calculator to solve.

$$\frac{2}{3} = 0.667$$

$$\frac{1}{2} = 0.5$$

$$0.667x = 0.5$$

$$\frac{0.667x}{0.667} = \frac{0.5}{0.667}$$

$$x \approx 0.7496$$

The two answers are extremely similar to each other. There will be times when using fractions is easier than using decimals and vice versa. When finding an answer that is in fraction form, but the decimal strategy was used, convert the fraction answers to decimals until the closest match reveals itself.

Choice C is closest value to 0.7496.

 It is important to use a strategy that effectively manages the time to answer the test question.

Fraction Addition and Subtraction

When adding and subtracting fractions, a common denominator is necessary. To find a common denominator, find the least common multiple (LCM) of the denominators or multiply both parts of one fraction by the denominator of the other fraction for both fractions in the problem.

The following are examples of adding and subtracting fractions.

Addition

$$\frac{1}{2} + \frac{2}{3} =$$

First find the least common multiple of the denominators. For 2 and 3, the LCM is 6; use 6 as the common denominator for both fractions. If finding the least common multiple becomes too time consuming, multiply each fraction by the denominator of the other fraction. This may result in needing to reduce the final answer, so know which method will be more efficient for you.

$$\frac{3}{6} + \frac{4}{6} = \frac{7}{6}$$

Turn the fraction with a numerator greater than the denominator into a mixed number by dividing 6 into 7. The remainder after dividing becomes the numerator in the fraction of the mixed number; the denominator always stays the same.

$$\frac{7}{6} = 1\frac{1}{6}$$

Subtraction

$$2\frac{1}{5} - 1\frac{3}{4} =$$

Turning mixed numbers into fractions with a numerator greater than the denominator to subtract ensures that you will not have to borrow, potentially making the problem much simpler.

$$\frac{11}{5} - \frac{7}{4} =$$

The least common multiple of 5 and 4 is 20, so multiply both parts of the first fraction by 4 and both parts of the second fraction by 5 to get a common denominator for the fractions.

$$\frac{44}{20} - \frac{35}{20} = \frac{9}{20}$$

Working with Integers and Decimals

When working with decimals, use the calculator as much as possible. When entering numbers into the calculator, watch the calculator screen to make sure you are keying in the correct numbers.

Integers are positive and negative whole numbers. When working with integers, also use the calculator if you are not 100% confident in knowing the rules for adding, subtracting, multiplying, and dividing them. Also, know how to enter a negative number into the calculator. The calculator you are able to use is like the one shown. To enter a negative number, enter the number, then press the $\pm$ button.

Solve problems involving ratio and proportions

A ratio is a comparison of two numbers using a fraction, a colon, or the word "to". Rates are ratios with different units, while ratios have the same units. When two ratios are equivalent, they can be set equal to one another to form a proportion. It is important to recognize proportional relationships because they will appear on the *Praxis*® Core Mathematics subtest in several different forms.

Test items that contain proportional relationships may involve any of the following:

- a scale on a map or from a diagram

- descriptions of similar figures

- geometric shapes

- constant rates/equivalency statements

All questions with proportional relationships are set up and solved the same way; it is up to the problem solver to recognize when a question requires a proportion. Each example below highlights the "clues" in the problem that indicate a proportional relationship when it is not explicitly stated.

Proportions: Given a Scale

A scale is typically given using a colon and questions include a map or a model. The units may or may not be part of the scale, but they will be given in the problem or in an accompanying picture.

Examples:

1) A model of a new parking garage being built downtown has a height of 12.5 inches. If the scale of the model to the actual building is 2:15 and represents inches to feet, how tall is the actual parking garage?

How do you identify using a proportion?

✓ Contains a scale (2:15)
✓ Each of the numbers contains units
✓ There are three numbers with units, and the problem asks for a fourth number with units.

Solution:

Set up the first part of the proportion using the scale.

$$\frac{2 \text{ inches}}{15 \text{ feet}}$$

Next, finish setting up the proportion by using what we call ***matchy-matchy***. Match the units in the first fraction with the units in the second fraction; if inches are in the numerator in the first fraction, inches must also be in the numerator for the second fraction.

$$\frac{2 \text{ inches}}{15 \text{ feet}} = \frac{12.5 \text{ inches}}{x \text{ feet}}$$

Last, cross multiply and solve the equation to find the value of the variable.

$2x = 12.5(15)$ *Note: Once you cross-multiply, the fraction has been eliminated.*

$$\frac{2x}{2} = \frac{187.5}{2}$$

$x = 93.75 \text{ feet}$

2) On a map, one centimeter (cm) is equivalent to 5 kilometers (km). If the distance between two cities is 8 kilometers 20 meters, how many centimeters apart are the two cities on the map?

Solution:

Using the *matchy-matchy* strategy, set up the proportion accordingly. Note that 20 meters has to first be converted to kilometers prior to setting up the proportion. 20 meters = 0.02 km.

$$\frac{\text{cm}}{\text{km}} = \frac{\text{cm}}{\text{km}}$$

$$\frac{1 \text{ cm}}{5 \text{ km}} = \frac{x \text{ cm}}{8.02 \text{ km}}$$

$(5)(x) = (1)(8.02)$

$$\frac{5x}{5} = \frac{8.02}{5}$$

$x \approx 1.6 \text{ cm}$

The two cities are approximately 1.6 cm apart on the map.

> **Testing Tip!**
>
> Watch for competencies that overlap in a problem.
>
> Word problems often combine skills. It is common to have to convert units before being able to solve a problem.

Proportions: Given a Description of Similar Figures

Some word problems describe a situation that is proportional without explicitly giving this information. In this case, the situation may represent similar figures. The side lengths of similar figures are proportional, which is why the problem does not have to state anything about proportionality. If all the units are alike, this may indicate similar figures.

Example:

The height of a tree can be found using similar triangles. A 12-foot tall tree casts a 7-foot shadow. If a nearby tree casts a 5-foot shadow, how tall is the tree?

How do you identify using a proportion?

✓ Contains similar figures that can be drawn
✓ Each of the numbers contains units
✓ There are three numbers with units, and the problem asks for a fourth number with units.

Solution:

Draw a picture and label the lengths.

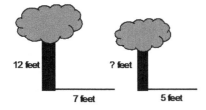

12 feet   ? feet

7 feet   5 feet

Next, use the picture to set up the proportion. Notice that the labels on the picture are already in the right place for a proportion.

$\frac{12}{7} = \frac{x}{5}$ *Note: The units are not included here because they are all the same.*

Last, cross-multiply and solve the proportion for the variable.

$7x = 12(5)$

$7x = 60$

$x = 8\frac{4}{7}$ feet

Proportions: Given Similar Figures in a Word Problem

Questions that contain a proportional relationship may also include a figure. Most often, these figures are triangles. In this instance, the picture may or may not contain labels. If the figure is not labeled, the first step is to label it.

Example:

A 22-ft. flagpole casts a shadow that is 30 feet long. A sign next to the flagpole casts a shadow that is 8 feet long. How tall is the sign? Round to the nearest tenth of a foot.

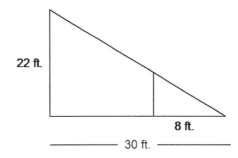

22 ft.

8 ft.

30 ft.

Solution:

Make sense of the picture. It may be easier to see the similar triangles by separating them as below. The larger triangle represents the flagpole and its shadow, and the smaller triangle represents the sign and its shadow. Once the similar triangles have been identified, the proportion can be set up and solved as in the previous question.

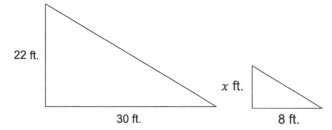

$$\frac{22}{30} = \frac{x}{8}$$

$$30x = 22(8)$$

$$30x = 176$$

$x = 5.9$ feet   *Note: Remember to round to the nearest tenth.*

Proportions: Given Similar Figures

Questions that contain a proportional relationship may simply contain two figures with a statement that indicates they are similar. In this instance, the shapes should be the same shape but a different size.

Example:

The rectangles below are similar. What is the length of the missing side, x?

How do you identify using a proportion?

✓ The problem stated the figures are similar.
✓ There are three numbers with units, and the problem asks for a fourth number with units.

Solution:

Be careful when setting up the proportion for this question because the second rectangle is rotated so that the shorter side is the length. When setting these up, think about matchy-matchy. If the first fraction in the proportion is set up as the shorter side over the longer side, make sure the second fraction is set up the same way.

$$\frac{5}{8} = \frac{x}{5}$$

$$8x = 25$$

$x = 3.125$ cm

3) An artist made a scale drawing of a mural he is painting on the side of a building that is 10 feet tall and 80 feet wide. The scale of inches to feet used to make the drawing is 3:40. How wide is the scale drawing?

double
6:80

A. 6 inches

B. 0.75 inches

C. 24 inches

D. 18 inches

E. 5 inches

Solution: A

The scale is one side of the proportion, and since the question is asking for the width of the scale drawing, the width of the actual building should be used. The length, in this case, is additional information.

$$\frac{3}{40} = \frac{x}{80}$$

$$40x = 240$$

$$x = 6 \text{ inches}$$

4) A small puddle reflects the top of building AB so that a person standing on the top of building ED can see the reflection of AB in the puddle. Using the information in the sketch below, find the height of building AB.

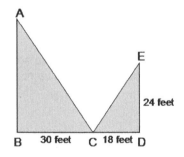

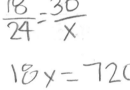

A. 36 feet

B. 39 feet

C. 40 feet

D. 45 feet

E. 48 feet

Solution: C

Use the information from the picture to set up a proportion.

$$\frac{x}{30} = \frac{24}{18}$$

$$18x = 720$$

$$x = 40 \text{ feet}$$

Solve problems involving percent

Realistic problems involving operations with real numbers often include fractions, decimals, and percents. The following are examples of problems with real numbers that may be on the *Praxis®* Core Mathematics subtest exam:

- Percent of increase/decrease

- What percent

- Percent of a number

- What fraction

- Sales tax, tip, commission

Percent of Increase/Decrease

Questions that require finding the percent of increase or decrease will either ask for percent of increase/decrease or the percent of change. To find the percent of change, first find the fraction that represents the change:

$$\frac{\text{new number} - \text{original number}}{\text{original number}}.$$

Next, convert the fraction to a decimal and then to a percent. If the percent is positive, the change was an increase. If the percent is negative, the change is a decrease.

 The negative sign is not included in the answer of a percent decrease. It is instead denoted with the word, decrease.

Example:

5) Last month the local gas station sold 18,590 gallons of gas. This month, the same gas station sold 20,230 gallons of gas. Find the percent of change to the nearest tenth and identify it as an increase or decrease.

    A. 8.1% increase

    B. 8.1% decrease

    C. 8.5% increase

    D. 8.8% increase

    E. 8.8% decrease

$$\frac{20,230 - 18,590}{18,590} = \frac{1,640}{18,590}$$
$$= 0.0882$$
$$= 8.8\%$$

Solution D:

$$\frac{20,230 - 18,590}{18,590} = \frac{1640}{18590} = 0.0882 = 8.8\% \text{ increase}$$

The result is an increase because the original number 18,590 increased to 20,230.

What Percent

When a question asks what percent a situation represents, this requires finding the fraction associated with the problem, converting the fraction to a decimal, and then converting the decimal to a percent.

Example:

6) At a local baseball tournament of 1,500 players, 476 of the players did not record a strikeout at the plate. What percent of the players, to the nearest whole percent, did record a strikeout during the tournament?

   A. 68%

   B. 69%

   C. 32%

   D. 46%

   E. 54%

Solution: A

First find the number of those striking out: $1500 - 476 = 1,024$

Next, write this number as a fraction out of the total number of players: $\frac{1024}{1500}$

Convert to a decimal and then a percent: $\frac{1024}{1500} = 0.6827 \approx 68\%$.

The correct answer choice is A, 68%.

Percent of a Number

The percent of a number asks for a specific percent. When a problem is asking for the percent of a number, convert the percent to a decimal by moving the decimal point two places to the left, and then multiply this decimal by the number given. Percent of a number questions are often embedded in data questions, requiring you to extract information from a table or graph (often a pie chart) to solve the problem.

Example:

7) A pizza restaurant gets an average of 250 orders on a weekend night. Of those orders 24% are for pickup, and the rest are for delivery. How many orders, to the nearest whole number, does the restaurant get for delivery on a weekend night?

   A. 60

   B. 100

   C. 180

   D. 185

   E. 190

Solution: E

If 24% of the orders are for pickup, therefore, 76% are for delivery ($100\% - 24\% = 76\%$). To find 76% of 250, multiply the two values.

$0.76 \times 250 = 190$

The correct answer choice is E, 190 orders are for delivery.

What Fraction

A question sometimes may want to know what fraction, usually in simplest form, represents a situation. Determine the two numbers for the fraction and reduce. If you are unable to reduce, change your answer and all the answer choices to decimals.

Example:

8) A married couple each make $40,000 per year salary. Any additional income they earn is from investments. At the end of the year, their gross earnings were $85,000. What fraction of their income was from investments?

A. $\frac{1}{16}$

B. $\frac{1}{17}$

C. $\frac{1}{2}$

D. $\frac{8}{17}$

E. $\frac{16}{17}$

$$\frac{5,000}{85,000} = \frac{5}{85} = \frac{1}{17}$$

Solution: B

Together the couple grossed $80,000. From investments they earned $85,000 - $80,000 = $5,000.

The fraction of investments for their total income is $\frac{5,000}{85,000}$. Reducing the fraction, $\frac{5,000}{85,000} = \frac{5}{85} = \frac{1}{17}$. The correct answer choice is B, $\frac{1}{17}$.

Sales Tax, Tips, Commission

Sales tax, tips, and commission are all the same as finding the percent of a number. Often an additional step is required in these instances, for example, once the tip is found, the question may ask for the total amount paid.

Example:

9) Charlie makes $20 per hour plus 8% commission on all his sales. This week he worked 30 hours and sold $11,000 worth of product. How much did he gross this week?

A. $9,400

B. $5,440

C. $1,480

D. $880

E. $600

Solution: C

To solve, determine how much Charlie made hourly, then find the amount of commission he earned. Last, add these two values together.

$20 \times 30 = $600 hourly wage for the week; $11,000 \times 0.08 = $880 commission

Total for the week: $600 + $880 = $1,480; The correct answer is answer choice C.

Proportions: Given a Constant Rate

Recall that a rate is a ratio that includes units, such as a number of envelopes stuffed every 20 minutes or the number of chaperones needed for every 15 students. A constant rate is a rate that does not change. For example, the car gets 32 miles per gallon of fuel, is a statement with a constant rate. Because rates in real world examples are often constant, or do not change, expect to see them throughout the exam.

Example:

10) A pie crust making machine can press 15 pie crusts into pie tins in 20 minutes. How many pie crusts can be pressed into pie tins in 4 hours?

How do you identify using a proportion?

✓ Contains an equivalency statement that represents a rate
✓ Each of the numbers contains units
✓ There are three numbers with units, and the problem asks for a fourth number with units.

Solution:

Set up the first part of the proportion using the equivalency statement, $\frac{15 \text{ crusts}}{20 \text{ minutes}}$.

Next, finish setting up the proportion, remembering ***matchy-matchy***. Be careful because the time for the second fraction is in hours. Convert hours to minutes so that the units are the same.

4 hours = $4 \cdot 60$ minutes = 240 minutes

$$\frac{15 \text{ crusts}}{20 \text{ minutes}} = \frac{x \text{ crusts}}{240 \text{ minutes}}$$

Last, cross-multiply and solve the equation to find the value of the variable.

$20x = 240(15) \rightarrow 20x = 3600$

$x = 180$ pie crusts

Additional Examples:

11) A factory produces 10 pillows every 45 minutes. If the factory produces pillows 8 hours each day, how many pillows will it produce in a 5-day work week?

A. 36

B. 45

C. 106

D. 533

E. 888

Solution: D

The rate for this problem is 10 pillows every 45 minutes. The question asks for the final answer in hours, so first convert 45 minutes to hours, which is $45 \div 60 = 0.75$ hour.

The final answer also asks for the number of pillows over 5 days. This problem can be solved by either using 40 hours in the proportion or using 8 and multiplying the answer by 5. To speed up the problem solving and not forget the last step, we suggest using 40 in the original problem.

$$\frac{10}{0.75} = \frac{x}{40}$$

$0.75x = 400$

$x = 533.\overline{3}$

Because the company cannot make $0.\overline{3}$ of a pillow, 533, answer choice D, is the correct solution.

12) In a pet shop, for every 3 cats there are 5 dogs. How many dogs are there if there are 12 cats total in the pet shop?

Solution:

$$\frac{\text{cats}}{\text{dogs}} = \frac{\text{cats}}{\text{dogs}}$$

$$\frac{3}{5} = \frac{12}{x}$$

$$(3)(x) = (5)(12)$$

$$\frac{3x}{3} = \frac{60}{3}$$

$$x = 20$$

There are 20 dogs in the pet shop.

13) On a farm, the ratio of pigs to cows is 1:3. If there are 100 animals on the farm, how many are pigs? How many are cows?

Solution:

First, notice the phrase "ratio of pigs to cows is 1:3." This means the pigs correspond with 1, and the cows correspond with 3. For every 1 pig on the farm, there are 3 cows. If there are 2 pigs, then there are 6 cows, if there are 3 pigs, then there are 9 cows, and so on. Since the ratio is the rule, the fewest number of animals on the farm is 4. For every 1 pig there are 3 cows which means $1 + 3 = 4$. This forms the third subgroup in the problem, which is total animals.

For this problem, there are three subgroups: pigs, cows, and total animals. Let's solve for pigs first, using the subgroups pigs and total animals.

The fraction $\frac{1}{4}$ represents a ratio we can use to solve for pigs. Next, set up the proportion using the total number of animals, 100.

$$\frac{\text{pigs}}{\text{total animals}} \qquad \frac{1}{4} = \frac{x}{100}$$

$$(1)(100) = (4)(x)$$

$$100 = 4x$$

$$\frac{100}{4} = \frac{4x}{4}$$

$$x = 25$$

This means that on a 100-animal farm where the ratio of pigs to cows is 1:3, 25 of the animals are pigs.

To solve for cows, repeat the same procedure.

$$\frac{\text{matchy}}{\text{matchy}} = \frac{\text{cows}}{\text{total animals}} \qquad \frac{3}{4} = \frac{x}{100}$$

$$(3)(100) = (4)(x)$$

$$300 = 4x$$

$$\frac{300}{4} = \frac{4x}{4}$$

$$x = 75$$

This means that on a farm where the ratio of pigs to cows is 1:3 and there are 100 animals, 75 of them are cows. (You can also subtract 25 from 100 to get the number of cows.)

Ratios are not limited to two comparisons. In the event that there are multiple comparisons in a ratio, such as 1:2:5, treat this type of ratio just as above. Let's take the farm animal example and add another animal.

Example:

14) On a farm, the ratio of pigs to cows to chickens is 1:3:6. If there are 100 animals on the farm, how many are pigs? How many are cows? How many are chickens?

Solution:

The extra number represents the subgroup for chickens and changes the number of animals in each subgroup and also changes the total of the ratio from 4 to 10 ($1 + 3 + 6 = 10$).

$$\frac{\text{pigs}}{\text{animals}}$$
$$\frac{1}{10} = \frac{x}{100}$$
$$(1)(100) = (10)(x)$$
$$100 = 10x$$
$$\frac{100}{10} = \frac{10x}{10}$$
$$x = 10$$

$$\frac{\text{cows}}{\text{animals}}$$
$$\frac{3}{10} = \frac{x}{100}$$
$$(3)(100) = (10)(x)$$
$$300 = 10x$$
$$\frac{300}{10} = \frac{10x}{10}$$
$$x = 30$$

$$\frac{\text{chickens}}{\text{animals}}$$
$$\frac{6}{10} = \frac{x}{100}$$
$$(6)(100) = (10)(x)$$
$$600 = 10x$$
$$\frac{600}{10} = \frac{10x}{10}$$
$$x = 60$$

This means that on a 100-animal farm where the ratio of pigs to cows to chickens is 1:3:6, 10 animals are pigs, 30 animals are cows, and 60 animals are chickens.

Demonstrate an understanding of place value, naming of decimal numbers, and ordering of numbers

The value of a certain digit is determined by the place it resides in a number. In our number system, each place has a value of ten times the place to its right. Take the following number as an example:

2,487,905.631

This number should read as two million, four hundred eighty-seven thousand, nine hundred five, and six hundred thirty-one thousandths.

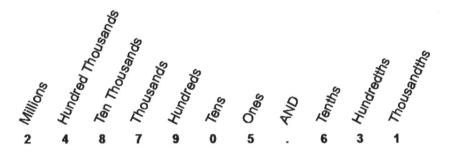

It is important to know how to manipulate a number using the base 10 system. Moving the decimal point to the left (to create a smaller number), is the same as dividing by increments of 10 or multiplying by fractional increments of $\frac{1}{10}$. Conversely, moving the decimal point to the right (to create a larger number) is the same as multiplying by increments of 10. Increments of 10 include 10, 100, 1,000, 10,000…etc.

Examples:

15) $2,487,905.631 \div 10 =$

    248,790.5631

    The decimal point moves one space to the left, reducing the original number.

16) $2,487,905.631 \times 100 =$

    248,790,563.1

    The decimal point moves two spaces to the right, increasing the original number.

When comparing and ordering numbers in a variety of forms, convert all numbers to decimals. Take all decimal numbers out three places (to the thousandths place). Add zeros at the end of any decimal numbers that only extend to one or two decimal places (tenths or hundredths). The table that follows includes numbers in a variety of forms and explains how to convert them to decimals if ordering or comparing them.

Number	Conversion	Decimal Representation
$\sqrt{25}$	A square root means you are looking for the factor of 25 that was multiplied by itself 2 times to get 25. For 25, the square root is ± 5 because $5 \times 5 = 25$ and $(-5) \times (-5) = 25$. When solving an equation, you will need both answers, but when the question asks for the square root of 25, you will only need the positive answer.	5
$\lvert -0.575 \rvert$	The absolute value of a number is how far away from zero on the number line the number in the absolute value bars is. Because this is referring to distance, the number will always be positive.	0.575
$\dfrac{3}{8}$	To convert a fraction to a decimal, divide from the top down. $\frac{3}{8} = 3 \div 8 = 0.375$.	0.375
$\dfrac{1}{9}$	Ninths are good to memorize in order to save time. Any fraction with 9 in the denominator is the number in the numerator repeating. $\frac{1}{9} = 1 \div 9 = 0.1111\ldots$	$0.\overline{111}$
$\dfrac{3}{4}$	Fourths are also good to memorize in order to save time. Standardized tests often use a variation of fourths and ninths throughout test questions. $\frac{3}{4} = 3 \div 4 = 0.75$. When ordering or comparing numbers, it is good practice to add zeros at the end of a decimal like this to bring it out 3 places.	0.750
2.01	Already in decimal form, 2.01 may only need zeros at the end if comparing or ordering.	2.010
4.5%	Percents are numbers out of 100. Thus, to change a percent to a decimal, we are dividing by 100, which moves the decimal point 2 places to the left. $$4.5\% = 04.5 = 0.045$$	0.045

Demonstrate an understanding of the properties of whole numbers

Numbers are classified into various groups based on their properties. Numbers used on the *Praxis®* Core Mathematics subtest exam are all part of the Real Number System. Numbers in the Real Number System are classified further into the groups shown in the table below.

CLASSIFICATION OF NUMBERS	
Real Number System	
Counting Numbers	$1, 2, 3, 4, 5, 6, ...$
Whole Numbers	$0, 1, 2, 3, 4, 5, 6, ...$
Integers	$..., -5, -4, -3, -2, -1, 0, 1, 2, 3, 4, 5, ...$
Rational Numbers	Any number that can be written as a fraction $^a/_b$, where a and b are any integer. Rational numbers include all terminating and repeating decimals. Ex: 0.2, $4\frac{1}{2}$, $7, \frac{1}{3}$
Irrational Numbers	Any number that cannot be written as a fraction. Ex: $\pi, \sqrt{3}$
Additional Classifications	
Prime	A positive integer that only has 1 and itself as factors. Ex: 2, 3, 13, 29 *Note: 1 is neither prime nor composite*
Composite	A positive integer that has factors other than 1 and itself. Ex: 4, 12, 27, 44
Even	A number that is divisible by 2
Odd	A number that is not divisible by 2

Terms used to classify real numbers may be sprinkled throughout the test. Know what type of number each of these terms represent in the event the term is used in a problem. For example, a question may ask to find the probability of a spinner landing on an even integer. In order to determine the solution, it is likely that test takers need to know the definitions of both even and integer.

Prime Factorization

Prime factorization refers to finding all the prime numbers multiplied together that result in a composite number. For example, the prime factorization of 24 is $2 \cdot 2 \cdot 2 \cdot 3$ or $2^3 \cdot 3$. A common method for finding the prime factorization of a number is using factor trees. Using a factor tree to find the prime factorization of 24 is shown below.

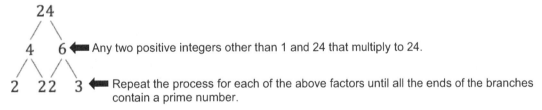

Knowing the prime factorization of common numbers will make simplifying or solving problems requiring factors easier.

Numbers to know the prime factorization of include:

- $4 = 2 \cdot 2$
- $9 = 3 \cdot 3$
- $25 = 5 \cdot 5$
- $49 = 7 \cdot 7$
- $81 = 3 \cdot 3 \cdot 3 \cdot 3$
- $100 = 2 \cdot 2 \cdot 5 \cdot 5$
- $121 = 11 \cdot 11$
- $125 = 5 \cdot 5 \cdot 5$
- $169 = 13 \cdot 13$

While this list is not all inclusive, it does represent the numbers most often used in math problems where prime factorization is part of the solution process.

Example:

17) Which of the following is the prime factorization of 28×42?

    A. $2^4 \times 3^2 \times 7^2$

    B. $2^3 \times 3^2 \times 7^2$

    C. $2^3 \times 3 \times 7^3$

    D. $2^3 \times 3^2 \times 7$

    E. $2^3 \times 3 \times 7^2$

Solution: E

To find the prime factorization of numbers being multiplied, find the prime factorization of each individual number, then combine factors.

$28 = 2 \times 2 \times 7$

$42 = 2 \times 3 \times 7$

Prime factorization of $28 \times 42 = 2 \times 2 \times 2 \times 3 \times 7 \times 7 = 2^3 \times 3 \times 7^2$, which is answer choice E.

Least Common Multiple and Greatest Common Factor

For the *Praxis*® Core Mathematics Subtest exam, you will most likely be applying knowledge of least common multiple (LCM) and greatest common factor (GCF), not necessarily finding these values as a final answer. Knowing both divisibility rules and times tables through the 12s is useful when finding both the LCM and the GCF.

Word problems that include these concepts include ideas such as 12 people per ride or every 50th person through the door winning a prize.

Using the least common multiple also allows fraction denominators to be as small as possible. This is useful when calculating, because it is always easier to compute with smaller numbers, and it also helps with being able to understand the relative size of fractions. Visualizing $\frac{3}{4}$ is easier than visualizing $\frac{16}{32}$, even though they are the same size. Being able to visualize or have an understanding of the size of the fraction helps to determine if the solution makes sense.

Knowing how to find the greatest common factor allows for reducing a fraction to simplest terms. Because answers will most likely be in simplest form, being able to simplify a fraction is a useful skill. The greatest common factor will be the largest number that divides into both the numerator and denominator of a fraction. While identifying the GCF when reducing fractions saves time, there is nothing wrong with taking an extra step or two when reducing. Converting the answer and all the answer choices to decimals is an acceptable strategy as well; this method will just take a little longer.

DIVISIBILITY RULES

A Number is Divisible by…	If…	Examples	
2	The last digit is an even number (ends in 0, 2, 4, 6, 8)	248	ends in 8
		12,550	ends in 0
3	The sum of the digits is divisible by 3	18	$1 + 8 = 9$; 9 is divisible by 3
		312	$3 + 1 + 2 = 6$; 6 is divisible by 3
4	The last two digits is divisible by 4	416	16 is divisible by 4
		1,912	12 is divisible by 4
5	The last digit is 0 or 5	435	ends in 5
		2,220	ends in 0
6	The number is divisible by 2 and 3	204	ends in even number and $2 + 0 + 4 = 6$; 6 is divisible by 3
		66	ends in even number and $6 + 6 = 12$; 12 is divisible by 3
8	The last three digits are divisible by 8	1,088	088 is divisible by 8
		5,800	800 is divisible by 8
9	The sum of the digits is divisible by 9	5,445	$5 + 4 + 4 + 5 = 18$; 18 is divisible by 9
		81	$8 + 1 = 9$; 9 is divisible by 9
10	The last digit is 0	400	ends in 0
		8,720	ends in 0

Example:

18) Select all of the following that are true about 12,033.

    I.   The number is divisible by 2.
    II.   The number is divisible by 3.
    III. The number is divisible by 6.
    IV. The number is divisible by 9.

A. II only

B. I and II

C. II and IV

D. II, III, and IV

E. I, II, and III

Solution: C

12,033 does not end in an even number, so I does not work. The sum of the digits is 9, so II works. Option III is not possible because I does not work. The sum of the digits is 9, so IV also works. Therefore, the correct answer choice is C.

19) Lynn and Monica each made the same snack mix that they are combining and then splitting into 16 separate $\frac{3}{4}$ lb. bags for the basketball team. Lynn made $5\frac{5}{6}$ pounds and Monica made $6\frac{3}{4}$ pounds. After they make all 16 bags of snack mix, how many bags of snack mix remain?

A. $\frac{7}{9}$ bag

B. $\frac{10}{11}$ bag

C. $\frac{151}{192}$ bag

D. $11\frac{4}{5}$ bags

E. $16\frac{7}{9}$ bags

Solution: A

First, find the amount of snack mix Lynn and Monica made together. Knowing the GCF of 4 and 6 is 12 will keep the fractions as small as possible when adding.

$$5\frac{5}{6} + 6\frac{3}{4} = 5\frac{10}{12} + 6\frac{9}{12} = 11\frac{19}{12} = 12\frac{7}{12}$$

Next, the $12\frac{7}{12}$ pounds of snack mix need to be divided into $\frac{3}{4}$ lb. increments because Lynn and Monica are making $\frac{3}{4}$ lb. bags.

$$12\frac{7}{12} \div \frac{3}{4} = \frac{151}{12} \div \frac{3}{4} = \frac{151}{12} \times \frac{4}{3} = \frac{604}{36} = \frac{151}{9} = 16\frac{7}{9}$$

Last, to find how many $\frac{3}{4}$ – pound bags of snack mix remain after the bags are made, subtract 16 from $16\frac{7}{9}$. The correct answer is A, $\frac{7}{9}$ bag.

Identify counterexamples to statements using basic arithmetic

A **counterexample** is an example that proves that the original statement is incorrect. Only one counterexample is needed to prove a statement is wrong, although there may be more than one. These types of problems are testing your knowledge of number sense rather than do you understand the concept of a counterexample.

Examples of the types of statements that may ask for a counterexample may look similar to the following:

- The quotient of a decimal number divided by a decimal number will always be a decimal number.

- The sum of two odd numbers is also odd.

- The product of two fractions is always a number less than 1.

- The difference of two numbers is always smaller than the greatest number in the problem.

Because the skill is finding a counterexample using arithmetic, the statement will involve an operation between numbers.

Example:

20) Which of the following answer choices is a counterexample to the statement, *"Whenever you divide two numbers, the result is always less than both of the numbers?"*

    A. 2 and 3

    B. 4 and 5

    C. −1 and 8

    D. 10 and 3

    E. −2 and −5

Solution: E

For this problem, dividing the numbers given in options A through D either way produces a smaller number than either of the numbers listed. For option E, a negative divided by a negative is a positive, so the solution will be greater than either of the numbers in the answer choice.

Solve real-life problems by identifying relevant numbers, information, or operations

Real-life problems often require the application of multiple skills, especially in the number and quantity content category because the category can include so many different concepts. Be prepared to apply the following skills when solving these types of problems:

- Identifying relevant information from a table

- Identifying relevant information from a graph or diagram, including line graphs, scatter plots, bar graphs, timelines, and circle graphs

- Converting between units

- Combining data to find a value needed as part of solving a problem.

Although this list is most likely not comprehensive, it gives an idea of the skills needed to gather the necessary information to solve a problem. Questions on the exam may even ask what information is missing in order to solve the problem.

Example:

21) What additional information is needed in the scenario below to be able to answer the question?

Joanie drove at a constant rate for 6 hours to get to her mother's house. What was Joanie's rate of speed?

    A. In what city Joanie's mother lives

    B. What time Joanie left home

    C. How many gallons of gas were in Joanie's car

    D. How many miles Joanie drove

    E. How many other cars were on the road

Solution: D

In order to determine Joanie's rate of speed, or miles per hour, the formula $d = rt$ would be used which means the number of miles she drove are needed (distance, d) since the scenario already includes the amount of time (t) it took her.

Solve problems involving units, including unit conversion and measurements

On the Praxis® Core Mathematics Subtest exam, values are given in different units of measure and need to be converted. Using a ratio method to do this streamlines the process and minimizes errors.

For example, instead of thinking 1 foot=12 inches, use a ratio. 1 foot for every 12 inches is the same as $\frac{1 \text{ foot}}{12 \text{ inches}}$. The same is also true for 12 inches=1 foot, or $\frac{12 \text{ inches}}{1 \text{ foot}}$. Using a ratio when converting is a good visual to ensure numbers and units are lined up correctly for canceling units.

Examples:

22) Convert 14 feet to inches.

Solution:

First, take the value being converted (14 feet) and put it over 1.

$$\frac{14 \text{ feet}}{1}$$

Next, write the ratio for feet to inches or inches to feet, depending on the initial ratio. Because feet are in the numerator (top of fraction) of the initial ratio, the only way to eliminate them is to have feet in the denominator (bottom of fraction) of the second fraction as shown below.

$$\frac{14 \text{ feet}}{1} \times \frac{12 \text{ inches}}{1 \text{ foot}}$$

Cancel units as conversion ratios are added. If done correctly, the only unit that remains is the one that was specified in the question.

$$\frac{14 \text{ \sout{feet}}}{1} \times \frac{12 \text{ inches}}{1 \text{ \sout{foot}}} = \frac{14}{1} \times \frac{12 \text{ inches}}{1} = 168 \text{ inches}$$

The value of a certain digit is determined by the place it resides in a number. In our number system each, place has a value of ten times the place to its right. Take the following number as an example:

23) Convert 8 kilometers per hour to meters per minute. (1 km=1000 m)

Solution:

When setting up the first ratio for this problem, pay particular attention to the units. Kilometers per hour is its own ratio.

$$\frac{8 \text{ kilometers}}{1 \text{ hour}}$$

Next, create the conversion ratios that will eliminate unwanted units until only meters per minute are left.

$$\frac{8 \text{ km}}{1 \text{ hr}} \times \frac{1000 \text{ m}}{1 \text{ km}} \times \frac{1 \text{ hr}}{60 \text{ min}}$$

Finally, cancel out units accordingly and simplify.

$$\frac{8 \text{ \sout{km}}}{1 \text{ \sout{hr}}} \times \frac{1000 \text{ m}}{1 \text{ \sout{km}}} \times \frac{1 \text{ \sout{hr}}}{60 \text{ min}} = \frac{8000 \text{ m}}{60 \text{ min}} \approx 133.3 \text{ }^{m}/_{min}$$

24) What are the closest dimensions to the dimensions given of Sandy's blanket?

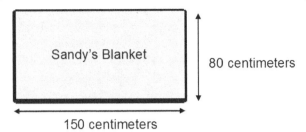

A. 59 inches by 32 inches

B. 59 inches by 80 inches

C. 75 inches by 40 inches

D. 75 inches by 32 inches

E. 80 inches by 150 inches

Solution: A

Using the conversion for centimeters to inches, 1 cm = 0.39370 inches, estimate that $1 \text{ cm} \approx 0.40$ inches. Therefore, $0.40 \cdot 80 \approx 32$ inches. Repeat this process for 150 centimeters, $0.40 \cdot 150 \approx 60$ inches. The closest measurements to Sandy's blanket are 59 inches by 32 inches, option A.

Metric Conversions		
1 cm	=	10 mm
1m	=	100 cm
1km	=	1000 m
Standard Conversions		
1 ft	=	12 in
1yd	=	3 ft
1 yd	=	36 in
1 mile	=	1760 yds
Metric → Standard Conversions		
1mm	=	.03937 in
1 cm	=	.39370 in
1 m	=	39.370 in
1 m	=	3.28084 ft
1 m	=	1.09362 yds
1 km	=	1093.6133 yds
1 km	=	.062137 miles
Standard → Metric Conversion		
1 in	=	2.54 cm
1 ft	=	30.48 cm
1 yd	=	91.44 cm
1yd	=	.9144 cm
1 mile	=	1609.344 m
1mile	=	1.60934 km

This page is intentionally left blank.

Data Interpretation and Representation, Statistics, and Probability

Statistics and probability questions on the *Praxis®* Core Mathematics Subtest exam include reading various types of graphs and diagrams, extracting and interpreting data from graphs and diagrams, and applying knowledge of number sense and algebra to arrive at a final answer. In addition, questions from this content category will include questions about simple probability and the counting theory. Expect many questions from this category to contain multiple steps.

Work with data and data representations to solve problems

Graphs that you should be familiar with for the *Praxis®* Core Mathematics Subtest exam include:

- Venn diagrams
- Bar graphs
- Histograms
- Stem-and-leaf plots
- Timelines
- Scatter plots
- Pictographs.

Testing Tips!

Because the exam is multiple choice, no question requires making a graph, but a question may ask for the graph that correctly displays a data set.

A test question may ask for a specific statistical value, such as the range or median, from the graphical representation of a data set.

Venn Diagrams

Venn diagrams are useful for depicting the likelihood of an event occurring and for making comparisons. Data in a Venn diagram is **categorical data**, meaning that the data falls into specific categories. Venn diagrams are used to show relationships among sets, using overlapping circles to depict relationships. Any relationships that overlap are counted in the region where the circles of the diagram also overlap (Overlapping data is when data falls in more than one category).

In lower grades two categories of data is common. In upper grades, 3 or more categories are often present in Venn diagram questions, so be prepared for 3 sets of data as well as values that fall outside all the categories in the diagram. Sometimes data does not fall into the categories used to make the Venn diagram. In this case, a number is placed outside the circles, and the entire set is enclosed in a rectangle.

Data in Venn diagrams is often referred to using the terms union and intersection.

Union, represented by the symbol ∪, is all of the data in the sets put together.

Intersection, represented by the symbol ∩, is only where data sets overlap.

DATA	GRAPH

Math only certification: 42
Science only certification: 28
Math & science certification: 8

To graph, create a circle for each category. Data that does not overlap stays outside the overlap. Data that includes both categories should be in the overlap section.

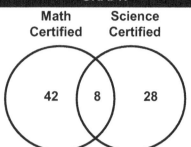

Math Certified   Science Certified

SAMPLE QUESTION:

A survey of 100 families found that 34 of the families have a cat, 41 families have a dog, 26 families have fish, 10 have a dog and fish, 12 have a cat and fish, 8 have a dog and a cat, and 3 have all three animals. How many families surveyed have none of the animals?

A. 1   B. 11   C. 20   D. 35   E. 38

Solution: D

To solve, draw three overlapping circles, and fill in all the categories that overlap.

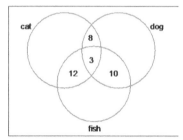

Next, fill in the numbers for families that have only one type of animal. Be careful; this information was not given in the problem. Subtract the families with overlaps from the totals given in the problem to find families with only one type of animal. For fish, there are 12, 3, and 10 families that lie inside the fish circle as part of an overlap. Add these values and subtract from 26, which is the total number of families with a fish tank. Repeat for cats and dogs.

Fish: $26 - (12 + 3 + 10) = 26 - 25 = 1$

Cats: $34 - (12 + 3 + 8) = 34 - 23 = 11$

Dogs: $41 - (8 + 3 + 10) = 41 - 21 = 20$

Add these numbers in the nonoverlapping part of the circles.

Last, add all the numbers in the Venn diagram to see how many families have one of the three types of pets. Be careful to only add each number once, not the total in each circle. Subtract this answer from 100 to find the number of families surveyed that don't have any of the three pets. This number will be in the rectangle but not in any of the three circles in a Venn diagram.

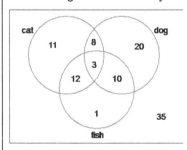

$100 - (11 - 8 - 20 - 12 - 3 - 10 - 1) = 100 - 65 = 35$

There are 35 families with none of the pets in the survey.

Bar Graphs

Data in a bar graph is also categorical data. A bar graph is typically used to track or compare change over time. Examples of when a bar graph might be used to display data include:

- Total electric bill for each high school in the county during the month of June

- Number of students enrolled in 7th grade advanced math over the last 6 years

- Students' grade in a course each quarter during the school year

A bar graph may be used to compare the same categorical data for more than one set of data on the same display. In the last bullet point, students' grade in a course each quarter during the school year, more than one student could be tracked on the same graph, providing both data that can be compared over time and data that compares one student to others.

DATA			GRAPH

	Paul	Ruben
Q1	$5,500	$5,200
Q2	$6,000	$6,400
Q3	$4,000	$4,000
Q4	$8,250	$8,500

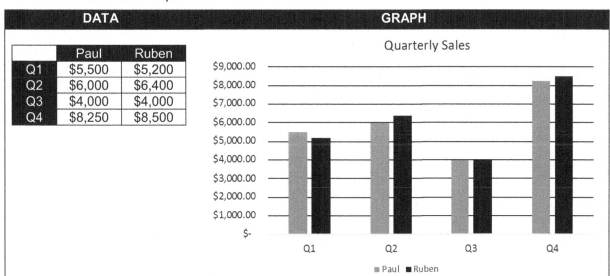

To graph, draw a bar to the height of each of the data points for Paul. Repeat for Ruben, keeping bars in the same category grouped together.

SAMPLE QUESTION:
What is the range in Paul's quarterly sales?

A. $500

B. $2,750

C. $3,750

D. $4,250

E. $4,550

Solution: D

To find the range, subtract the smallest value, $4,000, from the largest value, $8,250.

$8,250 - 4,000 = 4,250$

Be careful not to subtract Q1 from Q4.

Line Plots / Dot Plots

A line plot, sometimes called a dot plot, is a graph that uses numerical data and displays where all the values in a set lie in relation to one another. A line plot is often used to find the range, median, mode, and mean. The visual representation of data on a line plot allows for quick identification of the mode, range, and outliers.

DATA	GRAPH
Number of Hours Spent Studying 1, 3, 7, 2, 2, 1, 1, 1, 3, 10, 5, 2, 7, 1, 3, 4, 7, 5, 1, 4, 3, 3, 1, 1 *To graph, place an x or dot above the number each time it appears.*	(line plot with x marks above numbers 0 through 10)

SAMPLE QUESTION:

The line plot shows the number of hours teachers spent studying over a two-week period for the Math 5-9 Certification exam. Find the median number of hours studied.

A. 10   B. 9   C. 5   D. 3   E. 1

Solution: D

The values are already in order on the graph. Cross off numbers on both ends until the middle number is reached. Be careful not to count the blank spaces.

Example:

1) A small business collected data on how customers are finding out about the business to determine where money for advertising should be focused. The number of contacts by method is listed in the table.

	June	July	August	September
Internet Search	42	50	78	63
Radio Advertisement	18	22	11	21
Friend Referral	10	15	25	32

Which of the following types of graphs would be best for displaying the data for comparison?

A. Line plot

B. Three individual bar graphs

C. Triple bar graph

D. Stem-and-leaf plot

E. Frequency table

Solution: C

The data is categorical because the company is analyzing advertising methods. This eliminates a line plot and stem-and-leaf plot because they use numerical data. Because the data includes three methods of advertising, a triple bar graph would be best to compare the three methods.

Pictographs

A pictograph is a graph that uses pictures to represent numerical data. The visual representation of data on a pictograph allows for quick identification of the mode and distribution of the data set. A key is important for a pictograph so that the reader of the graph knows what each picture, or image, represents.

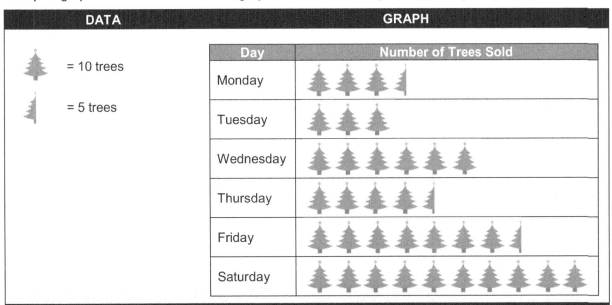

DATA	GRAPH

SAMPLE QUESTION:

How many more people bought a tree on Friday than on Tuesday?

A. 5.5

B. 8.5

C. 45

D. 55

E. 60

Solution: C

If each whole tree represents 10 trees sold and each half tree represents 5 trees sold, 75 trees were sold on Friday and 30 trees were sold on Tuesday. Thus, 45 more trees were sold on Friday than Tuesday.

Frequency Tables

A frequency table counts or tallies how many times a value falls within a defined range of values in a data set. Some frequency tables display the frequency of individual values while others display the frequency of a range of values occurring in a data set. An example of a range of values would be the number of students in a class scoring an A, scoring a B, scoring a C, or scoring a D on a quiz. Because an A may range from 91-100, the individual scores are unknown, but the number of scores falling within the A-range are known.

Example:

SAT Math Score Range	Frequency
200-299	1
300-399	0
400-499	1
500-599	8
600-699	7
700-799	2

Histograms

Although a histogram looks similar to a bar graph, that is where their relationship ends. A histogram uses numerical data instead of categorical data and displays the frequency or distribution of data that falls within equally spaced ranges of values. In addition, the bars of a histogram touch each other.

DATA	GRAPH
Class test grades 91, 88, 100, 82, 73, 88, 52, 76, 95, 55, 85, 65, 99 87, 90, 65, 93, 75, 92, 66, 78, 80, 68, 84, 85, 91, 98 <table><tr><th>Grade Range</th><th>Frequency</th></tr><tr><td>51-60</td><td>2</td></tr><tr><td>61-70</td><td>4</td></tr><tr><td>71-80</td><td>5</td></tr><tr><td>81-90</td><td>8</td></tr><tr><td>91-100</td><td>7</td></tr></table> *Determine equally created ranges. Determine the number of data points that fall within each range. Create a bar chart, making sure that bars touch, to show the frequency within each range.*	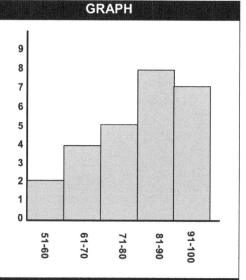

SAMPLE QUESTION:

Which of the following can be found using only a histogram?

A. mean

B. median

C. mode

D. range

E. none of the above

Solution: E

A histogram does not display values, only a range of values, so a single value cannot be found from the display.

Example:

2) Which of the following graphs would best display the results of students' favorite electives?

    A. Bar Graph

    B. Histogram

    C. Venn diagram

    D. Table

    E. Line Graph

Solution: A

A bar graph would best display the results because a bar graph compares data that is sorted by category, which is the favorite elective in this example. Option B would not be best because the survey was not looking for the frequency of a data range. Option C is not the best choice because the survey asked for one response (favorite elective), so there is no overlapping data. Option D is not best because the data could be written in a table, but the results of the data would not be as clear as with a bar graph.

Circle Graphs / Pie Charts

A circle graph, sometimes called a pie chart, visually shows how categories, or categorical data, is broken up into percentages. All the percentages for the categories should equal 100%.

 Circle graphs are good items for test questions because items can test your knowledge at reading a graph, identifying missing information, and finding a percent of a number.

DATA	GRAPH
200 female students at a college were surveyed about their favorite type of shoe. The results of the survey are listed in the table.	To make a circle graph, find the percent of 360° that each shoe type is and draw an angle that size from the center of the circle. 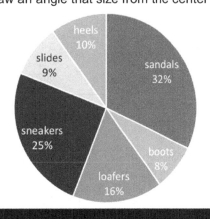

Favorite Shoe Type	
sandals	32%
boots	8%
loafers	16%
sneakers	25%
slides	9%
heels	10%

SAMPLE QUESTION:

How many students responded that either heels or loafers were their favorite type of shoe?

A. 10   B. 16   C. 26   D. 35   E. 52

Solution: D

Add the two categories together, $16 + 10 = 26$. Find 26% of 200 students, $200 \cdot 0.26 = 52$ students.

Example:

3) In a recent survey of 120 people at a grocery store, 20% said they were there to buy snacks, 45% said they were there for their weekly shopping, 15% said they were there to buy lunch, and the remaining people were there to purchase nongrocery items. How many people surveyed are buying nongrocery items?

A. 3

B. 20

C. 24

D. 25

E. 72

Solution: C

Subtract the percents given from 100 to get the percent of people shopping for nongrocery items, $100 - 45 - 15 - 20 = 20$. Next, find 20% of 120 people, $0.20 \cdot 120 = 24$

Stem-and-Leaf Plots

A stem-and-leaf plot organizes numerical data in a way that allows the reader to quickly calculate the mode and range of a data set. The mean and median can also be found from a stem-and-leaf plot, but it just may take more than a glance or quick calculation. A stem-and-leaf plot is best for data with stems that are no more than 10 numbers apart from one another. This is because the value of the stems must only increase by 1.

DATA and GRAPH	HOW TO GRAPH
Number of participants a in study group for the last 10 meetings: 20, 27, 22, 24, 28, 32, 35, 51, 22, 50 Stem | Leaf 2 | 0 2 2 4 7 8 3 | 2 5 4 | 5 | 0 1 key 2 | 0 = 20	• Organize the data from least to greatest. • Create a table with two columns and label the first column stem and the second column leaf. • Each leaf can only contain a single digit. If all the numbers in a data set have two digits, the stem and leaf will both contain one digit. If the values contain three digits, like 341, then each stem will have two digits and each leaf will still only have one digit. • Identify the smallest and largest stems in the data set. In the table, list the first stem and continue listing stems, going up by increments of one until reaching the largest stem. Do NOT skip any values in the list of stems. • list each leaf with its corresponding stem, in order, with no commas or decimal points. • Include a key to show how to read each value in the table. Visit https://youtu.be/9SyFUIrs05U for a comprehensive video on stem-and-leaf plots.

SAMPLE QUESTION:

Find the mode of the data set from the stem-and-leaf plot above.

A. 22   B. 10   C. 20   D. 28   E. 2

Solution: A

The number 22 is repeated twice, which can be seen in the row starting with the stem of 2.

The following table summarizes the information that each type of graph displays.

Data Display	Purpose
Venn Diagram	Compares categories of data, including overlaps; likelihood of events
Bar Graph	Compares categories of data, sometimes over time
Pictograph	Uses visuals related to the data to compare categories
Table	Organizes a list of data
Line Graph	Best to show change over time; two categories of data, e.g., time and distance
Stem-and-Leaf Plot	Useful for organizing decimal values and larger sets of data that are somewhat close together
Histogram	Determine the range or frequency where most data falls
Frequency Table	Organize data in a table by how frequently it occurs
Circle Graph	Visual representation of proportional relationships; comparison of parts to a whole
Scatterplot	Shows the correlation between two sets of data

Solve problems involving measures of central tendency and spread

Measures of center, or **measures of central tendency**, include mean, median, and mode. These statistical values are referred to as measures of center because they are symbolic of the middle values in the data set. Test questions that ask for the value of the mean, median, or mode may have data sets presented in a table, in a graph, or in a list, which may out of order.

MEASURES OF CENTER/CENTRAL TENDENCY	
Mean	Find the average; add all the numbers and divide by how many numbers were added. *We think of the mean as "mean" because it's mean to make you do so much work to get an answer.*
Median	Place numbers in order; find the middle number. If there are two middle numbers, add them and divide by 2. *Remember, median is in the middle, just like the median in the road.*
Mode	The number or numbers that occur the most. *Mode and most both start with MO...__MO__DE __MO__ST.*

Examples:

4) On a quiz in Mrs. Fingal's class, 8 students scored a 70%, 12 students scored an 80%, and 4 students scored a 95%. What is the mean score for the quiz? Round to the nearest whole number.

   A. 79

   B. 82

   C. 80

   D. 85

   E. 86

Solution: A

To find the mean of a list that groups values in sets, it is not necessary to list out all the numbers. Instead, find the sum of each like group of values, then add the sums together and divide by the total number of values.

Partial Sums:	Total sum:	Mean:
$8 \times 70 = 560$	$560 + 960 + 380 = 1,900$	$1,900 \div 24 = 79$
$12 \times 80 = 960$		
$4 \times 95 = 380$		

Therefore, the correct answer choice is A.

5) Find the mode of the data: $\{3, 3, 5, 6, 4, 5, 6, 2, 4, 5, 1, 10\}$

    A. 7

    B. 5

    C. 4

    D. 3

    E. 2

> **Testing Tip!**
>
> When finding the median and mode, make sure the data is in order first.

Solution: B

To find the mode, first put the numbers in order, then find the number that is repeated the most.

$\{1, 2, 3, 3, 4, 4, 5, 5, 5, 6, 6, 10\}$. The number repeated the most is 5, so the correct answer choice is B.

Range

To find the range, arrange the numbers in the data set in order, then subtract the smallest value from the largest value.

Examples:

To find the range, arrange the numbers in the data set in order, then subtract the smallest value from the largest value.

Examples:

6) Find the range of the data set. $\{6, 3, 1, 10, 12, 4, 9\}$

    A. 3

    B. 10

    C. 11

    D. 11.5

    E. 12

Solution: C

Place the values in order, $\{1, 3, 4, 6, 9, 10, 12\}$, then subtract the smallest from the largest, $12 - 1 = 11$. The correct answer is C.

7) Find the mode of the data: $\{3, 3, 5, 6, 4, 5, 6, 2, 4, 5, 1, 10\}$

    A. 7

    B. 5

    C. 4

    D. 3

    E. 2

Solution: B

To find the mode, first put the numbers in order, then find the number that is repeated the most.

$\{1, 2, 3, 3, 4, 4, 5, 5, 5, 6, 6, 10\}$

The number repeated the most is 5, so the correct answer choice is B.

> **Testing Tip!**
> An **outlier that is much greater** than the other numbers will skew the value of the **mean** so that it **is higher**.
> An **outlier that is much smaller** than the other numbers will skew the value of the **mean** so that it **is lower**.

Examples:

8) Find the median age given the table.

Age	Frequency
25	4
30	7
35	3
40	2

A. 30

B. 32.5

C. 35

D. 37

E. 38

Solution: A

The frequency in the table refers to how many times the number repeats in the list. Age 30 appears 7 times, with 4 numbers to the left, and 5 numbers to the right. Without writing out the entire list, we can deduce that 30 is the middle number (if this is not apparent, write out the list if small enough).

9) The range for data set A is 8, and the range for data set B is 15. What do these range values indicate about the data sets?

A. The data sets contain similar values.

B. The data sets contain several values that are the same.

C. The values in set A are closer together than the values in set B.

D. The values in set A are all different than the values in set B.

E. No comparison can be made from the range values.

Solution: C

The range indicates how far apart the data is, so a smaller range indicates values that are closer together.

10) The graph of the data below shows the number of bagels a company buys for its employees each month.

If the outlier is removed, how does this effect the mean of the data set?

A. The mean increases.

B. The mean decreases.

C. The mean stays the same.

D. There is no longer a mean.

E. There is no effect on the mean.

Solution: B

An outlier that is much higher than the rest of the data increases the mean, so removing the outlier decreases the value of the mean.

11) Five friends all go to a farm to pick blueberries. At the end of an hour, the number of berries picked was 78, 273, 312, 287, and 301. If the outlier is removed, which best describes the change in the data set?

A. The mean and median both increase, with the mean having a greater increase.

B. The mean and median both increase, with the median having a greater increase.

C. The mean increases, and the median stays the same.

D. The mean decreases, and the median stays the same.

E. Nothing in the data set changes.

Solution: A

Both the mean and the median will increase. The mean will have a greater increase because the outlier was much lower than the other data points. The median will shift, but only slightly because the remaining data points are close together.

Use data from a random sample to draw inferences about characteristics of a population

Because a survey is a sampling of a population, questions may ask for a prediction to be made about the whole population based on survey results or data gathered from a sampling of people. To solve these types of problems, identify the information needed from the sampling, then use a proportion to predict for the entire population.

Example:

12) Of the 45,500 students who attend a university, 1,500 were surveyed about the number of credit hours of courses they take each semester. The results are in the table below.

Number of Credit Hours	Number of Students
8	180
9	300
12	600
15	420

Based on the information in the table, predict how many students at the college enroll in 15 credit hours each semester.

A. 108

B. 420

C. 1,270

D. 12,470

E. 12,740

Solution: E

To predict the number of students who enroll in 15 credit hours each semester, set up a proportion and solve for x. The ratios in the proportion represent the partial number of students to total number of students.

$$\frac{420}{1,500} = \frac{x}{45,500}$$

Cross-multiply, then solve for x.

$1,500x = 420(45,500)$

$1,500x = 19,110,000$

$x = 12,740$

Identify positive and negative linear relationships in scatterplots

A scatter plot is a graph that contains bivariate data, or two data sets. An easy way to identify data as univariate or bivariate is if the information is graphed on a single number line or a coordinate plane, which contains two number lines (one vertical and one horizontal). Points graphed on a scatter plot create a visual representation of the correlation between the two sets of data. Data points on a scatter plot have a **positive correlation**, **negative correlation**, or **no correlation**.

A trendline is often drawn on a scatterplot to help visualize the relationship between the data and to make future predictions about the data.

GRAPHS

Positive Correlation	Negative Correlation	No Correlation
A trendline with a positive slope can be drawn to model the direction of the data.	*A trendline with a positive slope can be drawn to model the direction of the data.*	*No trendline can be drawn to model the direction of the data.*

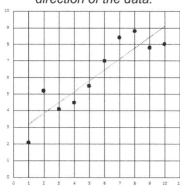 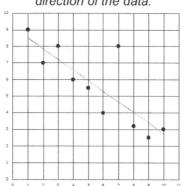 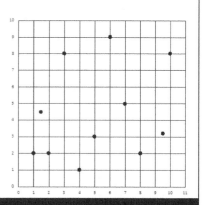

SAMPLE QUESTION:

Naomi surveyed 11 teachers in her school about the number of pets and the number of televisions each of them has at home. The graph of the data is shown below. What kind of correlation between these two data sets is most likely?

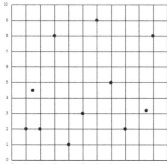

Solution: C

A. Positive correlation

B. Negative correlation

C. No correlation

D. Dual Correlation

E. Not enough information

There is no correlation on the graph between the number of pets a person has and the number of televisions they have in their home.

Examples:

13) How do you know when the data in a scatter plot has no correlation?

A. When a trendline can be drawn to show the data is increasing

B. When a trendline can be drawn to show the data is decreasing

C. When two trendlines can be drawn

D. When no trend in the data is apparent enough to say that it is increasing or decreasing

E. When the trendline is curved

Solution: D

If there is no apparent overall trend of the data increasing or decreasing, there is no correlation between the data.

14) The scatter plot displays the relationship between a person's arm span and their height. Based on the graph, what type of correlation exists between the two data sets?

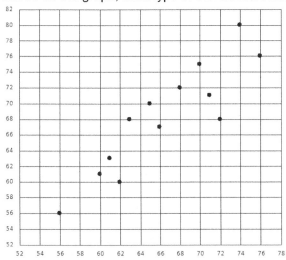

A. High, positive correlation

B. Weak, positive correlation

C. Negative correlation

D. No correlation

E. Low, positive correlation

Solution: A

The data is close together and increasing, so there is a high positive correlation. If it appeared that the data was increasing but was spread out, or far from a trendline, the data would indicate a loose or weak positive correlation.

Use a linear model for a data set to make predictions

A linear model is the comparison of two data sets that are increasing or decreasing at a constant rate of change. Linear models are often given in a graph or as a scenario in a word problem. Real-life examples of linear models include scenarios such as:

• Total pay after working a number of hours

• Amount left after paying the same payment each month

• The number of items at one cost and the number of items at another cost

• Miles traveled after a number of hours

• Height after a number of months.

Linear models require that you understand the rate of change (slope), the x-intercept of the graph, the y-intercept of the graph, and how to predict or read the graph of the situation. Test questions may ask to identify the correct graph of a situation or to identify or interpret the x- or y-intercept or rate of change in relation to the scenario.

15) Once a seedling has sprouted 2 cm, Randy begins measuring its growth over several weeks and finds that the plant grows at a constant rate of 3 cm per week over 8 weeks. Which of the following graphs correctly represents this situation?

A.

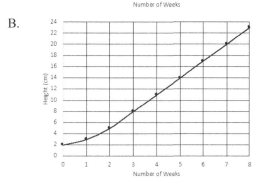

D.

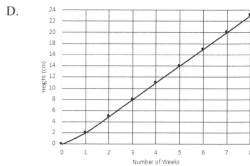

B.

E.

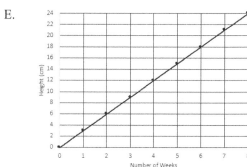

C.

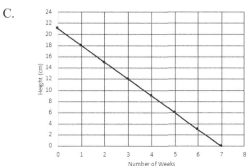

Solution: A

The plant height is increasing, which means the line should also be increasing from left to right, so option C can be eliminated. Randy begins measuring the plant when it is 2 cm. The height of the plant is on the y-axis, so the graph should start at 0 weeks and a height of 2 cm. This eliminates choices D and E because they both start at a height of 0 cm. Option B for week 1 has the height of the plant at 3 cm, but the plant grew 3 cm and should be at 5 cm. This leaves option A as the correct answer choice.

Differentiate between correlation and causation

Correlation and causation are two options of how two separate sets of data relate to one another. Questions dealing with correlation and causation are often accompanied by a scatterplot because scatterplots display two sets of data on one graph.

A **correlation** in a data set shows that there is some sort of pattern in the data such that as one set changes the other set changes as well. A correlation in the data does NOT mean that one set of data is the reason for the other set of data changing. While this may be the case, a correlation does not confirm it to be true. When reading scatterplots, be careful not to assume that because both sets of data are increasing that one was caused by the other. For example, test scores may appear to increase as the number of hours studied increases, but it may not be the cause. Although it is likely, there may be other factors that affected the test scores.

A **causation** means that one set of data causes the other set of data to change. For example, if you work more hours at an hourly rate, you will earn more money. The amount you work changes the total you earn.

 Data in scatterplots show a correlation. Keep this in mind when test questions ask for a description in the data set.

Compute simple probabilities, and use probabilities to solve problems

Probability is the likelihood that an event will occur. Regardless of the scenario, the method for finding probability is always the same. All probability must be put in its simplest form or as a percentage.

$$\text{Probability} = \frac{\text{Desired number of outcomes}}{\text{Total number of possible outcomes}}$$

When there is more than one opportunity or consecutive events, each probability is generated and then multiplied together. When there is more than one event, the probability is referred to as compound probability.

Sometimes when consecutive events occur the total number of possible outcomes changes with the occurrence of each event. An example of this would be drawing a name out of a hat and then NOT replacing the name and drawing another name. When this occurs, it is important to change the total number of possible outcomes in all the individual probabilities that occur after the first one.

Examples:

16) What is the probability of selecting a queen from a standard deck of 52 playing cards?

Solution:

To calculate the probability of selecting a queen, recall that are 4 queens in every deck and a total of 52 cards from which you are choosing. Thus, the probability is the number of cards that have a queen on them over the total number of cards.

$$\frac{\text{number of queens}}{\text{total number of cards}} \qquad \frac{4}{52} = \frac{1}{13} \text{ or } 8\%$$

17) What is the probability of rolling a 6 on a standard die for two consecutive rolls?

Solution:

To calculate the probability of rolling a 6 two times in a row, first determine the probability for each individual event.

$$\frac{\text{Rolling a 6}}{\text{Rolling 1, 2, 3, 4, 5, 6}} = \frac{1}{6}$$

Next, multiply each of the probabilities together for the probability of the two events together.

$$\frac{1}{6} \times \frac{1}{6} = \frac{1}{36} \text{ or } 3\%$$

18) The principal of a school is randomly choosing volunteers for a project. Out of a group of 5 freshman and 10 juniors, what is the probability of the principal choosing a junior in his first two picks?

Solution:

First determine the probability of selecting a junior for the principal's first pick. Because there are 10 juniors and 15 total students, the probability of the first selection is $\frac{10}{15}$.

Next, determine the probability of the second selection. After the first selection, there are only 9 juniors left and 14 total students. Thus, the probability of this event is $\frac{9}{14}$.

Last, now that the individual probabilities have been determined, multiply them to find the probability of the compound event.

$$\frac{\text{Juniors}}{\text{Freshman and Juniors}} \qquad \frac{10}{15} \times \frac{9}{14} = \frac{90}{210} = \frac{3}{7} \approx 43\%$$

Experimental probability is what happens when an experiment is performed.

Theoretical probability is what is expected to happen when the experiment occurs.

For example, when flipping a coin, we expect that it will land on heads 50% of the time. When a quarter is flipped 10 times, it may actually land heads up 6 times, or 60% of the time. What we expected, 50%, is the theoretical probability, and what actually happened, landing on heads 6 times, is the experimental probability.

When an experiment is conducted for a limited number of trials, the results can be used to predict what will happen if a much larger experiment were conducted. The same principle is true for theoretical probability. What is expected to happen in a small sampling can be used to predict what should happen in a much larger sample. For either type of probability, proportions are used to make predictions.

Examples:

19) Mel and Thomas spun a spinner that was divided evenly into 4 colors, blue, red, green, and yellow. Find the number of times the spinner will theoretically land on green after 80 spins.

A. 4   B. 12   C. 16   D. 20   E. 25

Solution: D

To make a prediction using theoretical probability, determine the probability of the spinner landing on green. Because there is 1 green section out of 4 total sections, the probability is $\frac{1}{4}$. Next, set up and solve a proportion to predict how many times the spinner lands on green after 80 spins.

$$\frac{1}{4} = \frac{x}{80}$$

$$4x = 80$$

$$x = 20$$

20) After conducting the experiment in problem 19, Mel and Thomas found the spinner landed on blue 18 times. Use this information to predict how many times the spinner will land on blue after 1,000 spins.

A. 56

B. 225

C. 280

D. 360

E. 388

Solution: B

In the last problem, the spinner was spun 80 times. Set up and solve a proportion using the fact that the spinner landed on blue 18 out of 80 times.

$$\frac{18}{80} = \frac{x}{1,000}$$

$$80x = 18,000$$

$$x = 225$$

Algebra and Geometry: Algebra

Algebra and geometry concepts are integrated throughout the math portion of the exam. For questions falling under this competency, you are expected to be able to write linear equations and inequalities from word problems, graphs, and tables. You should also be able to solve linear equations and simple quadratic equations. Geometry questions include concepts about angle pairs, angles formed by parallel and intersecting lines, properties of two-dimensional figures, and formulas for perimeter, area, and volume. Questions in this competency will be both math problems and word problems that include the application of multiple skills.

ALGEBRA

Seeing Structure in Expressions

Understanding how problems are structured helps when having to deconstruct a problem to answer a question. Math is versatile in that there are multiple ways to solve a problem. Knowing various properties that create structure will save time and increase the amount of correctly solved problems on the exam.

Demonstrate an understanding of the properties of the basic operations without needing to know the names of the properties

Several properties exist that allow for simplifying algebraic expressions and equations. Knowing the names of the properties is not required; you only need to know how to apply the properties and identify mistakes made when solving based on these properties. The properties of operations are described in the following table.

Property of Operations	Rule	Description
Commutative Property of Addition	$a + b = b + a$	Changing the order of two numbers being added does not change the sum.
Commutative Property of Multiplication	$a \cdot b = b \cdot a$	Changing the order of two numbers being multiplied does not change the product.
Associative Property of Addition	$(a + b) + c = a + (b + c)$	Changing the grouping of the addends does not change the sum.
Associative Property of Multiplication	$a \cdot (b \cdot c) = (a \cdot b) \cdot c$	Changing the grouping of the factors does not change the product.
Additive Identity Property of 0	$a + 0 = 0 + a = a$	Adding 0 to a number does not change the value of that number.
Multiplicative Identity Property of 1	$a \cdot 1 = 1 \cdot a = a$	Multiplying a number by 1 does not change the value of that number.
Inverse Property of Addition	For every a, there exists a number $-a$ such that $a + (-a) = (-a) + a = 0$	Adding a number and its opposite results in a sum equal to 0.
Inverse Property of Multiplication	For every a, there exists a number $1/a$ such that $a \cdot \frac{1}{a} = \frac{1}{a} \cdot a = \frac{a}{a} = 1$	Multiplying a number and its multiplicative inverse results in a product equal to 1.
Distributive Property of Multiplication over Addition	$a \cdot (b + c) = a \cdot b + a \cdot c$	Multiplying a sum is the same as multiplying each addend by that number, then adding their products.
Distributive Property of Multiplication over Subtraction	$a \cdot (b - c) = a \cdot b - a \cdot c$	Multiplying a difference is the same as multiplying the minuend and subtrahend by that number, then subtracting their products.

Demonstrate the ability to follow an arithmetic or algebraic procedure by carrying it out or analyzing it

Questions that fall in this category require an understanding of verbal/written steps for solving a problem. Because the steps are typically all written out, knowing how to work backwards from a solution is the key to being able to correctly answer these types of questions.

Example:

1) Kelvin told his friends that he is thinking of a perfect square, x. He states that following the steps below will help find the number.

- Double the sum of the number and 2.

- Subtract 6.

- Divide by 2.

- Add 4.

The result should be 28. What is the perfect square that Kelvin is thinking?

A. 5

B. 6

C. 25

D. 36

E. 49

Solution: C

There are a couple of ways to find the number. Working backwards from 28 is the easiest way to arrive at the original number. To work backwards, perform the inverse operation on the final number for each step, starting from the bottom.

- Starting with 28,

- Subtract 4 to get 24.

- Multiply 24 by 2 to get 48.

- Add 6 to 48 to get 54.

- Divide 54 by 2 to undo the doubling to get 27.

- Subtract 2 from 27 to get the original number, 25.

Therefore, the correct answer is C, 25. Be careful not to take the square root of 25 because the problem mentions perfect square. The perfect square is 25, and its square root is 5.

Use properties of operations to identify or generate equivalent algebraic expressions

Applying properties of operations to expressions to generate other equivalent expressions and recognizing when two expressions are equivalent are foundational skills in mathematics. When generating equivalent expressions, the commutative, associative, and distributive properties are often used for operations. On the *Praxis®* Core Mathematics Subtest exam, be prepared to recognize equivalent expressions through the use of these properties.

Examples:

2) Which property should be used first to rewrite the expression so that like terms can be combined?
$3(x + 7) - 8x + 1$

   A. Associative Property of Multiplication

   B. Commutative Property of Multiplication

   C. Distributive Property

   D. Inverse Property of Addition

   E. Additive Identity Property

Solution: C

For this example, you need to distribute the 3 to both terms inside the parentheses in order to add the terms with like variables (the *x* terms) and the constants (numbers without a variable).

$3(x + 7) - 8x + 1$

$= 3x + 21 - 8x + 1$

$= 3x - 8x + 21 + 1$

$= -5x + 22$

Can you identify the property that was used in the third line? If you said Commutative Property of Addition, you're right!

3) Which of the following is an equivalent expression to $(2x - 8 - 4x) - (3x + 2 - 5x)$?

   A. -10

   B. $-6x - 6$

   C. $-10x - 10$

   D. $14x - 10$

   E. $-10x - 6$

Solution: A

To simplify this expression, first "distribute" the minus sign to each of the terms in the second set of parentheses.

$(2x - 8 - 4x) - (3x + 2 - 5x)$

$= 2x - 8 - 4x - 3x - 2 + 5x$

Next, rearrange the expression, using the commutative property, to make it easy to combine like terms.

$2x - 8 - 4x - 3x - 2 + 5x = 2x + 5x - 4x - 3x - 8 - 2$

Last, combine like terms to get -10. Therefore, the correct answer choice is A.

4) Which of the following is an equivalent expression, $3 - (5y + 9 - 8y) - 2(-2 - 3y) - 7$?

   A. $3y + 10$

   B. $9y - 9$

   C. $-16y + 7$

   D. $-3y - 2$

   E. $-16y$

Solution: B

Distribute, paying attention to negative signs, then rearrange to collect like terms, and last, simplify.

$3 - (5y + 9 - 8y) - 2(-2 - 3y) - 7$

$= 3 - 5y - 9 + 8y + 4 + 6y - 7$

$= -5y + 8y + 6y + 3 + 4 - 9 - 7$

$= 9y - 9$

The correct answer choice is B.

Note that for this answer choice, the 9 can be factored out creating another equivalent expression. This may happen on the exam, so don't get worried if you do not see your answer. It may be there but just in a different form.

$9y - 9 = 9(y - 1)$

Write an equation or expression that models a real-life or mathematical problem

Although there is an endless number of examples that represent questions requiring an expression or equation, a general pattern exists when writing them. Be prepared to write algebraic equations, inequalities, and expressions from a table, a description, and a word problem.

Writing Linear Equations Given Key Features

One of the more advanced skills on the *Praxis®* Core Mathematics Subtest exam is being able to identify, write, and manipulate linear equations in various forms. The following table lists the forms of a linear equation you'll need to know and what each form reveals about the graph of the equation.

Form of Equation	Equation	What the Equation Reveals
Slope-intercept form	$y = mx + b$	slope (m) and y-intercept (b)
Standard form	$Ax + By = C$	x-intercept ($Ax = C$) and y-intercept ($By = C$)
Point-slope form	$y - y_1 = m(x - x_1)$	slope (m) and a point on the graph (x_1, y_1)

Knowing the formal name for the form of the equation is not necessary, but you should be able to recognize what the equation reveals and also know how to get from one form to another to reveal a key feature or determine if an answer written in another form is correct.

Slope-Intercept Form

Equations in slope-intercept form always start with $y =$. The slope of the line (which identifies the **constant rate or rate of change** in a real-life scenario) is always the number with x. Be careful not to think that it is the first number because sometimes equations are switched around so that the x term is second instead of first after the equal sign.

Example (Quick Check):

5) Identify the slope, m, and the y-intercept, b, for each of the equations below.

    a) $y = -3x$

    b) $y = 2 + 5x$

    c) $y = x + \frac{1}{2}$

Solution:

a) $m = -3, \ b = 0$

b) $m = 5, \ b = 2$

c) $m = 1, \ b = \dfrac{1}{2}$

Point-Slope Form $y - y_1 = m(x - x_1)$

Equations in point-slope form will contain both a point and a slope. Most likely, this form will not appear very often on the test because it is used most often for writing equations from a graph when the y-intercept is not visible. If a question on the test is in this form, you may have to identify the slope or point, or you may have to rewrite the equation in another form.

The point-slope form of an equation is the formula for slope rearranged.

Slope: $m = \dfrac{y_2 - y_1}{x_2 - x_1}$

Point-slope form: $y - y_1 = m(x - x_1)$

Example:

6) Identify a point on the line and the slope for the equation, $y - 4 = -(x + 2)$.

   Solution:

   Point on the line: $(-2, 4)$; Slope: -1

Standard Form $Ax + By = C$

Writing an equation in standard form is most likely to occur with word problems. More often than not, equations you write from word problems will be in slope-intercept form, but there is a chance they may be in standard form as well. You may also have to identify the x- or y-intercept of an equation in standard form. The x-intercept is the point where the line of the equation crosses the x-axis. The y-intercept is the point where the line of the equation crosses the y-axis.

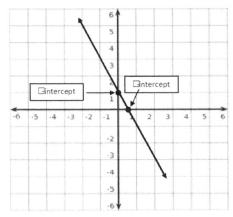

To find the x-intercept in standard form, remove the y term from the equation and solve for x. To find the y-intercept, remove the x term from the equation and solve for y. (This works because the terms we are removing have a value of 0 when they are part of an intercept.)

Examples:

7) Find the x-intercept and the y-intercept for the equation of the line $5x + y = 10$.

   Solution:

   x-intercept: $5x = 10$, so $x = 2$; y-intercept: $y = 10$

8) What is the equation of a line with a slope of $\frac{2}{5}$ and a y-intercept of $(0, 3)$?

    A. $2x - 5y = -15$

    B. $2x - 5y = -3$

    C. $2x + 5y = 3$

    D. $5x + 2y = -3$

    E. $2x + 5y = 15$

Solution: A

When given the y-intercept and the slope, substitute into slope-intercept form, $y = mx + b$, to get the equation of the line. Doing so, we get $y = \frac{2}{5}x + 3$. Looking at the answer choices, they are all in standard form, $Ax + By = C$, which requires converting $y = \frac{2}{5}x + 3$ to standard form as well. Equations in standard form do not contain fractions, and usually the x-term is positive.

To convert,

    1. Get x and y terms on the same side of the equal sign.

    2. Multiply each term in the equation by the denominator of the fraction to eliminate the fraction.

    3. Multiply all terms by a -1 so the x term is positive.

$$y = \frac{2}{5}x + 3$$
$$-\frac{2}{5}x + y = 3$$
    — Step 1

$$5\left(-\frac{2}{5}x + y = 3\right)$$
$$-\frac{10}{5}x + 5y = 15$$
    — Step 2
$$-2x + 5y = 15$$

$$-1(-2x + 5y = 15)$$
    — Step 3
$$2x - 5y = -15$$

The correct answer choice is A.

9) Which of the following equations could the slope of a line be found just upon inspection?

    I. $y - 8 = 4(x + 6)$

    II. $y = -\frac{2}{3}x$

    III. $2x + 4y = 10$

    A. I only

    B. I and II

    C. II and III

    D. I and III

    E. I, II, and III

Solution: B

Option I is in point-slope form, and 4 is the slope. Option II is in slope-intercept form, and $-\frac{2}{3}$ is the slope. Option III is in standard form, so some manipulation would need to occur before being able to identify the slope. Therefore, the correct answer choice is B.

Equation of a Line from a Word Problem

Equations you'll write from a word problem will either be in slope intercept form, $y = mx + b$, or standard form, $Ax + By = C$. For standard form, there are two values changing, and a total amount. In this scenario, it is likely there is a number of items, like bracelets and necklaces, that are changing along with their prices, which is constant, and a total which will also be constant.

Slope-intercept form ($y = mx + b$) in a Word Problem

If the question gives one value that changes and one value that never changes, the equation will be in slope-intercept form. In this scenario, a total value is unknown and is represented by y. The value that changes based on another value is the slope, and the value that does not change is the y-intercept.

Examples:

10) As a car salesman, Henry earns $300 each week plus a 3% commission on each car he sells. Write an equation to determine his salary for one week, S, if he sells c number of cars.

   Solution:

   Amount that does not change: $300, 300 = b$

   Amount that changes: 3% commission per car, $0.03 = m$

   Because his salary, S, is <u>dependent</u> on the number of cars he sells, c, S is the dependent variable, or is substituted for y, and c is the independent variable, substituted for x.

   Therefore, the equation is $S = 0.03c + 300$.

11) Carlos has already read 72 pages in his required summer reading. He plans to read 20 pages a day until he has finished reading the book. Write an equation that represents the total number of pages, p, Carlos has read after d number of days.

   Solution:

   Amount that does not change: 72, $72 = b$

   Amount that changes: total number of additional pages read at 20 pages per day, $20 = m$

   Equation: $p = 20d + 72$

> **Testing Tip!**
>
> It is not important that you know the math vocabulary associated with different forms of linear equations, such as slope-intercept form or standard form. What you need to know is how to write equations when situations presented lend themselves to each form.

Standard Form ($Ax + By = C$) in a Word Problem

Usually equations for word problems will be in slope-intercept form, but sometimes a question will give two values that are unknown and a total value that is known. In this case, the equation will be in standard form with the first unknown as Ax and the second unknown as By. The total that is given will be substituted for C.

12) Sarah sells two types of bracelets. One costs her $4 to make and the other costs her $5 to make. Write an equation that could be used to find how many of each bracelet she can make with $50.

   Solution:

   Amount 1 that varies: $4 bracelet, $Ax = 4x$

   Amount 2 that varies: $5 bracelet, $By = 5y$

   Total amount: $50, $C = 50$

   Equation: $4x + 5y = 50$

13) Preston wants to spend $30 on music downloads from two different websites. Site A charges $0.50 per song, and site B charges $1 per song. Write an equation to represent how many songs he can download.

Solution:

Amount 1 that varies: $0.50, $Ax = 0.50x$

Amount 2 that varies: $1, $By = 1y = y$

Total amount: $30, $C = 30$

Equation: $0.50x + y = 30$

 When an equation is in standard form, it does not matter which constant replaces A and which constant replaces B.

Equation of a Line from a Table

Use slope-intercept form, $y = mx + b$, to write an equation of a line from a table. When writing an equation of a line from a table, two different scenarios may occur, one where the y-intercept is part of the table, and one where it is not. In both cases, find the slope of the line, then determine the y-intercept based on the information given.

To find the equation of a line when the y-intercept is included:

Write the equation of a line for the table below.

x	y
−1	3
0	1
3	−5
8	−15

Slope:

To find the slope from a table, use any two points, stack them vertically, and subtract.

$$(-1, 3)$$
$$-$$
$$\underline{(0, 1)}$$
$$-1 \quad 2$$

Last, use the two differences to write the slope, $\frac{\text{change in } y}{\text{change in } x} = \frac{2}{-1}$. Be careful to write the y value for the numerator of the fraction.

Before finding the y-intercept, look to see if one of the x values is 0. If so, its y value is the y-intercept, and no further solving is required.

From the table above, the y-intercept is part of the table and is 1.

The equation of the line for this table is $y = \frac{2}{-1}x + 1$, or simplified, $y = -2x + 1$.

 Note: Answer choices may be in standard form. You still need to find the equation of the line in slope-intercept form, then convert the equation you wrote into standard form.

To find the equation of a line when the y-intercept is NOT included:

Write an equation of the line for the table.

x	y
−3	−6
3	−2
6	0
18	8

First find the slope:

$(-3, -6)$

$\underline{- \quad (6, \quad 0)}$

$-9 - 6$

Slope: $\frac{-6}{-9} = \frac{2}{3}$

Next, choose a point, and substitute this point and the slope into $y = mx + b$.

x	y
−3	−6
3	−2
6	0
18	8

Point: $(3, -2)$ Slope: $\frac{2}{3}$ (from above)

$y = mx + b \quad \rightarrow \quad -2 = \frac{2}{3}(3) + b$

Solve the equation for b.

$-2 = \frac{2}{3}(3) + b$

$-2 = 2 + b$

$-4 = b$

Once b is found, substitute b and m, the slope, back into $y = mx + b$, $y = \frac{2}{3}x - 4$.

Example:

14) Which of the following is an equation of the line represented by the table?

A. $y = -2x - 1$

B. $y = x - 1$

C. $y = -2x - 3$

D. $y = 2x - 1$

E. $y = \frac{1}{2}x - 1$

x	y
−1	−3
0	−1
1	1
2	3
3	5

Solution: C

Knowing that the y-intercept is in the form $(0, y)$, we can see that the table includes the y-intercept, $(0, -1)$, which is not always the case. When the y-intercept is included in the table, we can find the slope of the line and use slope-intercept form to write an equation.

To find the slope, choose two points from the table, and find the difference of the y-coordinates and the difference of the x-coordinates. We like to take two points and stack them to subtract. Doing so avoids subtracting mistakes.

$$\begin{array}{r} (3, 5) \\ -\underline{(2, 3)} \\ 1 \quad 2 \end{array}$$

Because slope is $\frac{\text{change in } y}{\text{change in } x}$ the slope for the equation of the line represented by the table is $\frac{2}{1}$.

Therefore, we have: $m = \frac{2}{1}$ and $b = -1$. Substituting into $y = mx + b$ we get,

$y = \frac{2}{1}x - 1$ or $y = 2x - 1$, which is answer choice C.

Solve word problems, including problems involving linear relationships and problems that can be represented by Venn diagrams

Venn diagrams are used to show the relationship between two or more sets of data. Each set of data is represented by a circle which may or may not overlap onto one another. The following diagram will be used to explain the concept of Venn diagram.

In the diagram, information is classified into sets. Each set has a title and includes the elements inside brackets { }.

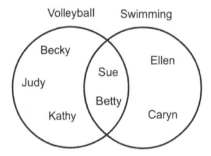

Volleyball: {Becky, Judy, Kathy, Sue, Betty}

Swimming: {Ellen, Caryn, Sue, Betty}

Set notation defines parameters about the information. The union (∪) symbol means to combine sets together.

Volleyball ∪ Swimming = {Becky, Judy, Kathy, Sue, Betty, Ellen, Caryn}

The intersection (∩) symbol means only the elements that are in both sets.

Volleyball ∩ Swimming = {Sue, Betty}

Example:

15) On a Friday night at the movie theater, movies A and B were both showing. If the movie theater sold a total of 53 movie tickets and 13 people watched both movies, how many people were at the movies on Friday night?

Solution:

Since 13 people saw both movies, 13 belongs in space where the circles overlap. The rest of the people saw only either Movie A or B. Since there is not enough information to determine how many people were in A and in B, and the question only asks for total people, subtract 13 from 53.

The reasoning behind this is that a person can only be counted once. Even though they attended two movies, it was the same person.

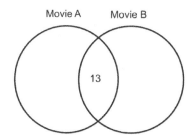

> **Testing Tip!**
> When finding the total number of elements from a Venn diagram, only include numbers that are part of an overlap ONE time!

Solve linear equations in one variable algebraically

Solving linear equations may include one-step equations, two-step equations, multi-step equations, and equations that include variables on both sides of the equal sign. Luckily, solving linear equations all have the same process, some just requiring an extra step or two.

To solve an equation, isolate the variable by using inverse operations. Remember that what you do to one side of the equation, you must do to the other side to keep the statement equal. Work using a reverse order of operations.

Linear Equation with Variables on Both Sides

Example: Solve $4x - 5 = x + 13$

STEP 1: Distribute and combine like terms on the same side of the equal sign if needed (not required for this problem)

STEP 2: Move all the variables to one side.

$$4x - 5 = x + 13$$
$$-x \qquad -x \qquad \text{Subtract } x \text{ from both sides of the equation.}$$

STEP 3: Move all the constants (numbers) to the other side of equation (not with x).

$$3x - 5 = 13$$
$$+5 \quad +5 \quad \text{Add 5 to both sides (this is an application of the addition equality property).}$$

STEP 4: Divide by the number with the variable.

$$3x = 18 \qquad \text{Divide both sides of the equation by 3.}$$
$$x = 6$$

Multistep Linear Equations

To solve multistep linear equations, isolate the variable using inverse operations, remembering what is done to one side has to be done to the other to keep the expressions equal. The steps below outline one way to approach multistep equations.

1. Distribute any numbers outside of parentheses on both sides of equation, if necessary.

2. Combine like terms **on the same side** of the equal sign.

3. Move variables to one side of the equation using inverse operations (add or subtract).

4. Isolate the variable term using inverse operations (add or subtract).

5. Divide both sides by the coefficient with the variable.

6. Look out for no solution or infinitely many solutions.

When an equation has **no solutions** or **infinitely many solutions**, the variable terms are eliminated when moved to one side. This leaves only numbers on both sides of the equation.

- No solutions: equation in the form $a = b$

  Ex: $2 = 3$; There are no solutions because 2 does not equal 3.

- Infinitely many solutions: equation in the form $a = a$

  Ex: $2 = 2$; There are infinitely many solutions because 2 equals 2; any solution will work for the equation.

Examples:

16) Solve: $-2(2x + 3) - 5 = -(5 - x)$

   Solution:

   $$-2(2x + 3) - 5 = -(5 - x)$$

   $-4x + (-6) - 5 = -5 + x$ 1. Distribute on both sides of the equation.

   $-4x + (-11) = -5 + x$
   $-4x - 11 = -5 + x$ 2. Combine like terms on the same side.
                                   Inverse operations not needed when combining on the same side.

   $-4x - 11 = -5 + x$ 3. Move variables to one side of the equation by adding or
   $+4x \quad\quad\quad\quad +4x$ subtracting. *It is always best to move smaller variables to avoid negative values.*

   $-11 = -5 + 5x$ 4. Isolate the variable term by adding or subtracting.
   $+5 \quad\quad +5$

   $\dfrac{-6}{5} = \dfrac{5x}{5}$ 5. Divide both sides by the coefficient with the variable.

   $$x = -\frac{6}{5}$$

17) Solve: $2(x + 3) = 2x - 8$

   Solution:

   $$2x + 6 = 2x - 8$$
   $$\underline{-2x \quad\quad\quad -2x}$$
   $$6 = -8$$

   Because 6 does not equal -8, **there are no solutions.**

18) Solve: $-2x + 3 - 6x = -8x + 3$

   Solution:

   $$-8x + 3 = -8x + 3$$
   $$\underline{+8x \quad\quad\quad +8x}$$
   $$3 = 3$$

   Because 3 equals 3, any solution will work for x, so there are **infinitely many solutions**.

Solve simple quadratic equations

Although solving simple quadratic equations sounds like a complicated process, these equations require a lot fewer steps than solving larger linear equations. **The one BIG idea you need to know when solving a quadratic equation is that there are two solutions, not just one.**

When finding the square root of a number, for example $\sqrt{25}$, the answer is either 5 or -5 because $5 \cdot 5 = 25$ and $-5 \cdot (-5) = 25$. We typically only give the positive answer, but there is a negative answer as well, and when solving simple quadratic equations, both solutions are required.

Solving a simple quadratic equation

1. Take the square root of both sides.

2. Divide the equation into two equations, one that equals a positive number and one that equals a negative number.

3. Solve for the variable, if needed.

Examples:

19) Ellie says the answer to the equation below is 6. Is Ellie correct?

$x^2 = 36$

A. Yes, because $\sqrt{36} = 6$.

B. Yes, because when you substitute 6 in for x, the equation is true.

C. No, because $\sqrt{36} = 18$.

D. No, because $\sqrt{36} = 6$ and $\sqrt{36} = -6$, so Ellie is missing part of the answer.

E. No, because $\sqrt{36} = 18$ and $\sqrt{36} = -18$, so Ellie is missing part of the answer.

Solution: D
To solve the equation, $x^2 = 36$, remember to rewrite the equation into two equations after taking the square root of both sides.

$x^2 = 36$

$\sqrt{x^2} = \sqrt{36}$

$x = 6$ and $x = -6$

No more solving is required, so the answers are 6 and -6. Ellie is missing part of the solution.

20) Solve the equation.

$(x + 10)^2 = 81$

Solution:

Follow the steps listed above.

$(x + 10)^2 = 81$

$\sqrt{(x + 10)^2} = \sqrt{81}$

$x + 10 = 9$ and $x + 10 = -9$
$\underline{-10 \quad -10} \qquad \underline{-10 \quad -10}$
$\qquad x = -1 \qquad\qquad x = -19$

This page is intentionally left blank.

Algebra and Geometry: Geometry

To be successful in the geometry section, it is important to be able to visualize each scenario. Geometry questions involve 2-dimensional shapes, 3-dimensional shapes, lines, points, and angles. Being able to visualize figures and having an understanding of the geometric properties of these figures and how they are related in a problem will increase your success in answering these types of questions.

Utilize basic properties of common two-dimensional shapes to solve problems

Triangles

Properties of triangles are useful when solving a variety of problems. On exam questions, characteristics of different triangles do NOT need to be stated in a problem if the type of triangle is named. The tables that follow provide definitions, characteristics, and examples of possible ways triangle types may be displayed in an exam question.

Triangle	Definition & Characteristics	Examples
Classification by Sides		
SCALENE	A triangle with no congruent sides	
ISOSCELES	A triangle with two congruent sides Angles opposite the congruent sides are also congruent	
EQUILATERAL	A triangle with all sides congruent Angles in an equilateral triangle are all congruent, equal to 60°	

Triangle	Definition & Characteristics	Examples
Classification by Angles		
ACUTE	A triangle with all angle measures less than 90°	
RIGHT	A triangle with one angle equal to 90°	
OBTUSE	A triangle with one angle greater than 90°	

Example:

21) What is the BEST way to classify the triangle below?

    A. Right, scalene

    B. Right, isosceles

    C. Acute, scalene

    D. Acute, equilateral

    E. Obtuse, isosceles

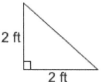

Solution: B

Because the triangle has two congruent sides, it is isosceles, and because it contains a right angle, it is also a right triangle. The correct answer choice is B.

Triangle Inequality Theorem

The **Triangle Inequality Theorem** states that the sum of the lengths of any two sides of a triangle is always greater than the length of the third side.

$$AB + BC > AC$$

$$BC + AC > AB$$

$$AC + AB > BC$$

> **Quick Tip**
>
> To determine if 3 side lengths form a triangle, check ALL three combinations of sides. Two combinations may work, so it is always necessary to check them all.

Examples:

22) Select all of the following that are a possible combination of side lengths for a triangle.

- ❑ 4 inches, 7 inches, 10 inches
- ❑ 2 inches, 3 inches, 5 inches
- ❑ 6 inches, 5 inches, 6 inches
- ❑ 4 inches, 4 inches, 4 inches

Solution: 1st box, 3rd box, 4th box

Use the Triangle Inequality Theorem to check all three combinations of sides for each answer choice.

$4 + 7 > 10, \ 11 > 10 ✓$ $2 + 3 > 5, \ 5 > 5 ✗$ $6 + 5 > 6, \ 11 > 6 ✓$ $4 + 4 > 4, \ 8 > 4 ✓$
$7 + 10 > 4, \ 17 > 4 ✓$ $6 + 6 > 5, \ 12 > 5 ✓$
$4 + 10 > 7, \ 14 > 7 ✓$

　　　YES　　　　　　　　　NO　　　　　　　　　YES　　　　　　　　　YES

23) Which of the following is NOT a possible third side of a triangle with lengths 8 centimeters and 7 centimeters?

- A. 1 centimeter
- B. 2 centimeters
- C. 3 centimeters
- D. 4 centimeters
- E. 10 centimeters

Solution: A

For option A, $1 + 7 > 8$ is not true, so 1 centimeter cannot be a possible side length. All the other side lengths work as possible sides because the sum of two sides is greater than the third side for all possible combinations.

Quadrilaterals

A quadrilateral is any polygon with four sides. There are special types of quadrilaterals because of unique properties describing their sides and angle measures. When a special quadrilateral is named, its unique properties are understood to be true. Each special quadrilateral and its properties are given in the tables that follow.

Note: *Because special quadrilaterals can have up to 3 defining characteristics, common marks are used to show sides and angles that are congruent and sides that are parallel.*

Congruent Sides	A single small slash on two or more sides means the sides are **congruent**, or the same measure.	
	Double small slash marks on two sides means the sides are congruent to one another but not to the sides without the double slash marks.	
Parallel Sides	A single arrowhead on two sides means those two sides are parallel.	
	A double arrowhead on two sides means those two sides are parallel to one another but not to the sides without the double arrowheads.	
Congruent Angles	A single arc in two or more angles means the angles are congruent.	
	A double arc in two angles means the angles are congruent to one another but not to the angles without the double arcs.	

Name	Figure	Definition
Parallelogram		A quadrilateral with • Opposite sides and opposite angles congruent • Opposite sides parallel
Rhombus		A parallelogram with • All sides congruent • Opposite angles congruent (1 pair obtuse, 1 pair acute)
Rectangle		A parallelogram with • Opposite sides congruent • All angles congruent
Square		A parallelogram with • All sides congruent and all angles congruent (90°)
Trapezoid		A quadrilateral with • One pair of parallel sides
Kite		A quadrilateral with • 2 pairs of adjacent sides congruent

Examples:

24) Choose all of the following that are not a parallelogram.

❑ Rectangle

❑ Rhombus

❑ Kite

❑ Square

❑ Trapezoid

Solution: kite, trapezoid

A kite and a trapezoid are not types of parallelograms because they do not have 2 pairs of parallel sides with opposite sides and opposite angles congruent.

25) If $\angle B$ in parallelogram $ABCD$ measures $65°$, what are the measures of all the other angles?

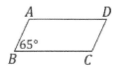

A. $\angle A = 65°, \angle C = 115°, \angle D = 115°$

B. $\angle A = 115°, \angle C = 65°, \angle D = 65°$

C. $\angle A = 115°, \angle C = 115°, \angle D = 65°$

D. $\angle A = 65°, \angle C = 65°, \angle D = 115°$

E. $\angle A = 115°, \angle C = 115°, \angle D = 115°$

Solution: C

Opposite angles have the same measure in a parallelogram, so if $\angle B = 65$, then $\angle D = 65$. Because a parallelogram is a quadrilateral, all four angles add to $360°$. Subtract the measures of angles B and D from 360 to get the sum of A and C.

$360 - 65 - 65 = 230$

Because A and C are congruent, divide their sum by 2 to get the measure of each angle.

$230 \div 2 = 115$

Therefore, the correct response is C.

Circles

The most important information about a circle is understanding how to find the radius and diameter and to understand where these values are in the circumference and area formulas for a circle.

• The diameter goes through the center of the circle to the edge of the circle.

• The radius starts at the center of the circle and ends on the edge of the circle.

• The radius is half the length of the diameter.

Remember that the radius of a circle can be drawn from the center of the circle to anywhere on the circle.

Another circle part that is useful when working with circle graphs is a central angle. A **central angle** in a circle is an angle with its vertex at the center of the circle. The part of the circle intercepted by the angle is called an **arc**. If several central angles were drawn in a circle, like a pizza, the sum of these angle measures would be $360°$.

 Central angle  Arc 360°

Arcs are measured two different ways, in degrees based on the measure of the central angle, and in a unit of length, based on the circle's circumference.

- *Arc measure* is equal to the degree of the central angle.

- *Arc length* is equal to the fractional part of the circumference of the circle represented by the arc.

To find the arc length of an arc created by a central angle, set up a proportion using the two ways arcs can be measured:

$$\frac{\text{arc measure}}{\text{degrees in a circle}} = \frac{\text{arc length}}{\text{circumference of circle}}$$

OR

$$\frac{\text{arc measure}}{360°} = \frac{\text{arc length}}{2\pi r}$$

Example:

26) A circle with a radius of 3 inches has a central angle that measures 40°. What is the length of the intercepted arc?

A. π

B. $\frac{2}{3}\pi$

C. 2π

D. 6π

E. 9π

Solution: B

To solve, use the proportion, $\frac{\text{arc measure}}{360°} = \frac{\text{arc length}}{2\pi r}$, filling in missing values to solve for arc length.

$$\frac{40}{360} = \frac{\text{arc length}}{2\pi(3)}$$

Simplifying the fractions before cross-multiplying,

$$\frac{1}{9} = \frac{x}{6\pi}$$

$$9x = 6\pi$$

$$x = \frac{6}{9}\pi = \frac{2}{3}\pi$$

The correct answer choice is B.

Quick Tip

When solving formulas that include π, look at the answer choices BEFORE working out the problem. If the π symbol is part of all the answers, you do not need to multiply by 3.14.

Utilize facts about angles to solve problems

Angles are two rays with a common endpoint, called the **vertex**. Angles may be named using only the vertex if there are no other angles. Otherwise, angles are named with a point from one ray, the vertex, then a point from the other ray. Below are examples of naming angles.

Note: The order of the points on the rays does not matter for naming. $\angle CAB$ is the same as $\angle BAC$.

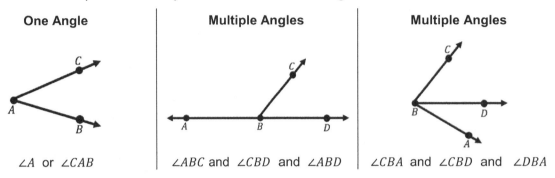

One Angle	Multiple Angles	Multiple Angles
$\angle A$ or $\angle CAB$	$\angle ABC$ and $\angle CBD$ and $\angle ABD$	$\angle CBA$ and $\angle CBD$ and $\angle DBA$

When lines intersect, the resulting angles have special names and properties that help to identify the measure of the angle(s). Angles formed by intersecting lines are defined in the following table.

Angle Name	Example	Definition
Complementary Angles		**Two angles that add to 90°** *Note:* The angles may share a side, as pictured, or may be two separate angles.
Supplementary Angles		**Two angles that add to 180°** *Note:* The angles may share a side, as pictured, or may be two separate angles.
Vertical Angles		Pairs of angles that are opposite or across from one another when two lines intersect **Vertical angles always have the SAME measure.**

 The terms complementary angles, supplementary angles, and vertical angles may appear in problems without an accompanying sketch, so knowing their names is important.

Corresponding Angles	*A line that intersects parallel lines is called a transversal.*	Angles on the same side of the transversal and the same side of their respective line on a pair of parallel lines; if the parallel lines were slid on top of one another, corresponding angles would also be on top of one another. **Corresponding angles always have the SAME measure.**
Alternate Interior Angles		Angles inside, or between, the parallel lines and on alternate sides of the transversal **Alternate interior angles always have the SAME measure.**
Same Side Interior Angles		Angles inside, or between, the parallel lines and on the same side of the transversal **Same side interior angles always add to 180°.**
Same Side Exterior Angles		Angles outside of the parallel lines and on the same side of the transversal **Same side exterior angles always add to 180°.**

 For angles formed by parallel lines and a transversal, it is not important to remember their names, only their angle measure properties.

Examples:

27) The complement to angle A is 42°. What is the measure of angle A?

    A. 42°

    B. 48°

    C. 58°

    D. 138°

    E. 180°

Solution: B

Complementary angles add to 90°. Therefore subtract $90 - 42$ to find the measure of angle A. The measure of angle A, $m\angle A = 48$.

28) Which of the following angle pairs is NOT equivalent?

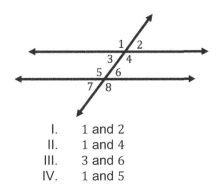

	I.	1 and 2
	II.	1 and 4
	III.	3 and 6
	IV.	1 and 5

A. I

B. II

C. III

D. IV

E. III and IV

Solution: A

Angles 1 and 2 are supplementary and add to $180°$. The only time two angles that are next to each other are equivalent is when both angles equal $90°$. If angles are equal to $90°$, they must be marked or must say so. Angles 1 and 4 are vertical, angles 3 and 6 are alternate interior, and angles 1 and 5 are corresponding, all of which have the same measure.

Utilize facts about congruence and similarity of geometric figures to solve problems

When two figures are congruent, all corresponding angle measures and all corresponding sides are congruent. Therefore, if a side measure or an angle measure is missing from a figure, the values from the congruent figure may be substituted. The images below are congruent, therefore, side a in the figure on the right is 5 cm.

Similar figures have corresponding sides that are proportional and corresponding angle measures that are equal. To find the missing length of a side when similar figures are given, use a proportion. (This skill was covered in the Number and Quantity section of the textbook.)

Use the formulas for area and circumference of a circle to solve problems

Circumference

The circumference of a circle is the measurement around the outside of a circle. To find the circumference of a circle use either formula, $C = \pi d$ or $C = 2\pi r$, depending on whether the diameter or radius is given (recall the radius is two times the diameter).

The area of a circle measures the amount of space inside a circle. To find the area of a circle, use the formula, $A = \pi r^2$. You may need to find the radius before finding the area if only the diameter of the circle is given.

Test questions about circles often expect that you can manipulate or extract information from one formula to use in another. These types of problems require less computational work but a better understanding of the formulas.

Example:

29) The area of a circle is 49π inches^2. What is the circumference of the circle?

    A. 7π inches

    B. 14π inches

    C. 28π inches

    D. 49π inches

    E. 98π inches

Solution: B

If the area of the circle is 49π inches^2, then 49 represents r^2 in the formula for area. Therefore, $r = 7$ inches. Using this to find the circumference,

$C = 2\pi r$

$C = 2 \cdot \pi \cdot 7$

$C = 2 \cdot 7 \cdot \pi$

$C = 14\pi$

Use the formulas for the perimeter and area of a triangle and a rectangle and the formula for the volume of a rectangular prism (box) to solve problems

Solving real-life problems involving perimeter, circumference, area, and volume are also known as **geometry word problems.**

Geometry word problems often require more than one step to solve. It is important to organize the information you are given, determine the steps needed to find missing information, and answer what the question is asking.

<u>Perimeter</u>

To find the perimeter of any figure, add all the sides.

Example:

30) The perimeter of a rectangle is 52 ft. If the length is 10 less than 2 times the width, what is the width?

    Solution:

    In this example, there are 3 clues: perimeter, length, and type of shape. Solve the problem using these three clues.

    First, determine the expressions for each of the sides of the rectangle. The problem states that the length is 10 less than 2 times the width, which is written algebraically as $2w - 10$. Make sure when you see the words *less than,* you write -10 in the correct position in the equation. The shape of the object is a rectangle, which means the widths are the same measure and the lengths are the same measure.

    Next, use the clue of perimeter to write an equation using the expressions for the sides.

    $2w - 10 + 2w - 10 + w + w = 52$

    Last, solve the equation for w.

$$2w - 10 + 2w - 10 + w + w = 52$$

$$6w - 20 = 52$$

$$6w = 72$$

$$w = 12 \text{ feet}$$

31) Stacey wants to plant one row of bushes along the length of her front yard. The length of Stacey's front yard is 6 less than three times the width. If the perimeter of her yard is 284 feet, what is the length of the yard where she is planting the bushes?

A. 37 feet

B. 39 feet

C. 74 feet

D. 105 feet

E. 210 feet

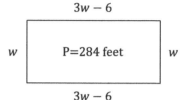

Solution: D

To solve, draw a picture and label the sides. The length is given in terms of the width. Therefore, the width is w, and the length is $3w - 6$ (remember less than switches the order).

The question gave the perimeter, which is a BIG hint that the perimeter of a rectangle formula is needed to solve. Substitute the expressions for the length and width into the perimeter formula and solve.

$$w + (3w - 6) + w + (3w - 6) = 284$$
$$8w - 12 = 284$$
$$8w = 296$$
$$w = 37$$

Be careful because solving the equation finds the width and the question asks for the length. Substitute into the expression for length, $3w - 6$.

$3(37) - 6 = 111 - 6 = 105$ feet. The correct answer choice is D.

Area

The area of all polygons (figures with straight sides such as a rectangle or triangle), can be found by using some combination of base times height. The base and height are always at right angles. When a figure is slanted, the height is drawn, usually by a dotted line. Most test questions involving area are word problems, which means you will usually be required to use the area of a rectangle.

Example:

32) A rectangular playground is being refurbished and covered in rubber mulch. Each bag of rubber mulch covers 1,500 square inches. If the playground measures 30 feet by 10 feet, how many bags of rubber mulch are needed?

A. 5 bags

B. 28 bags

C. 29 bags

D. 50 bags

E. 51 bags

Solution: C

To solve, find the area of the playground. Then, because the area the mulch covers is given in inches, the sides of the playground need to be converted to inches. Multiply each side by 12 to convert to inches. Last, find the area of the playground.

$30 \cdot 12 = 360$

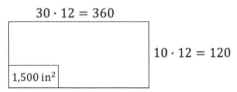

$10 \cdot 12 = 120$

1,500 in²

Playground area: $360 \cdot 120 = 43,200$

Each bag of mulch covers 1,500 square inches, therefore divide the total area by 1,500 to get the number of bags needed.

$43,200 \div 1,500 = 28.8$

Because bags of mulch cannot be split, 29 bags are needed to cover the playground, which is answer choice C.

Volume of a Prism (box)

The volume of box is the space inside the box. To find the volume, multiply the values for the length, width, and height together; $V = lwh$.

Example:

33) Sally bought a new box of almond milk. She estimates she will drink 500 cubic centimeters of the almond milk each day. How long will it take her to finish the almond milk?

A. 9 days

B. 10 days

C. 11 days

D. 12 days

E. 15 days

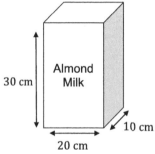

Solution: D

First find the volume of the carton.

$V = lwh$

$= 30 \text{ cm} \times 20 \text{ cm} \times 10 \text{ cm}$

$= 6,000 \text{ cm}^3$

Next, divide $6,000 \text{ cm}^3$ by 500 cm^3.

$6,000 \div 500 = 12$. The answer is answer choice D, 12 days.

34) Which of the following cereal boxes holds the most cereal?

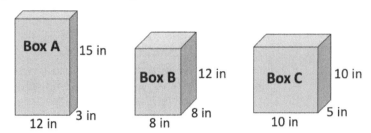

A. Box A

B. Box B

C. Box C

D. Both Boxes A and C

E. Both Boxes A and B

Solution: B

Find the volume of each box (rectangular solid).

Box A: $V = lwh = 12 \cdot 3 \cdot 15 = 540$ in^3

Box B: $V = lwh = 8 \cdot 8 \cdot 12 = 768$ in^3

Box C: $V = lwh = 10 \cdot 5 \cdot 10 = 500$ in^3

Box B will hold the most cereal, therefore the correct answer choice is B.

DIRECTIONS: Choose the answer choice that represents the best solution.

1. Kara's flower shop sells the most wedding bouquets from May through September. The number of bouquets she sold during each of these five months is shown below. How many more bouquets did she sell in June than in August?

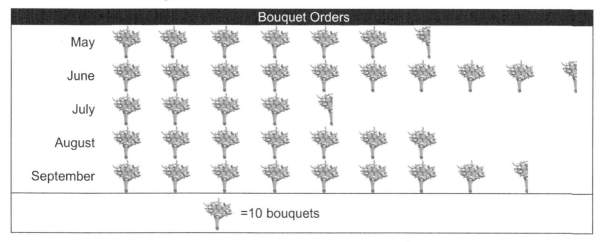

- O   15
- O   20
- O   25
- O   30
- O   35

2. On a popular live television program where the viewing audience votes on contestants, 28 million people voted during week one, 32 million voted week two, and 35 million voted during week three, which was the finale week. What percent of the total votes were the votes cast during the finale week?

- O   34%
- O   35%
- O   37%
- O   38%
- O   39%

3. If the number 23,489.6 is divided by 1,000, what digit would be in the tenths place?

- O   3
- O   4
- O   8
- O   9
- O   6

4. A painter paints $\frac{3}{5}$ of a square inch on a canvas per minute while creating an oil painting. How many minutes will it take the painter to paint $4\frac{1}{2}$ in² of the canvas?

     O   7.5

     O   6.8

     O   5.3

     O   3.9

     O   2.7

5. The price of apples was originally $2.98 per pound but dropped to $1.99 per pound as part of a promotion. What was the percent of decrease in the price of the apples to the nearest whole percent?

     O   32%

     O   33%

     O   50%

     O   68%

     O   71%

6. An arcade machine gives out colored tickets that can be redeemed for prizes. It gives out 2 white tickets, then 3 yellow tickets, then 4 red tickets, in that order. The pattern repeats until the game has produced the winning number of tickets. If Kelly won 75 tickets, and the first ticket was white, how many yellow tickets did she receive?

     O   8

     O   9

     O   11

     O   12

     O   25

7. A sequence of numbers occurs by subtracting three from the preceding number then adding two. If the fifth number is 88, what is the fourth number?

     O   41

     O   42

     O   44

     O   47

     O   170

8. A three-pack of paper towels costs $5.85. A 12-pack of paper towels costs $14.64. What is the difference in the cost of one roll when buying a 12-pack over one roll when buying a three-pack?

     O $0.62

     O $0.73

     O $1.22

     O $1.38

     O $1.95

9. The altitude of a plane during its descent at two different times is shown in the table. To the nearest tenth of a foot, how many feet per minute does the plane descend?

Time	Altitude (in feet)
2:16 P.M.	32,560
2:22 P.M.	16,980

- ○ 2,596.5
- ○ 2,596.7
- ○ 2,597.6
- ○ 2,759.6
- ○ 3,104.0

10. Which of the following shows 0.148, 0.099, 0.2, and 0.21 in order from least to greatest?

- ○ 0.099, 0.148, 0.2, 0.21
- ○ 0.099, 0.2, 0.148, 0.21
- ○ 0.21, 0.2, 0.148, 0.099
- ○ 0.2, 0.099, 0.148, 0.21
- ○ 0.148, 0.2, 0.21, 0.099

11. The football team is selling coupon cards for $20 each. For each card they sell, they make a $10 profit. Which answer choice represents how many cards they need to sell in order to raise at least $1,400?

- ○ $10x \geq 1,400$
- ○ $10x \leq 1,400$
- ○ $20x > 1,400$
- ○ $10x < 1,400$
- ○ $20x \geq 1,400$

12. Solve for x. Write the solution as a fraction in the boxes provided.

$$\frac{5}{9} + x = 7$$

13. How many solutions does the equation have?

$4 + 5x = x - 7 + 4x$

- ○ None
- ○ One
- ○ Two
- ○ Three
- ○ Infinitely many

14. Michael solved the equation $(x - 4)^2 = 25$ and got $x = 9$. What other solution for x should Michael have also gotten?

- ○ -1
- ○   1
- ○   2
- ○   3
- ○   4

15. A video streaming service charges a flat fee plus $0.10 per program watched. If the flat fee is $8 per month, and Megan's monthly bill totaled $12.50, how many programs did she watch?

- ○   34
- ○   35
- ○   45
- ○   125
- ○   205

16. A utilities worker earns $28 per hour for the first 8 hours he works in a day and h dollars for any hours over the regularly scheduled 8 hours. If a utility worker makes $260 in one 10-hour day, what is his hourly rate, h, in dollars, for working overtime?

- ○   8
- ○   18
- ○   19
- ○   36
- ○   64

17. Which of the following is equivalent to $-4a + 3b - 8 + 9a + 7b - 11$?

- ○ $5(a - 2b) - 19$
- ○ $15ab - 19$
- ○ $5(a + 2b) - 19$
- ○ $19 + 5a + 10b$
- ○ $-5a + 10b - 19$

18. Which of the following models the line of best fit for the scatterplot?

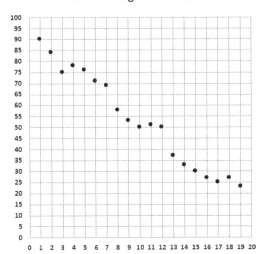

○ $y = \frac{1}{3}x + 100$

○ $y = -\frac{1}{3}x + 100$

○ $y = 3x + 100$

○ $y = -3x + 100$

○ $y = -3x$

19. The graph below gives the number of sales during a holiday sale. What is the range in the number of sales during the first 8-hour period?

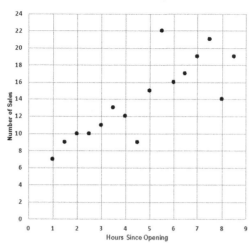

○   7.5

○   8.5

○   12

○   15

○   16

20. Given the scatterplot, which statement can be concluded?

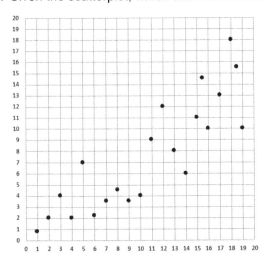

- ○ There is a strong positive correlation between x and y.
- ○ There is a weak positive correlation between x and y.
- ○ There is a negative correlation between x and y.
- ○ The number of x increases as the number of y decreases.
- ○ There is no correlation between the data sets.

21. Given the scatterplot, which statement can be concluded?

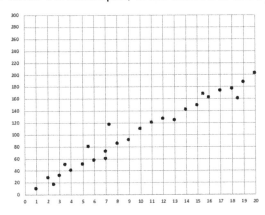

- ○ As x increases by 10, y increases by 10.
- ○ As x increases by 1, y increases by 10.
- ○ As x increases by 5, y increases by 10.
- ○ As x increases by 10, y increases by 1.
- ○ As x increases by 1, y increases by 1.

22. What can be concluded from the scatterplot?

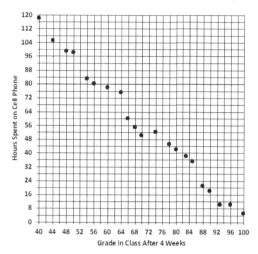

Grade in Class After 4 Weeks

- ○ As time spent on a cell phone increases, a student's grade in the class increases.
- ○ As time spent on a cell phone increases, a student's grade in the class decreases.
- ○ There is a strong positive correlation between a student's time spent on their cell phone and their grade in the class.
- ○ There is a negative correlation between a student's time spent on a cell phone and their grade in the class.
- ○ There is no relationship between a student's time spent on a cell phone and their grade in the class.

23. The total profits for a large pest control company are $5 million dollars per year. The company services individual homes, housing communities, and businesses. If the profits were graphed in a circle graph, the profits from the company represented by housing communities would be represented by a central angle of 108°. How much does the company make in profits from housing communities?

- ○ $15,000
- ○ $150,000
- ○ $500,000
- ○ $1,500,000
- ○ $2,500,000

24. The Smith's total monthly budget is $1,600. How much do they allocate to utilities and eating out?

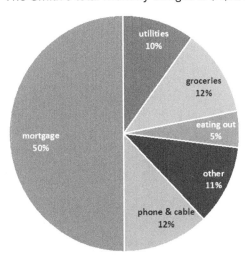

- ○ $120
- ○ $165
- ○ $220
- ○ $240
- ○ $265

25. Select all of the following that are equivalent to $10a^2$.

- ❑ $(2a)(5a)$
- ❑ $(4a)(6a)$
- ❑ $4a + 6a$
- ❑ $\frac{20a^3}{2a}$
- ❑ $10a(a)$
- ❑ $\frac{1}{2}a(20)^2$

26. The bar graph shows the number of pets each student in Mr. Singh's class has. How many students have fewer than 3 pets?

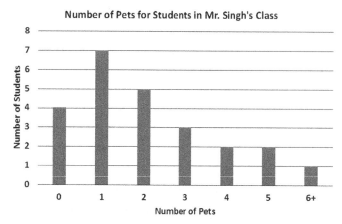

Number of Pets for Students in Mr. Singh's Class

- ○ 16
- ○ 11
- ○ 7
- ○ 4
- ○ 3

27. Find the average (arithmetic mean) of the numbers, $-5, 4, -2, 1, 0, 7, 4, -1$.

- ○ -1
- ○ 1
- ○ 0
- ○ 1.1
- ○ 8

28. The set M is a set that contains whole numbers from 12 to 28 exclusively. What is the median of the set of values for M?

- ○ 19
- ○ 19.5
- ○ 20
- ○ 20.5
- ○ 21

29. The timeline below shows major events that occurred during the creation of the Constitution of the United States. How many years after the Articles of Confederation were drafted did the states ratify the Constitution?

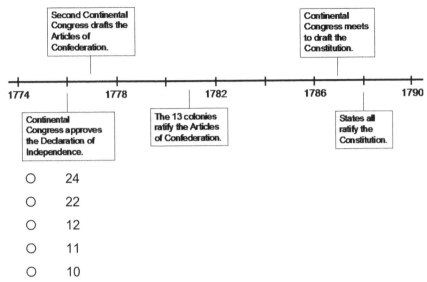

- ○ 24
- ○ 22
- ○ 12
- ○ 11
- ○ 10

30. The table below represents survey data from 8,000 people ages 22-50. The survey was used to measure how many people are dissatisfied with their jobs. If this is a representative sample of a population of 1.2 million people, predict how many people between the ages of 41 and 50 are currently unhappy with their employment.

Age Group	Percent
22-25	12%
26-30	24%
31-35	38%
36-40	10%
41-45	9%
46-50	7%

- ○ 1,280
- ○ 84,000
- ○ 108,000
- ○ 124,000
- ○ 192,000

31. A jar contains blue, pink, and yellow gumballs. There are 10 blue gumballs and 8 pink gumballs. If the probability of picking a yellow gumball is $\frac{1}{4}$, how many yellow gumballs are in the jar?

- ○ 3
- ○ 4
- ○ 5
- ○ 6
- ○ 7

32. There are 400 of both white and blue cards in a bag. If the probability of picking a white card is 0.64, how many more white cards than blue cards are in the bag?

- ○ 101
- ○ 102
- ○ 110
- ○ 112
- ○ 256

33. Given the information in the table below, what is the probability of selecting a student at random who is a female student attending the college part-time?

	Male	Female
Part-time	345	286
Full-time	590	872

34. Lines s and t are parallel, and line u is a transversal. Find the value of x.

- ○ 24
- ○ 26
- ○ 36
- ○ 56
- ○ 124

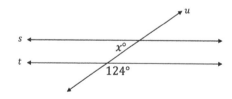

35. A snack mix has 2 cups of almonds, $\frac{3}{4}$ cup of raisins, and 1 cup of chocolate chips. Which of the following ratios represents a ratio of almonds to raisins to chocolate chips?

- ○ 8:3:4
- ○ 3:1:2
- ○ 4:2:3
- ○ 8:1:4
- ○ 2:3:4

36. Stocking up on snacks for a team road trip, Miguel bought 16 bags of chips for $0.75 each, 28 pieces of candy for $.20 each, 12 bottles of water for $1.25 each, and 4 packs of gum for $1.99 each. How much did Miguel spend on snacks for the team's road trip?

- ○ $40.50
- ○ $40.56
- ○ $41.56
- ○ $41.78
- ○ $41.98

37. What is the value of x?

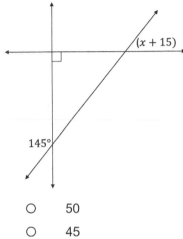

- ○ 50
- ○ 45
- ○ 40
- ○ 35
- ○ 30

38. A rectangular shipping box has a length of 12 inches and a width of 8 inches. If the volume of the box is 1,056 cubic inches, what is the height of the box in inches?

- ○ 11
- ○ 12
- ○ 13
- ○ 14
- ○ 15

39. A round clock has a diameter of 14 inches. What is the circumference of the clock face to the nearest hundredth of an inch?

- ○ 21.98 inches
- ○ 43.96 inches
- ○ 87.92 inches
- ○ 153.86 inches
- ○ 192.13 inches

40. The manager at an office supply store buys 3-gallon jugs of drinking water for the office. This month the office supply store staff drank $2\frac{1}{2}$ jugs of water. How many pints of water did they drink?

1 gallon = 4 quarts

1 quart = 2 pints

- ○ 7.5
- ○ 24
- ○ 30
- ○ 48
- ○ 60

41. The scale on a map is 2 centimeters for every 5 kilometers. If the actual distance between two locations is 12 kilometers 50 meters, what is the distance between the locations on the map?

- ○ 4.7 cm
- ○ 4.80 cm
- ○ 4.82 cm
- ○ 4.85 cm
- ○ 5.0 cm

42. Which of the following shapes has two sides that are parallel but not equal and two sides that are not parallel or equal?

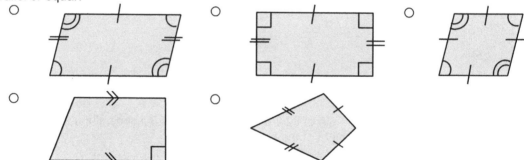

43. If there are 18 fiction books for every 3 autobiographies in the library. How many autobiographies are there in the library if there are 8,154 fiction books?

- ○ 453
- ○ 463
- ○ 579
- ○ 1,359
- ○ 2,718

44. To find a number, you are given the following directions.

Start with x
Add 5
Multiply by 2
Subtract 4
Divide by 10.

If the final number is 68, what is the value of x?

- ○ 7.8
- ○ 10.6
- ○ 337
- ○ 347
- ○ 680

45. Given the equation, $2x + 9y = 32$, what is y in terms of x?

- ○ $\frac{32+2x}{9}$
- ○ $\frac{-2x+32}{9}$
- ○ $9(32 - 2x)$
- ○ $-2x + \frac{32}{9}$
- ○ $-\frac{30x}{9}$

46. Given the graph, what is ratio of blue to red at 6 seconds?

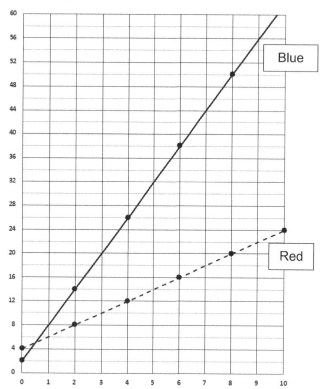

$$\frac{\boxed{}}{\boxed{}}$$

47. If $\frac{w}{x} = \frac{5}{6}$ and $\frac{y}{x} = \frac{7}{12}$, what is $\frac{w}{y}$?

○ $\frac{72}{35}$

○ $\frac{7}{10}$

○ $\frac{7}{5}$

○ $\frac{5}{7}$

○ $\frac{10}{7}$

October 2019

48. There are 1,240 people attending their company's year-end awards banquet. If 12 people can sit at a table in the banquet room, what is the minimum number of tables needed for the banquet?

   ○ 100
   ○ 101
   ○ 102
   ○ 103
   ○ 104

49. Which is the prime factorization of $25 \times 40 \times 48$?

   ○ $2^2 \times 3^1 \times 5^3$
   ○ $2^4 \times 3^2 \times 5^2$
   ○ $2^7 \times 3^1 \times 5^3$
   ○ $2^{12} \times 3^1 \times 5^2$
   ○ $2^7 \times 3^2 \times 5^3$

50. Read the scenario below and answer the question that follows.

   Jenna was the 300th person to get on the beach trolley from a community parking lot 2 miles from the beach. If the trolley picks up a new load of people every 5 minutes, and all the seats have been full for each trip, how many trips did the trolley make to the beach prior to Jenna getting on the trolley?

   What additional information is needed to answer the question?

   ○ The number of attendants on the trolley.
   ○ The number of people in line before Jenna.
   ○ How long Jenna waited in line.
   ○ The maximum number of people that can fit on the trolley at one time.
   ○ How long it takes the trolley to drive to the beach.

51. A survey of 500 people asked if they ate chicken or steak for dinner this past week. Of the respondents, 268 people said they ate both chicken and steak. If 322 ate chicken and 275 ate steak, how many respondents didn't eat either chicken or steak for dinner?

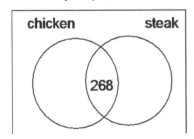

   ○ 61
   ○ 171
   ○ 201
   ○ 268
   ○ 329

52. Using the diagram, find the value of $a + b$.

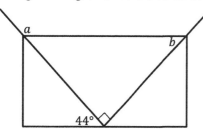

- ○ 182
- ○ 136
- ○ 92
- ○ 90
- ○ 88

53. If A is a point between -2 and -3 and B is a point between 0 and 1, which of the points on the number line could be the value of $A \cdot B$?

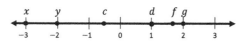

- ○ c
- ○ d
- ○ x
- ○ y
- ○ g

54. Omar bought a refrigerator for $800. If he doesn't put any money down and pays $50 per month, which of the following graphs represents how long it will take him to pay off the refrigerator?

○ 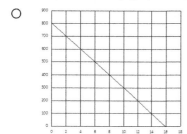   ○ 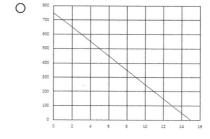   ○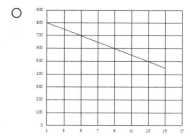

○ 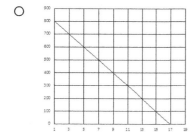   ○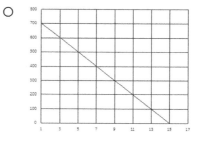

55. Olivia made a model of a statue that is in the courtyard of her school. What is the width of the model she made?

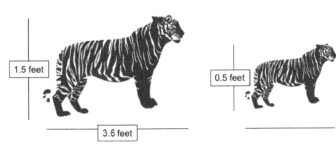

1.5 feet

0.5 feet

3.6 feet

- ○ 1.1
- ○ 1.2
- ○ 1.8
- ○ 2.1
- ○ 2.2

56. Minerva and Estrella are making a string art project. Minerva has used 32 feet of string, which is 64% of the amount of string Estrella has used. How many feet of string did the girls use in all to create both art projects?

- ○ 18
- ○ 32
- ○ 50
- ○ 68
- ○ 82

This page is intentionally left blank.

October 2019

Number	Answer	Content Category	Explanation
1.	25	II	Since the question is asking how many more bouquets were sold in June than August, subtract the number of bouquets sold in August from the number sold in June. Each symbol is worth 10, so in June 9 ½ symbols or $9.5 \times 10 = 95$ bouquets were sold. In August, $7 \times 10 = 70$ bouquets were sold. Find the difference by subtracting $95 - 70 = 25$. Another way to approach the problem is to see that there are 2 ½ more bouquets on the graph in June than August. Since each symbol is worth 10, $2.5 \times 10 = 25$.
2.	37%	I	To find the percentage use the following formula $\frac{\text{finale week votes}}{\text{total votes}}$. Note that even though the votes are tallied in millions, it is not necessary to input the values using all the zeros. Because all the values are in the millions, we can use $28, 32,$ and $35,$ making the problem more manageable. $\frac{35}{28+32+35} = \frac{35}{95} \approx .368 \approx 37\%$.
3.	4	I	Use your calculator and input $23,489.6 \div 1,000$. The result is 23.4896. The tenths place is the first number to the right of the decimal place, $23.\underline{4}896$, so 4 is in the tenths place. Another way to approach this problem is knowing that dividing by 1,000 moves the decimal point three places to the left. This eliminates the need to use the calculator and speeds up solving.
4.	7.5	I	Use your calculator to convert the fractions to decimals in order to make the problem more manageable $(\frac{3}{5} = 0.6, 4\frac{1}{2} = 4.5)$. Next, use a proportion to solve. Each ratio should be in the form $\frac{\text{in}^2}{\text{minutes}}$. Set up the proportion as follows: $\frac{0.6\text{in}^2}{1 \text{ min}} = \frac{4.5\text{in}^2}{x \text{ min}}$. Solve using cross-multiplication $0.6x = 4.5$ Last, divide to get the variable by itself. $\frac{0.6x}{0.6} = \frac{4.5}{0.6} \rightarrow x = 7.5$.
5.	33%	I	To find the percent decrease use the formula $\frac{\text{new price}-\text{old price}}{\text{old price}}$. Make sure to substitute the correct values; $\frac{1.99-2.98}{2.98} = \frac{-0.99}{2.98} \approx -0.332 \approx -33\%$. The negative is only significant to show that it was a percent decrease and is not necessary to keep for the final answer.

October 2019

Number	Answer	Content Category	Explanation
6.	25	II	The pattern of ticket dispensing is W-W-Y-Y-Y-R-R-R-R And the pattern continues to repeat itself. Since there were 75 tickets won, it is important to find out how many times the pattern repeats itself within those 75 tickets. Because there are 9 tickets in each repeating pattern, divide 75 by 9. $75 \div 9 = 8.33$, This means the pattern will fully repeat itself 8 times and then continue, 0.33 of the way. To fully understand this, multiply 8×9 to get 72. The last R (red ticket) in the pattern will be ticket number 72. Continue to count from the beginning of the pattern with the first W (white ticket) as 73, then the next one as 74, and finally the 75th ticket will be the first Y (yellow ticket). The pattern repeated itself 8 times plus the 75th ticket was also yellow, so $8 \times 3 + 1 = 25$ yellow tickets.
7.	47	I	This problem can be solved multiple ways. One way is to write an equation given the sequence. $(x - 3) \times 2 = 88$ $2x - 6 = 88$ $2x = 94 \rightarrow x = 47.$ The problem may also be worked backwards, but remember everything is opposite, divide instead of multiplying and add instead of subtracting. $88 \div 2 = 44 + 3 = 47.$
8.	$0.73	I	To solve this problem, first find the cost of a single roll for each pack. $\frac{\$5.85}{3} = \$1.95$ and $\frac{\$14.64}{12} = \$1.22.$ Next, find the difference between the two single roll prices. $\$1.95 - \$1.22 = \$0.73.$
9.	2,596.7	I	Use the chart to determine the difference in time and the difference in altitude. Finally, divide the altitude by time. Difference in time: $2:22 - 2:16 = 6$ minutes Difference in altitude: $32,560 - 16,980 = 15,580$ feet $15,580 \div 6 \approx 2,596.67 \approx 2,596.7$
10.	See answer explanation for solution	I	ANSWER: $0.099, 0.148, 0.2, 0.21$

Number	Answer	Content Category	Explanation
			Since all of the values are decimals, start with the tenths place (first value to the right of the decimal). The 0 in 0.099 is lower than any other value in that place, therefore it is the smallest number in the sequence. Process of elimination will rule out the last three answer choices. Continuing on, the 1 in 0.148 is next smallest value which solidifies that the first answer choice is correct without having to compare any other values. Just to be sure, the 2 in the last two are the same so move to the next place value where nothing is a 0 and is smaller than 0.21.
11.	$10x \geq 1,400$	I	One of the most important parts of this problem is the phrase, "at least." This means that the value has to be equal to or greater than 1,400 and the $\geq$ sign will be used in the expression. If every card represents $10 in profit, then $10x$ represents the amount made from sold, resulting in the inequality $10x \geq 1,400$.
12.	$\dfrac{58}{9}$	I	Because the answer calls for a fraction, write 7 as a fraction by putting it over 1, $\frac{7}{1}$. Next, rewrite this fraction with 9 as the denominator so that both fractions in the equation have the same denominator. The resulting equation will be $\frac{5}{9} + x = \frac{63}{9}$. Continue to solve for x by subtracting $\frac{5}{9}$ from both sides, getting $x = \frac{58}{9}$. Alternatively, you could subtract $\frac{5}{9}$ from both sides and get $7 - \frac{5}{9} = 6\frac{4}{9}$ and then convert this mixed number to a fraction greater than 1.
13.	None	I	First simplify the equation by collecting like terms on the right. $4 + 5x = x - 7 + 4x$ $4 + 5x = -7 + 5x$ Notice at this point the variables are going to be eliminated because the same term, $5x$, is on both sides. After eliminating the $5x$ from both sides, we are left with the statement $4 = -7$. When this happens, ask yourself, "Does 4 equal -7?" $4 \neq -7$ Since 4 will never equal -7, this equation has no solutions. No matter what is substituted for the x value, the equation will not be true.

Number	Answer	Content Category	Explanation
14.	−1	III	Guess and check is a viable strategy for solving this problem. Just be careful with negative signs when evaluating. Start with the first answer choice by substituting it for x. $$(-1-4)^2 = 25$$ $$(-5)^2 = 25$$ $$25 = 25$$ Remember that when a negative number is squared it becomes positive. A second method is to take the square root of each side of the equation and then break the equation into two answers, one positive and one negative because the square root of a number always has a positive solution and a negative solution. $$(x-4)^2 = 25$$ $$\sqrt{(x-4)^2} = \sqrt{25}$$ $x - 4 = 5$ and $x - 4 = -5$ $x = 9$ or $x = -1$, so −1 is the second solution.
15.	45	III	To solve this problem, work backwards starting with the total of the monthly bill. Take away the $8 flat fee first and then divide by $0.10 to figure out how many shows were watched. $$\$12.50 - \$8.00 = \$4.50$$ $$\$4.50 \div \$0.10 = 45$$
16.	18	III	First, because a 10-hour day is made up of the regularly scheduled 8 hours plus another 2 hours, we need to figure out how much the worker makes for his daily rate of $28 for the first 8 hours. $$\$28 \times 8 = \$224$$ Next, subtract that value from the $260 total for the day. $$\$260 - \$224 = \$36$$ Finally, divide that total by the 2 remaining hours to determine the overtime hourly rate. $$\$36 \div 2 = \$18$$

October 2019

Number	Answer	Content Category	Explanation
17.	$5(a + 2b) - 19$	III	First, simplify the expression by combining all like terms. Next, cross reference with the answer choices to see which one matches up. Be careful because the answer may not look exactly as the one that was simplified. $-4a + 3b - 8 + 9a + 7b - 11$ $5a + 10b - 19$ The third choice is the factored form of the simplified form above; the a and b terms were both divided by 5, and the 5 was placed outside the parentheses. This is an application of the distributive property. $\dfrac{5a}{5} + \dfrac{10b}{5} - 19$ $= 5(a + 2b) - 19$

The key to being able to identify a line of best fit on a scatterplot is to be able to find the y-intercept and/or the slope. Given the slope-intercept form of an equation, $y = mx + b$, where m is the slope and b is the y-intercept, determine these values on the graph and know where they are in the equation.

The answer choices may all have the same slope or same y-intercept, which means you won't have to find both values. Notice that in the answer choices given, the y-intercept is 100 in all the choices but the last one. Looking at the graph, if we sketched a line that modeled the points, then the line would most likely cross the y-axis at 100.

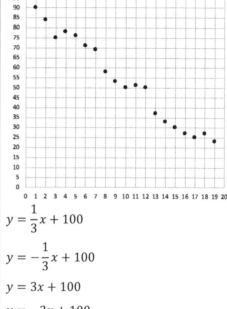

18.	$y = -3x + 100$	II	$y = \dfrac{1}{3}x + 100$
			$y = -\dfrac{1}{3}x + 100$
			$y = 3x + 100$
			$y = -3x + 100$
			~~$y = -3x$~~

This eliminates the last answer choice because the y-intercept is 0.

Next, by reading the points from left to right the pattern of points is sloping downward which indicates a negative slope. This will eliminate the first and third answer choices because the slopes, m, are positive for both equations.

Finally, it comes down to either a slope of $-\dfrac{1}{3}$ or -3. Slope is the change in y over the change in x, or rise over run, which means to go from one point to the next the direction is up or down (number in numerator) and left or right (number in denominator).

The scale on the y axis is in increments of 5, and the scale on the x axis is in increments of 1. Starting from 100 on the y axis, the slope of best fit is to go down 3 and right 1 for every point on the line which yields a line of best fit for this graph of $y = -3x + 100$.

Number	Answer	Content Category	Explanation
19.	15	II	In a set of data points, the range is the difference between the lowest and highest numbers in the set. Since the question asks for the first 8-hour period of the store doing business, only include the data points on the graph from 0 to 8 on the x axis. Each point represents a number in the set, the lowest being 7 and the highest being 22. $22 - 7 = 15$, therefore, the range in sales is 15.
20.	There is a weak positive correlation between x and y	II	The look fors on a scatterplot are whether the points are compact or spread apart as well as if all the points are generally following the same pattern. Looking at the data from left to right, the points move in an upward direction which indicates a positive correlation. This eliminates the third, fourth, and the fifth choice. The difference between the first and second answer is a strong vs. weak correlation. This depends on how compact the data points are, and in this case, they are not very compact and form a weak correlation.
21.	As x increases by 1, y increases by 10	II	Based on the answer choices, it is important to recognize the scale of the $x-$axis and $y-$axis. The $x-$axis is in increments of 1 while the $y-$axis is in increments of 20. According to the pattern of the plots, for every 1 shift to the right, there is a shift of 10 up. Thus, every x increase of 1 results in a y increase by 10.
22.	There is a negative correlation between a student's time spent on a cell phone and their grade in class.	II	When looking at the scatterplot it is important to recognize the labels on the $x-$ and $y-$axes. In this case the $y-$axis is time spent on cell phone and the $x-$axis is grade in the class. The plots go in a downward pattern from left to right which indicates a negative correlation. The plots are also compact indicating a strong relationship. The only statement that applies is the fourth answer choice. It is important to note that the second answer choice sounds correct, but based on the data points, a straight line is not created. Thus, this statement does not apply to every data point.
23.	$1,500,000	III	The key to this problem is that the information is being represented using a pie chart, which is a circle. Given the central angle measure of 108°, and knowing that a circle is 360°, the full amount of money allocated to housing developments is $\frac{108}{360}$ of the total value. $\$5,000,000 \times \dfrac{108}{360}$ $\$5,000,000 \times 0.3 = \$1,500,000$

October 2019

Number	Answer	Content Category	Explanation
24.	$240	II	Make sure to correctly identify which wedges of the pie chart are for "utilities" and "eating out." Combine both percents and multiply by the total monthly budget. $(0.10 + 0.05) \times \$1,600$ $(0.15)\$1,600 = \$240$
25.	$(2a)(5a)$ $\dfrac{20a^3}{2a}$ $10a(a)$	I	Solve each answer choice accordingly using the proper multiplication and exponent rules $(2a)(5a) = 10a^2$ ✓ $(4a)(6a) = 24a^2$ $4a + 6a = 10a$ $\dfrac{20a^3}{2a} = 10a^2$ ✓ $10a(a) = 10a^2$ ✓ $\dfrac{1}{2}a(20)^2 = \dfrac{1}{2}a(400) = 200a$
26.	16	II	The bars on the graph that count in this scenario are students with $0, 1,$ and 2 pets. Since 4 students have zero pets, 7 students have one pet, and 5 students have 2 pets, the sum will be answer. $4 + 7 + 5 = 16$
27.	1	I	To find the average, take the sum of all values in the set and divide by the number of values in the set. $\dfrac{(-5) + 4 + (-2) + 1 + 0 + 7 + 4 + (-1)}{8} = \dfrac{8}{8} = 1$
28.	20	I	The median in a set of values is the exact middle value of the set. In this case the numbers 12 to 28 are the set. Be careful if you are trying to use a shortcut by subtracting, $28 - 12 = 16$ and determining that there are only 16 numbers in the set, making the 8th number the median – because it is not! It may take extra time, but in order to be safe quickly write the numbers $12 - 28$ out in ascending order. $12, 13, 14, 15, 16, 17, 18, 19, 20, 21, 22, 23, 24, 2\,5, 26, 27, 28$ Notice that there are actually 17 numbers in the set. In order to find the place of the median in an odd numbered set, divide the amount of values by two and round up to the nearest whole number. That number will be the median. $\dfrac{17}{2} = 8.5 \approx 9$ This means that the 9th value in the set is the median which is 20.

Number	Answer	Content Category	Explanation
29.	11	III	When reading a timeline, first determine what the unmarked scales represent. In this case, the timeline increases in increments of 2 for each tick mark. Thus, the draft of the Articles of Confederation occurring in 1777 and the ratification of the Constitution in 1788 is separated by 11 years. Note: Read the events carefully to ensure you are choosing the correct events to solve the problem. Some events may sound similar, so make sure you've chosen the right ones.
30.	192,000	III	Using the chart notice that the values for people ages 41 to 50 are a combination of two age groups. The $41-45$ age group is 9% and the $46-50$ age group is 7%. Add these values and change to a decimal. $9\% + 7\% = 16\% = 0.16$ Next, multiply the decimal by the total population to predict the number of people expected. Note that 1.2 million written out is 1,200,000. $0.16 \times 1,200,000 = 192,000$
31.	6	III	It is important to have a good understanding of probability. Probability is found by taking the number of desired outcomes divided by the entire number of outcomes or $\frac{\text{number of desired outcomes}}{\text{total number of outcomes}}$. In this scenario the total number of gumballs are not given, but the probability of choosing a yellow gumball is. The probability should be set up as $\frac{\text{yellow}}{\text{total}}$. The only way to solve for yellow is to make a proportion using the probability for yellow. $\frac{Y}{10+8+Y} = \frac{1}{4}$ $\frac{Y}{(18+Y)} = \frac{1}{4}$ $4Y = 1(18+Y)$ $4Y = 18 + Y$ $3Y = 18$ $\frac{3Y}{3} = \frac{18}{3}$ $Y = 6$

October 2019

Number	Answer	Content Category	Explanation
32.	112	III	This is a multi-step problem involving probability given as a decimal. Usually probability is written as a fraction or a percentage, so don't let the decimal confuse you. Since 100% includes the total of any sample size, its decimal equivalent is 1. This problem states that 0.64 represents the probability of getting a white card which means that $1 - 0.64$ must equal the probability of getting a blue card. Therefore, $1 - 0.64 = 0.36$ represents the probability of getting a blue card. To find the difference between the two colors, the amount of each color must be found first. White $400 \times .64 = 256$ Blue $400 \times .36 = 144$ White $-$ Blue $= 256 - 144 = 112$
33.	$\dfrac{286}{2,093}$	III	For this problem the desired outcome is the number of part-time female students, which is the upper-right value in the chart. To find he total sample size, add all the numbers in the chart because this represents all the students at the school. $\dfrac{part - time\ female}{all\ students} = \dfrac{286}{2,093}$
34.	56	III	It is important to note that if lines s and t are parallel and are intersected by line u, the angles created by line u are special angle pairs. At the intersection of line t and u, the 124° angle creates a linear pair with the angle to its left. Thus, $180° - 124° = 56°$. The relationship with the newly found 56° angle and angle x is that they are corresponding angles, or equivalent to each other. Thus, $x = 56°$.
35.	8:3:4	III	The key to this problem is noticing that there is a fraction in the original ratio. In order to eliminate the fraction, multiply the value of the denominator to all values in the ratio. $2(4):\dfrac{3}{4}(4):1(4) = 8:3:4$
36.	$40.56	I	Use your calculator to compute the value of each item purchased and add them together for the total. $16 \times \$0.75 = \$12.00$ $28 \times \$0.20 = \$5.60$ $12 \times \$1.25 = \$15.00$ $4 \times \$1.99 = \$7.96$ $\$12.00 + \$5.60 + \$15.00 + \$7.96 = \$40.56$

October 2019

Number	Answer	Content Category	Explanation
37.	40	III	Use your knowledge of supplementary angles, vertical angles, and sum of the angles in a triangle to solve this problem. First, the 145° angle creates a supplementary pair (two angles that add up to 180°) with the angle to its right. Therefore, $180° - 145° = 35°$ for the bottom angle in the triangle. The triangle is a right triangle, denoted by the square, so find the last angle measure by subtracting the two known angles from 180°. $180° - 90° - 35° = 55°$. The new 55° angle makes a vertical pair with the angle $(x + 15)$. To solve for x, set the two angles equal to each other. $x + 15 = 55$ $x = 40$
38.	11	III	The formula for volume of a rectangular prism is $V = l \times w \times h$. Input all the values available and solve for the missing variable, in this case height (h). $1,056 = (12)(8)(h)$ $1,056 = 96h$ $h = 11$
39.	43.96 inches	III	There are two formulas to find the circumference of a circle: $C = \text{Diameter}(\pi)$ or $C = 2(\pi)(\text{radius})$. Since the diameter is given in the problem, use the first formula. A quick look at the answer choices will let you know if you have to use a value for pi (π). In this case because the answer is being rounded to the nearest hundredth, use $\pi = 3.14$. $C = (14)(3.14) = 43.96$

Number	Answer	Content Category	Explanation
40.	60	III	To solve, first convert the 3-gallon jugs to pints. A good rule to remember is anytime a conversion is going from a larger unit to a smaller unit, the amount is always multiplied by the conversion number. If 1 gallon = 4 quarts and the jugs are 3 gallons each, multiply 3 gallons by 4 to get the amount of quarts in 3 gallons. $3 \times 4 = 12$ quarts. The same reasoning applies for converting quarts to pints. Multiply the 12 quarts by 2 because for every 1 quart there are 2 pints. $12 \times 2 = 24$ pints. Therefore, every 3-gallon jug of drinking water is equivalent to 24 pints. The problem states there are 2 ½ jugs, so multiply 24 by 2 ½ to get the total amount of pints. $24 \times 2\frac{1}{2} = 24 \times 2.5 = 60$
41.	4.82	III	The easiest way to solve a scale problem is to create a proportion. Since this problem is talking about the distance on a map in relation to actual distance, the key to the proportion is setting up the ratio as follows: $\frac{\text{map distance}}{\text{actual distance}}$. Using the units given, setup the proportion to solve. $\frac{2 \text{ cm}}{5 \text{ km}} = \frac{x}{12 \text{ km } 50 \text{ m}}$ Make sure to realize that the denominators are not in the same units and must be converted. Convert km values to meters by multiplying by 1000, rewrite the proportion, and solve. $\frac{2 \text{ cm}}{5,000 \text{ m}} = \frac{x}{12,050 \text{ m}}$ $5,000x = (2)(12,050)$ $5,000x = 24,100$ $\frac{5,000x}{5,000} = \frac{24,100}{5,000}$ $x = 4.82$ Alternatively, you could convert 12 km 50 meters to kilometers. 12 km 50 m = 12.05 km. Then the proportion would be, $\frac{2 \text{ cm}}{5 \text{ km}} = \frac{x \text{ cm}}{12.05 \text{ km}}$ Use the conversion you feel most comfortable with.
42.		III	The only figure with one pair of parallel sides the trapezoid. The parallelogram, rectangle, and rhombus (first three choices) all have two pair of parallel sides. The kite (last choice) has no sides that are parallel.

Number	Answer	Content Category	Explanation
43.	1,359	III	To solve this problem setup a proportion using the following ratio: $\frac{\text{Fiction}}{\text{Autobiographies}}$. Using the numbers given in the problem, set up the proportion according to the ratio above. $\frac{18}{3} = \frac{8{,}154}{x}$ $18x = (3)(8{,}154)$ $18x = 24{,}462$ $\frac{18x}{18} = \frac{24{,}462}{18}$ $x = 1{,}359$
44.	337	I	Use the directions to set up an equation in order to solve for x. x $x + 5$ $(x + 5)(2)$ $(x + 5)(2) - 4$ $\frac{(x + 5)(2) - 4}{10} = 68$ Once the equation is set up correctly, solve for x. Start by eliminating the 10 in the denominator by multiplying both sides by 10. $10\left(\frac{(x + 5)(2) - 4}{10}\right) = (10)(68)$ $(x + 5)(2) - 4 = 680$ $2x + 10 - 4 = 680$ $2x + 6 = 680$ $2x = 674$ $\frac{2x}{2} = \frac{674}{2}$ $x = 337$ Alternatively, you could work backwards using inverse operations for each step.

Number	Answer	Content Category	Explanation
45.	$\dfrac{-2x + 32}{9}$	III	In this problem it is important to know that y in terms of x means that the equation needs to be solved for y, or be in the form $y =$. $2x + 9y = 32$ $9y = -2x + 32$ $\dfrac{9y}{9} = \dfrac{-2x + 32}{9}$ $y = \dfrac{-2x + 32}{9}$
46.	$\dfrac{19}{8}$	I	Make sure to understand the graph before beginning to solve this problem. The x axis is time in seconds and the $y-$axis is speed. Next, find the values for blue and red at 6 seconds. According to the graph, blue is 38 and red is 16. The problem is asking for a ratio so substitute the values in the order stated in the question. $$\text{Blue: Red} = \frac{38}{16} = \frac{19}{8}$$ (It is not necessary to reduce for fill in the blank types of questions. Either answer is correct.)
47.	$\dfrac{10}{7}$	III	In the numerators, there are two different variables being used, each with a unique value. In the denominator there are two different values for the same variable. The easy answer would be to choose $\frac{5}{7}$ because that is how the variables match up with the values, but that is incorrect. The key to the answer is finding the common denominator for x. In this case 12 is the common denominator which means 2 must be multiplied to both the 5 and the 6 in $\frac{5}{6}$. $\dfrac{5 \times 2}{6 \times 2} = \dfrac{10}{12}$ Once the denominators are the same, the corresponding variables in the numerators are now equivalent to each other. $\dfrac{w}{x} = \dfrac{10}{12}$ and $\dfrac{y}{x} = \dfrac{7}{12}$ $\dfrac{w}{y} = \dfrac{10}{7}$

October 2019

Number	Answer	Content Category	Explanation
48.	104	III	In order to find how many tables are needed for the banquet, divide the numbers of attendees by the number of people per table. $$\frac{1,240}{12} = 103.33$$ This means that 1,240 people with 12 people per table will completely fill 103.33 tables. Because tables are whole objects and cannot be broken into fractional parts, the answer needs to be a whole number. Do not make the mistake of rounding the 0.33 down to 103 because 103 tables are not enough tables to seat all people. Whenever dealing with whole objects, such as people or tables, always round based on what is needed in the question. Therefore $103.33 \approx 104$ tables.
49.	$2^7 \times 3^1 \times 5^3$	I	It is tempting to multiply all three numbers together and factor the total, 48,000. An easier method is to factor out each of the three factors given and combine them to find the answer. $25 \rightarrow 5 \cdot 5$ $40 \rightarrow 2 \cdot 20 \rightarrow 2 \cdot 2 \cdot 10 \rightarrow 2 \cdot 2 \cdot 2 \cdot 5$ $48 \rightarrow 2 \cdot 24 \rightarrow 2 \cdot 2 \cdot 12 \rightarrow 2 \cdot 2 \cdot 2 \cdot 6 \rightarrow 2 \cdot 2 \cdot 2 \cdot 2 \cdot 3$ Next, combine all the prime factors for the final answer. $2 \cdot 2 \cdot 2 \cdot 2 \cdot 2 \cdot 2 \cdot 2 \cdot 3 \cdot 5 \cdot 5 \cdot 5$ $2^7 \times 3^1 \times 5^3$
50.	The maximum number of people that can fit on the trolley at one time	I	Because the question states that additional information is needed to solve the problem, focus on how you would write an equation to solve this problem. If Jenna is the 300th person for the day, it is important to know the maximum number of people the trolley can hold during each trip. Therefore, the maximum number of people the trolley can hold is the missing information for this problem.

Number	Answer	Content Category	Explanation
51.	171	II	With the information given in the problem, fill out the remaining portions of the Venn diagram. To find out how many people ate only chicken and only steak, take the values given and subtract 268. Chicken only $\rightarrow 322 - 268 = 54$ Steak only $\rightarrow 275 - 268 = 7$ Next add all the values to find how many total people ate chicken, steak, or chicken and steak. $268 + 54 + 7 = 329$ Finally, subtract that value from 500, and the result is the number of respondents that did not eat chicken or steak. $500 - 329 = 171$
52.	182	III	To find the missing angles use your knowledge of angle pairs and properties of parallel lines to solve. Since the shape of the figure is a rectangle, the top and bottom lines are parallel to each other. The bottom line is cut into three angles: 44°, a right angle, and a missing angle. To find the value of the missing angle, set all three angles equal to 180° because they all lie on a straight line, or form a straight angle. $180° - 44° - 90° = 46°$ Using the 46° angle first, extend the top line of the rectangle to the left and the right and notice that angle b is the alternate interior angle to 46°. Therefore, angle $b = 46°$. Next, with the lines extended on the upper left side of the rectangle, notice that the 44° angle is supplementary to angle a. $180° - 44 = 136$ Therefore, angle $a = 136°$, and angle $b = 46°$. Last, take the sum of both values to solve the problem $a + b$. $136 + 44 = 182$
53.	c	I	This problem is testing your knowledge of number sense and what happens to a number greater than 1 when it is multiplied by a decimal less than 1. Eliminate all answer choices greater than 0 because the result of multiplying a negative by a positive is negative. The easiest way to solve this problem if the answer is not intuitive is to pick "middle of the road" values for A and B. Let's say $A = -2.5$ and $B = 0.5$. Then, $A \cdot B = -1.25$. Looking at the number line, the only option that aligns with this answer choice, is point c.

Number	Answer	Content Category	Explanation
54.	See answer explanation for solution	II	ANSWER: The first graph choice is the correct answer. Using the information in the problem, figure out how many months it will take to pay off the refrigerator. $800 \div 50 = 16 \text{ months}$ Next, notice that the $x-$axis represents months and the $y-$axis represents amount of money left to pay off. To correctly graph this information, the line must start on the $y-$axis at 800 and end on the $x-$axis at 16. The only graph that matches these requirements is the first choice. In the event that more than one graph had the same information, then the slope of the line would have to go down 50 for every 1 unit to the right.
55.	1.2	III	To solve this problem, use the information given to set up a proportion using the ratio $\frac{\text{height}}{\text{width}}$. $\dfrac{1.5}{3.6} = \dfrac{0.5}{x}$ $1.5x = (3.6)(0.5)$ $1.5x = 1.8$ $\dfrac{1.5x}{1.5} = \dfrac{1.8}{1.5}$ $x = 1.2$

Number	Answer	Content Category	Explanation
56.	82	III	First, we need to find the amount of string Estrella used. The problem states that Minerva used 64% of the amount Estrella used, so the problem we are solving is, "64% of what number is 32?" 64% of $(x) = 32$ $0.64x = 32$ $\dfrac{0.64x}{0.64} = \dfrac{36}{0.64}$ $x = 50$ Now that we know Estrella used 50 feet of string, to find the amount both girls used, add 50 and 32. $50 + 32 = 82$ feet

1. The following chart represents flowers in a garden.

	Red	White
Roses	4	8
Tulips	7	9

What is the probability that a flower picked at random is white, a rose, or a red rose?

- ○ $\frac{1}{7}$
- ○ $\frac{3}{4}$
- ○ $\frac{3}{7}$
- ○ $\frac{13}{28}$
- ○ $\frac{33}{28}$

2. How many non-congruent triangles can you make with the following segments?

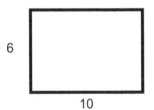 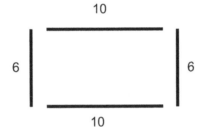

- ○ 0
- ○ 1
- ○ 2
- ○ 3
- ○ 4

3. The yearly spending budget for a family of four is shown in the pie chart below. If their total spending budget is $85,000 per year, how much money was spent on Entertainment?

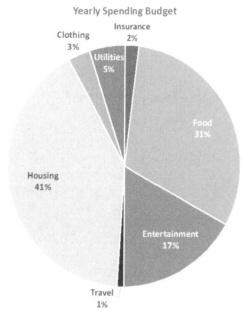

Yearly Spending Budget

Insurance 2%
Clothing 3%
Utilities 5%
Food 31%
Housing 41%
Entertainment 17%
Travel 1%

- ○ $1,445
- ○ $14,450
- ○ $17,000
- ○ $26,350
- ○ $31,300

4. A newlywed couple purchased their first house for $175,000. Six years later, the house was sold for $236,250. What was the percent increase in the sale price of the home?

- ○ 20%
- ○ 26%
- ○ 35%
- ○ 42%
- ○ 74%

5. How many solutions does the equation have?

$3(x + 4) + 2x = x + 12 + 4x$

- ○ None
- ○ One
- ○ Two
- ○ Three
- ○ Infinitely many

6. A researcher studying large-mouth bass catches, tags, and releases 200 bass from a local lake. Two weeks later the researcher catches 100 bass from the same lake and 20 have tags on them. What is the closest approximation of the total number of bass in the lake?

   - ○ 200
   - ○ 400
   - ○ 600
   - ○ 1,000
   - ○ 1,200

7. Rank the following numbers from least to greatest.

   $$\frac{1}{10}, -1, -\frac{1}{3}, \frac{1}{5}$$

   - ○ $-\frac{1}{3}, -1, \frac{1}{10}, \frac{1}{5}$
   - ○ $-1, -\frac{1}{3}, \frac{1}{5}, \frac{1}{10}$
   - ○ $\frac{1}{10}, -1, -\frac{1}{3}, \frac{1}{5}$
   - ○ $-\frac{1}{3}, -1, \frac{1}{5}, \frac{1}{10}$
   - ○ $-1, -\frac{1}{3}, \frac{1}{10}, \frac{1}{5}$

8. Solve for x:
   $$\frac{x}{5} = \frac{2x - 1}{9}$$

   - ○ $x = 5$
   - ○ $x = 1$
   - ○ $x = -1$
   - ○ $x = -5$
   - ○ $x = \frac{5}{19}$

9. The Venn diagram below represents three different sessions at an education conference. The attendance for sessions 1 and 2 totaled 235 teachers, with 40 teachers attending both sessions. In addition, 165 teachers only attended session 3. What is the total number of teachers in attendance at the educational conference?

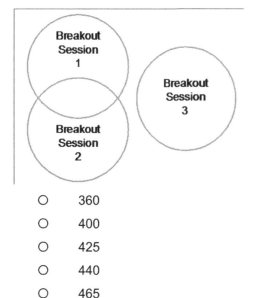

- ○ 360
- ○ 400
- ○ 425
- ○ 440
- ○ 465

10. In a school play, male and female members are represented by the variables m and f respectively. If half the males and $\frac{1}{3}$ of the females are sophomores, what does the expression $\frac{3m+2f}{6(m+f)}$ represent?

- ○ Number of sophomores in the play
- ○ Fraction of sophomores in the play
- ○ Number of students in the play
- ○ Fraction of males to females in the play
- ○ Number of students who are not sophomores in the play

11. The chart below represents the average rainfall for a town. Which two-month period has the highest average increase in rainfall?

RAINFALL

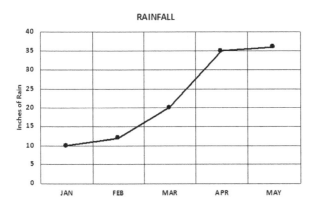

- ○ March-May
- ○ January-March
- ○ February-April
- ○ January-April
- ○ February-May

12. Find the median of the following hourly wages. Write your answer in the box.

$11.85	$7.50	$8.65	$12.14
$7.85	$9.75	$10.34	

13. A student solves the following problem step-by-step. In which step did the student make the mistake?

$$4(x - 1) + 3x = 14 - x$$

Step 1: $4x - 4 + 3x = 14 - x$

Step 2: $7x - 4 = 14 - x$

Step 3: $6x - 4 = 14$

Step 4: $6x = 18$

Step 5: $x = 3$

- ○ Step 1
- ○ Step 2
- ○ Step 3
- ○ Step 4
- ○ Step 5

14. In an inventory report for a school supply manufacturer, crayons make up 5 million units. When shown on a pie chart, the central angle measure for crayons is 60°. What is the total amount of inventory the company has?

   ○   830,000

   ○   1,500,000

   ○   3,000,000

   ○   8,000,000

   ○   30,000,000

15. A recipe for a cake calls for 18 cups of flour to be split between a small bowl and a large bowl in a ratio of 1:3. Using the ratio, how much flour should be in the large bowl?

   ○   3 cups

   ○ $4\frac{1}{2}$ cups

   ○   6 cups

   ○ $13\frac{1}{2}$ cups

   ○   17 cups

16. Given the number below, which of the following operations would result in the 9 being in the hundredths place?

   23,897.04

   ○   Multiply by 100

   ○   Multiply by 0.001

   ○   Divide by 100

   ○   Divide by 10

   ○   Multiply by $\frac{1}{100}$

17. Which of the following could result in a number between 0 and 1? Choose all that apply.

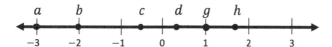

   ❑ $a + b$

   ❑ $\frac{c}{b}$

   ❑ $c + h$

   ❑ $a \times g$

   ❑ $d \times g$

18. A teacher purchases supplies for her classroom. She bought 75 pens at $0.25 each, 46 markers at $0.50 each, 22 erasers at $0.15 each, and 3 three-ring binders at $6.00 each. How much did all the school supplies cost?

    ○ $63.05

    ○ $65.15

    ○ $67.45

    ○ $68.00

    ○ $69.30

19. The mean of 5 test scores is 60. Which of the following scenarios will increase the range of all five scores?

    ○   Add 10 points to the highest test score

    ○   Add 10 points to the highest and lowest test score

    ○   Subtract 10 points from the highest score

    ○   Subtract 10 points from the highest and lowest score

    ○   Add 10 to the lowest and subtract 10 from the highest

20. A family's Labrador retriever grows at the following rate:

Month	Weight (lbs.)
1	7
2	11
3	15

If the pattern continues, how much will the dog weigh at month 6?

    ○   19 lbs.

    ○   22 lbs.

    ○   26 lbs.

    ○   27 lbs.

    ○   31 lbs.

21. Which inequality is represented by the number line?

    ○ $x < 1$

    ○ $x \leq 1$

    ○ $x > 1$

    ○ $x \geq 1$

    ○ $x = 1$

22. Which of the following can be concluded from the scatterplot?

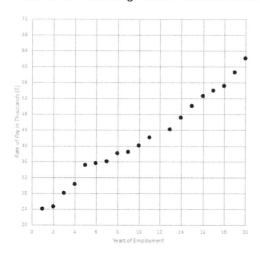

Years of Employment

○ There is a strong negative correlation between rate of pay and years of employment.

○ There is a strong negative correlation between rate of pay and years of employment.

○ There is a weak positive correlation between rate of pay and years of employment.

○ There is a strong positive correlation between rate of pay and years of employment.

○ There is no correlation between rate of pay and years of employment.

23. A random number generator creates 2-digit integers and is set to produce odd numbers 0.4 of the time. The first four numbers created are 12, 59, 73, and 44. What is the percentage that the fifth number will be an even number?

○ 0

○ 0.2

○ 0.4

○ 0.8

○ 1

24. A rectangular prism has base dimensions of 7 inches and 3 inches. If the volume of the prism is 420 in^3, what is the height of the prism?

○ 14 in.

○ 20 in.

○ 21 in.

○ 28 in.

○ 42 in.

25. If $\frac{x}{8} = 0$ and $\frac{5}{y} = 5$, what is the value of $x + y$?

○ -1

○ 0

○ 1

○ 4

○ 7

26. The chart below represents a town divided into square mile blocks. The number inside indicates the number of drug stores within the square mile. What is the average number of drug stores per square mile in the town?

0	1	2
8	4	5
1	0	1
5	6	3

- ○ 3
- ○ 12
- ○ 16
- ○ 36
- ○ 42

27. A jar contains colored gumballs. There are 12 red gumballs, 5 white gumballs, and some blue gumballs. How many of the gumballs are blue if the probability of picking a white gumball out of the jar is $\frac{1}{6}$?

- ○ 4
- ○ 13
- ○ 14
- ○ 24
- ○ 30

28. The area of a house floorplan can best be defined in which of the following units?

- ○ square centimeters
- ○ square inches
- ○ square yards
- ○ square feet
- ○ square kilometers

29. Find the value of x.

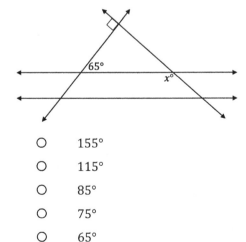

- ○ 155°
- ○ 115°
- ○ 85°
- ○ 75°
- ○ 65°

30. Which of the following is the correct action to take in order to convert 26 miles per hour to feet per minute?

  ○   Multiply 26 by 5,280

  ○   Divide 26 by 60

  ○   Multiply 26 by 88

  ○   Divide 26 by 88

  ○   Multiply 26 by 176

31. The area of a circle is 16π. What is the circumference of the circle?

  ○ 4π

  ○ 8π

  ○ 16π

  ○ 32π

  ○ 64π

32. A recent study found that a student's grades in high school has a strong positive correlation to their grades as a freshman in college. Which of the following statements can be deducted from the study? Check all that apply.

  ❑   Students with good grades in high school tend to have good grades as freshman in college.

  ❑   Students with good grades in high school will cause students to have good grades as a freshman in college.

  ❑   Students with bad grades in high school tend to have bad grades as freshman in college.

  ❑   Students with bad grades in high school will cause students to have bad grades as freshman in college.

  ❑   Students with good grades in high school will tend to have bad grades as freshman in college.

33. Find the value of x.

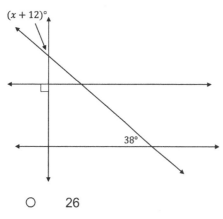

  ○   26

  ○   38

  ○   40

  ○   90

  ○   116

34. In a sequence of numbers, the pattern from one number to the next is defined as three less than five times a number. If the fifth term is 187, what is the value of the fourth term?

- ○ 37
- ○ 38
- ○ 39
- ○ 42
- ○ 45

35. Each child dressed in a costume at a Halloween party received 2 bags of candy. In each bag there were 3 lollipops, 5 chocolates, and 7 pieces of gum. Which of the following expressions shows the total amount of candy per child? Check all that apply.

- ❑ $3 + 3 + 5 + 5 + 7 + 7$
- ❑ $2 + 3 \times 2 + 5 \times 2 + 7$
- ❑ $2 + (3 + 5 + 7)$
- ❑ $2(3 + 5 + 7)$
- ❑ $3 \times 2 + 5 \times 2 + 7 \times 2$

36. How many years from incorporation did it take the company to reach $2,000,000 in sales?

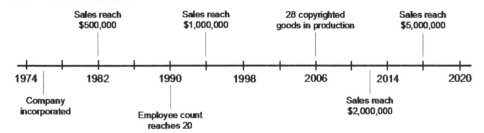

- ○ 24
- ○ 28
- ○ 30
- ○ 34
- ○ 36

37. Due to expansion in the neighborhood, High Street is being added to accommodate new construction. If High Street is parallel to Low Street, what are the angle measures of x and y?

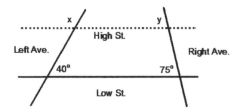

- ○ $x = 140°, y = 105°$
- ○ $x = 140°, y = 75°$
- ○ $x = 40°, y = 75°$
- ○ $x = 40°, y = 105°$
- ○ $x = 50°, y = 15°$

October 2019

38. Select all the quadrilaterals that have at least one pair of opposite sides parallel.

☐ Square

☐ Rectangle

☐ Rhombus

☐ Parallelogram

☐ Trapezoid

☐ Kite

39. The chart below shows sales for an electronics company for the first part of the year. What is the total number of sales from January to May?

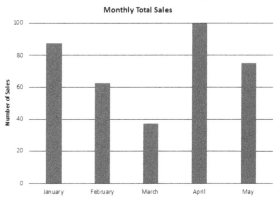

O 290

O 315

O 320

O 360

O 445

40. Based on the scatterplot, what is the trend in the data points?

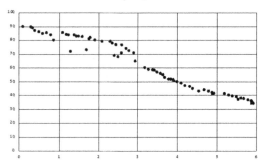

O Negative linear correlation

O Positive linear correlation

O Neutral linear correlation

O Inverse correlation

O No correlation

41. The pictograph shows the number of cars parked on each floor of a parking garage. Each symbol represents the same number of cars. If the 1st and 5th floor have a combined total of 72 parked cars, how many cars are parked on the 2nd floor?

| 1st floor |
| 2nd floor |
| 3rd floor |
| 4th floor |
| 5th floor |

- ○ 4
- ○ 8
- ○ 32
- ○ 40
- ○ 48

42. Given the following information, what is the equation of the line?

x	1	2	3	4	5
y	4	7	10	13	16

- ○ $y = x + 3$
- ○ $y = 3x + 1$
- ○ $y = 3x$
- ○ $y = 3x + 3$
- ○ $y = 4x + 1$

43. During a promotion at a craft store, every third person who walks through the door gets a 20% off coupon, every fourth person gets a 25% off coupon, and every tenth person gets a 50% off coupon. This pattern continues for the first 150 people. How many people received a 25% off coupon?

- ○ 36
- ○ 37
- ○ 38
- ○ 40
- ○ 50

44. Select all of the options that are solutions to the equation.

$(x + 2)^2 = 16$

- ❑ 4
- ❑ −2
- ❑ 2
- ❑ 6
- ❑ −6

45. What percent of 190 is 57?

     ○   0.30%

     ○   33%

     ○   3%

     ○   30%

     ○   0.33%

46. Jocelyn and Ella both left their houses to go shopping. Jocelyn drove 18 miles to the store, which was 60% of the distance that Ella had to drive. How many more miles did Ella have to drive to get to the store?

     ○   12

     ○   18

     ○   22

     ○   28

     ○   30

47. An odometer on an old truck reads 194,682. What is the value of the 9 in this number?

     ○   9 tens

     ○   9 hundred

     ○   9 thousand

     ○   9 ten thousand

     ○   9 hundred thousand

48. A $6,500 donation was made to a local recreation center. With the funds the center was able to purchase two basketball goals for $450 each, a resurfacing of the gym floor for $3,000, a new volleyball net for $1,500, and sporting goods for $775. If floor mats cost $25 each, how many mats will the recreation center be able to purchase with the remaining funds?

     ○   4

     ○   11

     ○   13

     ○   18

     ○   25

49. The product of 6 and a number is decreased by the quantity of 3 plus the same number can be written algebraically as which of the answer choices?

     ○ $6n - 3 + n$

     ○ $6 + n - (3 + n)$

     ○ $(3 + n) - 6n$

     ○ $(6n - 3) + n$

     ○ $6n - (3 + n)$

50. Three children received an inheritance in the ratio of 3:5:6. If the smallest share was $150,000, what was the total amount of the inheritance?

    ○ $150,000

    ○ $250,000

    ○ $300,000

    ○ $500,000

    ○ $700,000

51. A line passes through the points $(-4, 4)$ and $(2, -3)$. What is the slope of the line?

    ○ $m = \frac{6}{7}$

    ○ $m = -\frac{7}{6}$

    ○ $m = -\frac{2}{7}$

    ○ $m = \frac{7}{6}$

    ○ $m = -\frac{2}{1}$

52. The three angles in a triangle are named $a, b,$ and c. What is the measure of angle a if $b + c = 85°$?

    ○   5°

    ○   30°

    ○   85°

    ○   95°

    ○   100°

53. The base of a rectangular prism measures 2 inches by 3 inches, and it has a height of 6 inches. What is the volume of the prism?

    ○   36 cubic inches

    ○   30 cubic inches

    ○   40 cubic inches

    ○   28 cubic inches

    ○   45 cubic inches

54. What is the probability of rolling a pair of regular six-sided dice and having the numbers facing up total 7?

    ○ $\frac{7}{36}$

    ○ $\frac{1}{6}$

    ○ $\frac{1}{7}$

    ○ $\frac{7}{12}$

    ○ $\frac{7}{18}$

55. A bowl of candy contains 7 mints, 5 pieces of gum, and 10 caramels. What is the probability of picking a caramel, not putting it back, and then picking a mint?

- ○ $\frac{17}{462}$
- ○ $\frac{17}{22}$
- ○ $\frac{5}{33}$
- ○ $\frac{70}{484}$
- ○ $\frac{35}{242}$

56. A local ice cream cart offers vanilla, chocolate, strawberry, and coffee ice cream flavors. Along with the ice cream, the toppings they offer are whipped cream, hot fudge, caramel, sprinkles, nuts, and fruit. If ice cream comes in a waffle cone, regular cone, or cup, and customers are only allowed one ice cream flavor and one topping, how many different ice cream order combinations are available?

- ○ 13
- ○ 24
- ○ 30
- ○ 48
- ○ 72

Number	Answer	Content Category	Explanation
1.	$\dfrac{3}{4}$	II	This problem deals with the probability of picking any one of three specified objects. With probability, put the total number of possible outcomes on the bottom of the fraction. The total number of outcomes is 28 because all the values in the table add to 28. $$(4 + 8 + 7 + 9 = 28)$$ $$\overline{}\over 28$$ In this case you can pick the rose, which is 12 possibilities, all of the white, which is 17 possibilities, and a red rose, which is 4 possibilities. Due to the fact that some of these picks overlap, it must be taken into consideration that values will repeat. For example, all roses and all white overlap with the number 8; therefore, 8 must only be factored in once. For all picks, use the numbers $4 + 8 + 9 = 21$. The probability of a rose, white flower, or a red rose is $\dfrac{21}{28} = \dfrac{3}{4}$. <table><tr><td></td><td>Red</td><td>White</td></tr><tr><td>Roses</td><td>4</td><td>8</td></tr><tr><td>Tulips</td><td>7</td><td>9</td></tr></table>
2.	2	III	Congruent means the sides, or angles are the same. Therefore, non-congruent means they are not the same. With four sides of the rectangle, there is a possibility of making four triangles. However, there are only 2 unique triangles out of the four. See below for the 4 different triangles that can be made. $\Delta\,6 - 10 - 6$ $\Delta\,10 - 6 - 10$ $\Delta\,6 - 10 - 6$ $\Delta\,10 - 6 - 10$ The stipulation given is that they must be **non-congruent** or not the same. Therefore, there are *only 2 non-congruent triangles*. $\Delta\,6 - 10 - 6$ $\Delta\,10 - 6 - 10$
3.	$14,450	I	To find the percent of a number use multiplication. In this case, the entire spending is $85,000. We are looking for the amount spent on entertainment, which is 17%. To find 17% of $85,000, multiply 17% or 0.17 by 85,000. $0.17 \times 85,000 = 14,450$

Number	Answer	Content Category	Explanation
4.	35%	I	To find percent increase use the formula: $$\frac{\text{original-new}}{\text{original}} = \% \text{ increase}$$ If the answer is negative, this is denoted by using the phrase, a percent decrease, instead of a negative sign. $$\frac{175,000-236,250}{175,000} = \frac{-61,250}{175,000} = \frac{-61,250}{175,000} = 0.35 = 35\% \text{ decrease}$$
5.	Infinitely many solutions	III	Linear equations can only have none, one, or infinitely many solutions. Therefore, the answer choices two and three can be eliminated. To solve the equation to determine the number of solutions, distribute the 3, then combine like terms on each side of the equation. $3(x + 4) + 2x = x + 12 + 4x$ $3x + 12 + 2x = x + 12 + 4x$ $5x + 12 = 5x + 12$ If the expression on the left is the exact same as the expression on the right, any value substituted for x will make the equation true, so no need to solve any further; there are infinitely many solutions.
6.	1,000	I	To solve, use a proportion. Make sure the top and bottom units for each fraction match. $$\frac{\text{tagged (1st sample)}}{\text{total (1st sample)}} = \frac{\text{tagged (2nd sample)}}{\text{total (2nd sample)}}$$ Notice, the proportion matches; **tagged over total = tagged over total**. Therefore: $$\frac{200}{x} = \frac{20}{100}$$ $$20x = 20,000$$ $$\frac{20x}{20} = \frac{20,000}{20}$$ $$x = 1,000$$

Number	Answer	Content Category	Explanation
7.	$-1, -\frac{1}{3}, \frac{1}{10}, \frac{1}{5}$	I	Ranking the numbers from least to greatest means to put them in order from the smallest to the largest. To make this easier, convert the fractions to decimals. $\frac{1}{10} = 0.1$ $-1 = -1$ $-\frac{1}{3} = -0.333$ $\frac{1}{5} = 0.2$ Finally, rank them accordingly. $-1, -\frac{1}{3}, \frac{1}{10}, \frac{1}{5}$ Use your answer choices. You can see that -1 is definitely going to be the lowest number, right away you can eliminate the first, third, and fourth answer choices. Then $\frac{1}{10}$ is less than $\frac{1}{5}$. Save time by being strategic.
8.	$x = 5$	III	To solve a proportion, cross-multiply and use algebra to solve for x. $\frac{x}{5} = \frac{2x - 1}{9}$ $5(2x - 1) = 9(x)$ distribute the 5 $10x - 5 = 9x$ subtract 10x from both sides $-5 = -1x$ $\frac{-5}{-1} = \frac{-1x}{-1}$ divide by -1 $5 = x$ Another method to use if the above method escapes you at test time is guess and check. To do this, substitute each answer in for x. The one that proves the equation true is the correct answer. The following example uses the first answer choice. $\frac{(5)}{5} = \frac{2(5) - 1}{9}$ $\frac{5}{5} = \frac{10 - 1}{9}$ $\frac{5}{5} = \frac{9}{9}$ $1 = 1$

Number	Answer	Content Category	Explanation
9.	360	II	In order to find the number of teachers who attended the education conference, you must identify how many attended sessions 1 and 2, not including the overlap.
			The key is to understand what to do with the number of teachers who attended both sessions of the conference (40). We cannot figure out how many teachers went to the individual sessions because there is not enough information.
			By subtracting the 40 teachers who attended both sessions from the 235 that attended gives you the total amount of teachers who attended sessions 1 and 2. The 40 represents the overlap in the diagram of teachers who attended both sessions. Since they would have been counted twice, one in each session, we must subtract 40 to correctly identify the total number of teachers.
			Number of teachers in sessions 1 and 2: $235 - 40 = 195$
			Add session 3, which 165 teachers attended, for the total number of teachers: $195 + 165 = 360$.
10.	Fraction of Sophomores in the play	III	The best method to use on this problem is guess and check. Based on the information given, it is important to choose numbers that are easy to work with. Since male sophomores represent $\frac{1}{2}$, pick a number that is divisible by 2. Female sophomores represent $\frac{1}{3}$ so pick a number that is divisible by 3.
			Since time is critical during the exam, choose numbers which are easily computed. For this problem let $m = 2$ and $f = 3$. Remember, use the smallest possible numbers you can because they are easiest to work with.
			When substituting the new values in the expression:
			$$\frac{3(2) + 2(3)}{6(2 + 3)} = \frac{6 + 6}{6(5)} = \frac{12}{30} = \frac{2}{5}$$
			It is important to understand what $\frac{2}{5}$ represents. Using 2 for males and 3 for females gives you a total of 5 students in the play. Since half of the males are sophomores, then $\frac{1}{2}$ of 2 is one. There is a total of one male sophomore. Since a third of the females are sophomores, then $\frac{1}{3}$ of 3 is one. This gives a total of 2 sophomores out of a combined 5 students which yields the fraction $\frac{2}{5}$. This expression represents the fraction of sophomores that are in the play.

October 2019

Number	Answer	Content Category	Explanation
11.	February – April	II	Do not overthink this question. Just because it uses the term *average*, doesn't mean you have to find an average. First, eliminate the last two choices because they are not a 2-month span. Next, figure out the change in rainfall for the remaining 2-month periods: March – May: $20 \rightarrow 36 = 16$ January – March: $10 \rightarrow 20 = 10$ February – April: $12 \rightarrow 32 = 20$ Therefore, the highest average increase occurred between February and April.
12.	$9.75	II	To find the median, put the values in order from least to greatest. The median is the number in the exact middle. $7.50, $7.85, $8.65, **$9.75**, $10.34, $11.85, $12.14
13.	Step 3	III	The mistake occurs in the third step of the problem. The student incorrectly subtracts the x from the right side of the equation to the left. The correct operation would have been to add the x, which causes the error.
14.	30,000,000	I	To solve this problem correctly, it is important to have an understanding of central angle measures in circles. For this problem, 60° represents only crayons. Since there is 360° in every circle, the 5,000,000 units of crayons represents $\frac{60°}{360°}$ of the pie chart. If you multiply the total units of inventory by $\frac{60°}{360°}$, it should yield 5,000,000. The following equation shows the solution: $$\frac{60°}{360°}(x) = 5,000,000$$ $$\frac{1}{6}(x) = 5,000,000$$ $$x = 5,000,000 \left(\frac{6}{1}\right)$$ $$x = 30,000,000$$

Number	Answer	Content Category	Explanation
15.	$13\frac{1}{2}$ cups	I	To solve this problem, set up a proportion. $\dfrac{\text{large bowl}}{\text{total flour}}$ Note: Remember the total flour combines the ratio 1 and 3 to make 4. $\dfrac{3}{4} = \dfrac{x}{18}$ $4(x) = 3(18)$ $4x = 54$ $\dfrac{4x}{4} = \dfrac{54}{4}$ $x = 13\frac{1}{2}$
16.	Multiply by 0.001	I	The hundredths place is two place values to the right of the decimal. In order for the 9 to be in the hundredths place, the decimal point would need to move 3 places to the left. This would happen if the number 23,897.04 were multiplied by 0.001.
17.	$\dfrac{c}{b}$ $d \times g$	I	For each of the answer choices, it is easiest to estimate the value of the point and substitute the estimated values in for the variables. $a = -3$ $b = -2$ $c = -0.5$ $d = 0.4$ $g = 1$ $h = 1.6$ $a + b = -3 + (-2) = -5$ $\dfrac{c}{b} = \dfrac{-0.5}{-2} = 0.25$ $c + h = -0.5 + 1.6 = 1.1$ $a \times g = -3(1) = -3$ $d \times g = 0.4(1) = 0.4$ The answer choices that fall between 0 and 1 are $\dfrac{c}{b}$ and $d \times g$.

Number	Answer	Content Category	Explanation
18.	$63.05	I	Make sure to calculate all the values correctly. $75(0.25) + 46(0.50) + 22(0.15) + 3(6)$ $18.75 + 23 + 3.30 + 18 = 63.05$
19.	Add 10 points to the highest test score	II	Range is the difference between the highest and lowest numbers. To help visualize the answer choices, substitute values in for the test scores. Let's use 50 and 70, this would make the range 20. Here are the scenarios: A. $70 + 10 = 80$, $80 - 50 = 30$, 30 is greater than 20; increase B. $50 + 10 = 60$, $70 + 10 = 80$, $80 - 60 = 20$; no change C. $70 - 10 = 60$, $60 - 50 = 10$, 10 is less than 20; decrease D. $50 - 10 = 40$, $70 - 10 = 60$, $60 - 40 = 20$; no change E. $50 + 10 = 60$, $70 - 10 = 60$, $60 - 60 = 0$, 0 is less than 20; decrease
20.	27 lbs.	III	Given the information in the chart, the constant rate of change in weight is 4lbs. To get to the sixth month, add 4 to 15 three times. $15 + 4 + 4 + 4 = 27$
21.	$x \leq 1$	III	Because the point is solid, or filled in, the symbol will include the "or equal to" line under the inequality. Because the arrow points towards numbers that are less than 1, the correct symbol is the less than or equal to symbol, $\leq$. All answer choices contain 1, so the symbol is all that needs to be determined.
22.	Strong positive correlation	II	Because the data is increasing from left to right and is very close to a line, there is a strong positive correlation between the data. Strong because the data points are close to forming a line, and positive because the data is increasing from left to right.
23.	1	II	Be careful on how you interpret this problem. It is important to know what 0.4 means (0.4 is the same as 40%). Therefore, this number generator will produce odd numbers 40% of the time. Since you know what four out of the five numbers are, you can determine what the fifth will be. 40% of five numbers is 2, which means two of the five numbers generated will be odd numbers. 59 and 73 have been created, and are odd, so the remaining three numbers have to be even. Since the fifth number has to be even, there is a 100% chance or 1 that this number is even.

Number	Answer	Content Category	Explanation
24.	20 in.	III	A rectangular prism is a three-dimensional shape with a rectangle as its base. The formula for volume is $v = l \times w \times h$. Substitute all the values and solve for the missing variable, height. $420 = (7)(3)(h)$ $420 = 21h$ $\dfrac{420}{21} = \dfrac{21h}{21}$ $20 = h$
25.	1	III	In order to solve this problem correctly you must first solve for x and y and then add them together. $\dfrac{x}{8} = 0$ $8\left(\dfrac{x}{8}\right) = (8)(0)$ $x = 0$ $\dfrac{5}{y} = 5$ $y\left(\dfrac{5}{y}\right) = (5)(y)$ $5 = 5y$ $\dfrac{5}{5} = \dfrac{5y}{5}$ $y = 1$ $0 + 1 = 1$
26.	3	II	To calculate the number of drug stores per square mile, find the sum of all stores and divide by the total number of square miles. $0 + 1 + 2 + 8 + 4 + 5 + 1 + 0 + 1 + 5 + 6 + 3 = 36$ $\dfrac{36}{12} = 3$

Number	Answer	Content Category	Explanation
27.	13	II	Use a proportion to solve this problem. $$\frac{\text{white gumball}}{\text{total gumballs}}$$ $$\frac{1}{6} = \frac{5}{12+5+b}$$ $$\frac{1}{6} = \frac{5}{(17+b)}$$ Next, cross-multiply and solve for b. $$(1)(17+b) = (5)(6)$$ $$17 + b = 30$$ $$b = 13$$ Another way to this problem is to use the ratio given and compare it to the number of gumballs given. A ratio of $\frac{1}{6}$ means 1 white gumball to the total number of gumballs. Since there are more than 6 total gumballs, as stated in the problem $(12 + 5) = 17$. This must mean the fraction has been reduced. The opposite of reducing a fraction is multiplying both parts by a common factor. The numerator of the ratio means 1 white gumball. The problem states there are 5 total white gumballs. This means to get from 1 to 5 you have to multiply by 5. Whatever you do to one part of a fraction has to be done to the other. Since you multiply the 1 by 5, you have to multiply the 6 by 5 to get 30. This means there are 30 total gumballs in the jar. If 12 are red and 5 are white, $30 - 12 - 5 = 13$ which is the number of blue gumballs in the jar.
28.	square feet	I	Area of a house floor plan, or living space, is commonly defined in square feet. Centimeters and inches are too small. Conversely, square kilometers are too big.

Number	Answer	Content Category	Explanation
29.	155	III	To find the value of x for the figure, it is important to be able to recognize the supplementary angles and also recall that three angles in a triangle add to 180°. The angle next to the right angle and inside the triangle is also 90° because the two angles are supplementary angles (labeled 90° in the image below). Next, because three angles in a triangle add to 180°, the angle now labeled a is equal to $180 - 115 - 90 = 25$. (Angle a was added in the explanation for clarification.) Last, angle a and x are supplementary, which means they add to 180, so $x = 180 - 25 = 155$.
30.	Multiply 26 by 88	I	To solve this problem, it is important to have an understanding of how to convert units using conversion factors. If converting miles to feet, for example, the conversion is 1 mile for every 5,280 feet. This can be written in fraction form as $\frac{1 \text{ mile}}{5,280 \text{ feet}}$. The following solution will show how to solve using this process. $$\frac{\text{miles}}{\text{hour}} \cdot \frac{5,280 \text{ feet}}{1 \text{ mile}} \cdot \frac{1 \text{ hour}}{60 \text{ minutes}}$$ As you can see, all of the ratios are multiplied together in order to cancel out miles per hour and leave only feet per minute. $$\frac{\cancel{\text{miles}}}{\cancel{\text{hour}}} \cdot \frac{5,280 \text{ feet}}{1 \cancel{\text{ mile}}} \cdot \frac{1 \cancel{\text{ hour}}}{60 \text{ minutes}} = \frac{5,280 \text{ feet}}{60 \text{ minutes}} = 88 \text{ ft/min}$$ Therefore, the conversion factor from miles per hour to feet per minute is to multiply by 88.
31.	8π	III	The formula for the area of a circle is $A = \pi r^2$. If the area of the circle is 16π, then $r^2 = 16$ and $r = 4$. If the radius of the circle is 4, use the equation, $C = 2\pi r$ to find the circumference. $C = 2\pi \cdot 4 = 8\pi$
32.	Statements 1 and 3	II	Since this is a study and not a fact, you are unable to determine the results of the information is universal. Statements 2 and 4 use the word "cause" and are therefore incorrect because this is not the case all the time. Statement 5 is incorrect because this represents a negative relationship. Statements 1 and 3 are positive relationships and use the word "tend" instead of cause showing that there is a relationship among the data.

Number	Answer	Content Category	Explanation
33.	40	III	Vertical angles are angles formed by intersecting lines; they are the angles across from each other and are equal in measure. Both $(x + 12)$ and the $90°$ angle have a vertical angle pair inside the triangle that is formed. Thus, we have two of the three angles in the triangle. 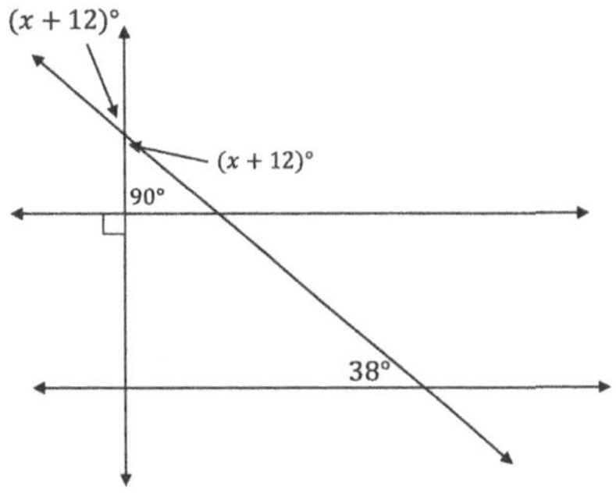 The third angle and the angle that is $38°$ are corresponding angles formed by parallel lines and a transversal, so they are congruent, or equal, to one another. In the diagram below, the third angle is marked a. 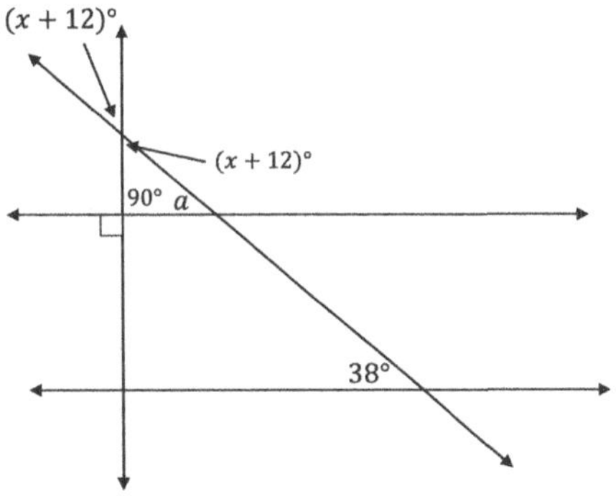 Now that we have the three angles in the triangle, we can add them together and set the sum equal to 180. $(x + 12) + 90 + a = 180$ $(x + 12) + 90 + 38 = 180$ $x + 12 + 128 = 180$ $x + 140 = 180$ $x = 40$
34.	$x = 38$	III	Since the pattern is given, work backwards to get the solution. The most important thing is to understand that three less than five times a number is $5x - 3$. Use this to solve. $5x - 3 = 187$ $5x = 190$ $\dfrac{5x}{5} = \dfrac{190}{5}$ $x = 38$

Number	Answer	Content Category	Explanation
35.	See answer explanation for solution	I	ANSWER: ☐ $3 + 3 + 5 + 5 + 7 + 7$ ☐ $2 \times (3 + 5 + 7)$ ☐ $3 \times 2 + 5 \times 2 + 7 \times 2$ Performing the operations in options 1, 4, and 5 yields the correct amount of candy per child. Options 2 and 3 have the multiplication and addition signs incorrectly placed.
36.	36	III	The first step to solving this problem is figuring out the scale on the timeline (how far apart from one another each mark is). From 1974 to 1982 is 8 years, so the unlabeled tick marks are 4 years from the years on either side. Therefore, the company was incorporated between 1974 and 1978. Because this date appears to be in the middle of this time span, assume that they were incorporated in 1976. Following the same assumption for when they reached $2,000,000 in sales, this appears to have happened in 2012. Thus, it took from 1976 to 2012 to reach $2,000,000 in sales, which is 36 years.
37.	$x = 140°$ $y = 75°$	III	Any time a line intersects two parallel lines it is called a transversal, and special angle pairs are formed. Since Left Ave. is a transversal, the two given angles are supplementary or equal to 180°. $180° - 40° = 140°$. Right Ave. is a transversal which means the given angles are corresponding or the same thus $y = 75°$.
38.	square rectangle rhombus parallelogram trapezoid	III	The quadrilaterals that have at least one pair of parallel sides include a square, rectangle, rhombus, parallelogram, and trapezoid.
39.	360	II	This problem is designed to test your skills of estimation. Because the values are difficult to pinpoint, estimate as closely as possible. The following are estimated values: January: 90 February: 55 March: 40 April: 100 May: 75. The sum of all these values is 360.

Number	Answer	Content Category	Explanation
40.	Negative linear correlation	II	To determine if a relationship exists among a set of points, first draw a line so that it is as close as possible to all or most of the points. If most of the points are close to, or somewhat close to, the line, the relationship is said to be linear. For the scatterplot in this problem, the data is linear because the points are all relatively close to the line. Next, the slope of the line determines if the relationship is positive or negative. From left to right the line decreases, meaning it is negative. Therefore, this is an example of a negative linear correlation.
41.	32	II	To solve you must determine how many cars the symbol represents. Since the 1st and 5th floors have a total of 9 symbols, which is 72 cars, divide 72 by 9 to get the value of each car symbol, which is 8. Because there are 4 car symbols for the 2nd floor, multiply 4 and 8 to get 32 cars.
42.	$y = 3x + 1$	III	There are a number of ways to find the equation of a line given the information in the chart. First, look at the answer choices to see what form they're in; in this case, they are in slope-intercept form. Next, look at the y row; Notice the pattern that every number increases by 3. Therefore, the slope of this line is 3. We can eliminate the first and last choices. Next, the y-intercept is found when the x-coordinate equals 0. Even though there is no 0 in the x-coordinate row, use the pattern to work backwards. Since x increases by 1, subtract one from 1 to get 0. The same must be done with the y-coordinate. If y increases by three, take 3 away to get 1. The new point is $(0, 1)$, which is the y-intercept. The line in this set of points crosses the y-axis at 1 with a slope of 3, so the correct answer is $y = 3x + 1$.
43.	37	I	This problem is an example of the application of multiples. If every fourth person gets a 25% off coupon for the first 150 people, divide 150 by 4, $150 \div 4 = 37.5$ Because we can't have half a person, 37 people will have received the 25% off coupon.

Number	Answer	Content Category	Explanation
44.	$2, -6$	III	Quadratic equations, equations where the x term is squared, may have none, one, or two solutions. For testing purposes, it is likely the equations given will have two solutions (there will never be more than 2). Recall that when taking the square root of a number, for example $\sqrt{16}$, the resulting solution can be positive or negative because $4 \cdot 4 = 16$ and $-4 \cdot (-4) = 16$. So, when we take the square root in order to solve an equation, the equation gets broken up into two smaller equations. The simplest way to solve this problem is to substitute the answer choices in the equation to determine which value(s) equal 16. $(4+2)^2 = 36 \neq 16$ NO $(-2+2)^2 = 0 \neq 16$ NO $(2+2)^2 = 16 = 16$ YES $(6+2)^2 = 64 \neq 16$ NO $(-6+2)^2 = 16 \neq 16$ YES Alternately, if you understand solving using algebra, use the following method. First, take the square root of both sides. Because squaring and taking the square root are opposite actions, this removes the squared exponent. $\sqrt{(x+2)^2} = \sqrt{16}$ $x + 2 = 4$ $x + 2 = -4$ $\underline{-2 \quad -2}$ $\underline{-2 \quad -2}$ $x = 2$ $x = -6$ Therefore, the solutions to the equation are 2 and -6.
45.	30%	I	Understanding how to set this problem up is the key. When asking for the percent **of** a number, in this case 190, the "percent of" number is going to be the denominator (bottom number) of the fraction. The remaining number, 57, or the "**is**" value, will be the numerator of the fraction. The fraction that represents the percent is $\frac{57}{190}$ and this equals 0.30. When converted to a percent, the final answer is 30%.

Number	Answer	Content Category	Explanation
46.	12 miles	I	The problem is asking how many <u>more</u> miles it was from one store to the other, which means finding difference between the two distances. To do this, find the total distance each girl drove, and then subtract. We know Jocelyn drove 18 miles, which is 60% of what Ella had to drive. If 18 miles is 60% of Ella's distance, we need to find 60% of a number that equals 18. $60\% \cdot x = 18$ $0.6x = 18$ $\dfrac{0.6x}{0.6} = \dfrac{18}{0.6}$ $x = 30$ Ella drove 30 miles to get to the store and Jocelyn drove 18 miles. Thus, the difference in the number of miles they drove is $30 - 18 = 12$. Ella had to drive 12 more miles than Jocelyn to get to the store. Another way to approach the problem is to estimate. If you know that 18 miles is 60% of what Ella drove, then she drove a little more than half the distance. If you were to double 18, you get 36. Knowing this is too high, estimate the distance to be approximately 32. The difference of 32 and 18 is 14. Knowing that this is just an estimate, look at all possible answer choices and you will notice the only one that is at or below 14 is the first answer choice, which is the correct answer.
47.	9 ten thousand	I	The fifth space to the left of the decimal is the ten thousands place. Therefore, the 9 represents ninety thousand.
48.	13	I	The last of the $6,500 donation needs to be distributed. In order to do this, subtract all of the purchases from 6,500. $6,500 - 450 - 450 - 3,000 - 1,500 - 775 = 325$ If each mat costs $25, divide this into 325 to find the answer. $325 \div 25 = 13$
49.	$6n - (3 + n)$	III	Product means to multiply the 6 with the variable. To decrease is to subtract, and quantity means to use parentheses. Inside the parentheses is the addition of 3 and n.
50.	$700,000	I	To solve, set up a proportion using the smallest share and the total inheritance. Note that the ratio of 3:5:6 means that the sum of the parts of the inheritance is $3 + 5 + 6 = 14$. $\dfrac{\text{smallest share}}{\text{total inheritance}} = \dfrac{3}{14} = \dfrac{150,000}{x}$ Cross multiply and solve to find the total inheritance, x. $3x = 14(150,000)$ $3x = 2,100,000$ $x = 700,000$

Number	Answer	Content Category	Explanation
51.	$m = -\dfrac{7}{6}$	III	Slope is the fraction that represents the change in the y values over the change in x values. The formula for slope is $\dfrac{y_2 - y_1}{x_2 - x_1}$. $\dfrac{-3-4}{2-(-4)}$ $= \dfrac{-7}{6} = -\dfrac{7}{6}$ Don't get hung up on the subscripts in the formula. Pick a point to be the first one, denoted by the subscript 1, and the other point will be the second point. It doesn't matter which one is the first point and which is the second.
52.	$a = 95°$	III	The three angles in a triangle add to 180°. If angles $b + c = 85°$, then $a + 85 = 180$. Subtract 85 from 180 and angle $a = 95°$.
53.	36 cubic inches	III	Volume of a prism is found by finding area of the base and multiplying by height or doing $length \times width \times height$. $2 \times 3 \times 6 = 36$.
54.	$\dfrac{1}{6}$	II	There are 6 possible ways for two dice to add to 7. 1-6, 2-5, 3-4, 6-1, 5-2, and 4-3 Since each die has 6 faces with one of the digits 1 through 6, there are 36 possible combinations ($6 \times 6 = 36$) when rolling two at the same time. Therefore, the probability of rolling a 7 is $\dfrac{6 \text{ desired outcomes}}{36 \text{ total outcomes}}$ or $\dfrac{1}{6}$.
55.	$\dfrac{5}{33}$	II	The important information in this problem is that the picks are consecutive without replacement, which means the total number of outcomes changes after the first pick. When finding the probability of multiple events, multiply the probability of the first pick by the probability of the second pick. Remember there is a total of 22 pieces of candy to choose from. After the first pick there will be only 21 pieces of candy left. Remember to always reduce when possible. $\dfrac{10}{22} \times \dfrac{7}{21}$ $= \dfrac{5}{11} \times \dfrac{1}{3} = \dfrac{5}{33}$
56.	72	I	Use of the counting principle to find the answer to this problem, which means multiply the number of options for each type of choice together. Count carefully as the number of items is not given because they are listed out. There are 4 ice cream flavors, 6 toppings, and 3 container choices. Thus, the number of ways to pick one of each is found by multiplying each of these numbers together. $4 \times 6 \times 3 = 72$

Made in the USA
Middletown, DE
08 June 2020